Mr. Quarter-to-Two
Life & Death with
Mother Nature's Misfits

Robert H. Miller
Rusty Baillie

Mr. Quarter-to-Two:
Life & Death with
Mother Nature's Misfits

Ebook & Paperback developed
by Cognitio Books & Apps.

ISBN 978-0-9990655-2-5
ISBN 978-0-9990655-3-2 (Ebook)

Table of Contents

One Cup to the Dead Already:

Charles D. Carpenter
Layton Kor
Mark Davis
Blair Griffiths
Pasang Sona
Dawa Dorje
Ang Tsultim
Ken North

Foreword

When the *Alpinist* accepted one of these essays for publication in 2015 we were (as they say in parts of Oklahoma) "shittin' in tall cotton". But it didn't take long for reality to set in. During the months-long editing process, the magazine incrementally excised all humor, politics, sex, religion, law-breaking and any other remotely possible controversial subjects, however ephemeral or past the statutes of limitation. When the bowdlerization became intolerable, we regretfully withdrew the essay from consideration.

And so began the idea for this book.

It grew apace when *Outerlocal*, an online outdoor adventure pursuits online magazine, which had published the essay "Mr. Quarter-to-Two", went under, with all its archives lost to the cloud. *Outerlocal* was the brain child of Christian Beckwith, founder of the *Alpinist* back in 2002. He sold the magazine in 2008 to found *Outerlocal*, what he imagined publishing would become in the internet age.

"Buying Gasoline in Ethiopia" was the essay that wouldn't die. Due to be published in *Outside* magazine, it just missed the presses: the editor who'd accepted it either quit or got fired. Budget cuts or politics nixed it. Merrill Lynch's corporate magazine, *Pursuits*, also accepted it. But, again, it died in production when the brokerage firm closed its high glossy publication. A scion of the piece, funded by National Geographic, died on the vine when famine hit Ethiopia and the magazine thought it inappropriate to publish during such a humanitarian disaster. It finally saw life as a short piece in *Liberty* magazine.

Another essay, "From Ayn Rand to...Hayduke Lives!"—in much abbreviated form—was also published by *Liberty* magazine. The other three are original pieces commissioned for this volume.

However, this is not a traditional anthology, where the essays are completely independent. In one sense they are—they can be read out of order and with no reference to the other essays. But in a deeper sense, they cohere to create a whole larger than the pieces. The theme concerning the choices the protagonists (eccentric characters all) make—what makes life living—build and reach a climax in the final essay, "Learning by Dying", with Rusty Baillie's meditation on the 1982 Canadian Everest Expedition.

Robert H. Miller, the editor of, and an author in, this anthology, has always been allergic to authority, probably due to growing up in Communist Cuba. In his quest to solo-kayak Cataract Canyon in flood—aka Satan's Gut—he declined to submit to the long and involved permit system (at that time not available to solo kayakers, anyway—especially in flood). To avoid detection, he had to unload his boat and gear at the launch site after dark, hide them in the tamarisk groves, park his pick-up miles away, and then walk back to his launch site. In the frenzied, stealthy launch preparations, he forgot his helmet. So he improvised: he lined his cooking pot with three-eighths inch ensolite, and attached parachute cord as a chin strap. Voila! A helmet.

It wasn't the first time he'd bucked permits or mandatory fees. To climb Kilimanjaro without incurring the expenses of having to hire a guide, porters, or pay the permit fee, he snuck onto the mountain via Oloitokitok, a route used only by the resident Outward Bound School. His plan was to move swiftly and furtively to avoid detection. But he had to detour around elephants, got lost and missed the bivouac hut he'd planned on sleeping in. Thinking it was still up ahead, he quickened his pace. After 15 hours he found himself on Kili's summit, inadvertently setting some sort of a solo record up to that time (1972). He spent a glorious night on the summit's black sands surrounded by stark, white glacier ice.

Two years later, he planted the first Cuban flag atop Mt. McKinley—as it was then known.

In the award-winning BBC documentary *The Great Climb* (1967) Rusty Baillie, an ex-pat from Rhodesia (as Zimbabwe was then known), and prolific African, European and North American first ascentionist, strips down to his skivvies, ties a rope around his waist and dives into the frigid maelstrom of surging swell and smashing waves to set up a rope traverse across to an unclimbed sea stack off the coast of Scotland.

Rusty throws himself wholeheartedly into all his projects. When he, Chris Bonnington and Tom Patey set their sights on the first ascent of The Old Man of Hoy, an impressively tall and chimney-like sea stack in the Orkneys, the BBC decided to film it.

But the film indulges in some poetic license. Due to a scheduling conflict, it missed the first ascent, and so resorted to a later re-enactment, which additionally included two entirely different climbs. A week before the staged first ascent of the Old Man, Rusty and Joe Brown, *the* outstanding pioneering English rock climber of the 1950s and '60s, decided to warm up on a first ascent of Yesnaby Castle, another sea stack, but one separated from Stromness Island by a raging North Sea. While the Old Man of Hoy is firmly anchored to the Orkney mainland, Yesnaby isn't. And in the film, Yesnaby does not take pride of place, being subtly segued with the climb up the Old Man.

As the youngest member of the team, Rusty didn't actually draw the short straw to dive into the waves that were smashing on the rocks to swim the 30 yards to the stack—he was jumping out of his clothes to do it. At the base of the Castle he set up a rope traverse for Brown and their gear. For some unknown reason, Rusty's climbing shoes never made it across. He climbed the route barefooted, a route rated Hard Very Severe+, or 5.10a in the American rating system—at that time, about the hardest in the world.

But he also has a spiritual side. On his trek into Everest Base Camp during the first Canadian Everest expedition (1982), his group stopped for lunch at a porters' rest spot next to a cluster of tall boulders incised with Buddhist Mani inscriptions. When a

young monk passed by he stopped to chat. "Headed for Sagamartha?" He asked. The answer was obvious, but the holy man
wanted to pass the time and engage the mountaineers. "Why
aren't you practicing climbing on these boulders?" He followed
up.

Rusty's group responded that out of respect for the Mani
petroglyphs, they'd left them alone, in order to simply bask in the
spiritual aura of the spot. The monk retorted that the inscriptions were part of the past, but that their climb was in the
present. They would be honoring the inscriptions by climbing on
them: Each time they touched a carved inscription-hold, a prayer
would be carried up to heaven by the Wind Horses...so long as
they climbed with a holy spirit. Rusty was the first to consecrate
the boulders' updated meaning, moving with care, wonder and
reverence...

Mani stone.

Introduction

A man who has been through bitter experiences and travelled far
enjoys even his sufferings after a time
—*Homer*, The Odyssey

In the fall of 1970, Warren Harding and Dean Caldwell, while enduring 27 days on their first ascent of El Capitan's 3,600 foot overhanging *Wall of the Early Morning Light* in Yosemite, ran out of food (and wine and brandy, a Harding staple). Half way through the ordeal, while waiting out a four-day winter storm, they refused a rescue from the National Park Service—a rescue they had not requested, but one that the authorities insisted was necessary.

In a note dropped in a tin can during the ascent, Caldwell wrote that a rescue was unneeded, unwanted and would not be accepted; while Harding piped in: "We must be the most miserable, wet, cold stinking wretches imaginable. But we're alive, really alive, like people seldom are."

Harding and Caldwell had planned this project and they were determined to see it through, in their way—come what may. Whatever Harding undertook, it was always laced through and through with *fun*. Contrary to some perceptions of endurance fests and extreme pursuits as grim trials of constant torture, there is a strong undercurrent—often merrily overt—of enjoyment, even if it sometimes approaches that old saw of hitting oneself with a hammer because it feels so good when you stop. The two saved a bottle of cabernet, some crackers and cheese for a celebration on their last night on the wall.

And then there's Freya Hoffmeister, the first woman to circumnavigate New Zealand's South Island, Iceland and Australia in a kayak—the last both a solo and a record-setting feat. In 2015 she became the first person to circumnavigate South America in a kayak. When planning her route around Australia she decided to cut across the Gulf of Carpentaria, that giant incursion of ocean at the top of the island continent. A distance across of 357 miles, it would take about 10 days in a tight kayak with no chance of relief from the constrained sitting position other than exiting the tiny, narrow boat in shark-, salt water crocodile- and poisonous sea snake-infested seas—and then attempting to reenter the kayak, a craft not much stabler than a round log floating in water. When advised of the near impossibility of such an endeavor, the German's retort was, "Vas da problum?" her usual response to perceived obstacles.

Hoffmeister finds extreme adventure not just fun, but something approaching the realms of carnal ecstasy: "Dancing blind in waves" during all-night paddles is "sensual;" rough water is "sexy, the rougher the better. I like it *big* out there." And she celebrates by showing off after particularly harrowing experiences. Following a long stint in the kayak without getting out, her legs wobbly, upon reaching shore Freya channeled her inner acrobat and walked around on her hands.

One character in this anthology, while descending the Upper Salt River in Arizona at a high water level, purposely plunges into a Class 6 rapid in his kayak: an unrunable, no-way-out, no rescue, double waterfall with a hole at the bottom capable of swallowing an articulated Peterbuilt semi—in other words, certain death—in spite of carefully analyzing the risks and weighing the consequences…just to find out what all the hoopla is about.

While on a two-day ascent of the Northwest Face of Half Dome my partner and I were awakened at dawn by a gut wrenching, other-worldly scream. We'd bivouacked on Big Sandy Ledges three-quarters of the way up the 2,000 foot route. Looking up we spotted a human body in mid-air, way off the dome's summit visor, a granite slab gang-plank that sticks horizontally out the top of the feature.

This was no way to welcome our day, a day that right off the bat presented the climb's toughest challenges—the notorious Zig-

Zags. Suddenly the body came to a halt in the middle of the void, bounced and swung a bit and let out a forced, manic laugh. It was enough—bizarre—consolation for us that we proceeded with our own mad pursuit, ignoring the denouement to the drama above us, but only after commenting, "How stupid! That guy's crazy! Totally insane!" Shaking our heads in disbelief.

For a short time, *rope jumping* had become a new, thrill-seeking pursuit; a bit like bungee jumping but without the stretch and bounce of a real bungee. Rock climbing ropes are meant to stretch when catching a fall. It's a safety feature. In a typical fall, they'll stretch about 7%. In a really big fall, say, the full 200-foot length, they may stretch as much as 30%. The fool who woke us up that morning went for the full Monty: a free-fall the full length of the rope.

Dan Osman, an extreme rock climbing free-solo practitioner—no ropes or safety gear—took rope jumping to an extreme, logging a record jump of over a 1,000 feet by tying ropes together. Oddly enough, when ropes are tied together, the weakest point is at the knot. On November 23, 1998, Osman went up to the top of the Leaning Tower, an overhanging feature in Yosemite, to dismantle ropes he'd used in previous rope jumps over the course of a month. But at the last minute he changed his mind and decided to jump again.

After a few short jumps, he went for (if memory serves me right) a 3-rope, 600-foot jump. The ropes broke at a knot. They had been exposed to rain and snow over the course of the previous month, losing precious strength.

There is a big difference between Osman, on the one hand, and Harding and Caldwell. Harding and Caldwell were extreme, plodding accomplishers. They planned on a 12-day climb seeking a high level of fulfilment through dogged determination—and verification that their imagination and planning were in sync with reality through a constant feed-back process, one that allowed for recalibration as the adventure unfolded. Osman sought an intense, instant thrill—an adrenaline rush, if you will—and certain recognition of his genius—or madness—depending on one's perspective, with no time to fine tune things if they started to go south (as in bull riding). While both exploits required fine calculation, Osman's unfolded at terminal velocity. In reality, the line between high octane plodding accomplishment and self-generated instant thrill-seeking is a continuum, with proportional doses of neurotransmitters generated by the instantaneity of the intensity.

Somewhere along that spectrum lies the late Dean Potter, a man who eschewed (in his own words, "didn't get") the very notion of "extreme sports." He termed his pursuits "arts." These included high difficulty free-solo rock climbing (the sort done without a rope—often with his dog Whisper in a pack on his back); wingsuit BASE jumping (ditto with his dog Whisper); and free-solo highline walking (tightrope/high wire walking across a natural chasm, such as between the Lost Arrow Spire and the canyon rim in Yosemite—or between two high-rise buildings). Potter reported that he had a "unique reaction to adrenaline," which probably explains his rejection of the term and notion "extreme":

> *I just found out recently that my brain functions differently than most people's. I have an opposite effect to drugs; adrenaline makes everyone feel amped up. But adrenaline makes me very calm. I feel really calm at my max exertion while flying through the air. The scarier things get, the more amped I should be, but I just get calmer.*

What about that 'madness' component in "mad pursuit"? Some adventurers seek to exorcise inner demons, or calm out-of-control restlessness. Though we all have a bit of madness in us, the individuals in these essays pursued their dreams, sought survival or prevailed in quite calculated ways. Perhaps we, like Alex Honnold—the climbing free-soloist profiled in the award winning documentary *Free Solo*—have under-functioning amygdalas: ones that allow our fear to be tempered by our intellect. After all, it's difficult to think straight when shaking in terror. Honnold averred that he does not experience a sensory rush: "There is no adrenaline rush. If I get an adrenaline rush, it means that something has gone horribly wrong."

A separate consequence of this condition is that the brain's reward system needs a higher level of stimulation to avoid boredom. As Fred Beckey, America's most prolific mountaineer—ever —observed about taking a cruise on a ship, "How dull!" (But then, he went through climbing partners as if they were one-night stands.)

Our endeavor to achieve the unique, the unusual, and the heretofore unimagined owes much to ego, a concept that has, in contemporary discourse, gotten a bad rap. Ego is the part of the mind that mediates between the conscious and the unconscious and is responsible for reality-testing and a sense of personal identity. It can be the source of much creativity.

One of our authors, Rusty Baillie, while participating in the first Canadian Everest expedition, knew exactly when his pursuit of the summit became too much: when one too many deaths showed that new dangers had changed the likelihood of death from possible to probable. At that point he called it quits. The summit had changed from a glorious childhood dream to a well trampled mound of rock and ice, much like any other spot in the high mountains.

Why do some people intentionally put themselves in what most consider harm's way (*pace* those attempting to save lives)? And sometimes, when given the chance, refuse an exit when conditions take a turn for the worse as in the case of Harding and Caldwell?

Generalizing as to exactly what drives such mad pursuits is often futile, usually shallow, inevitably obvious and beyond the scope of this anthology—the authors being averse to too much analytical navel gazing. Any answers inevitably approach George Mallory's quip as to why he sought to climb Everest: "Because it's there", an answer he provided perhaps out of exasperation with the question, or because it required too much introspection on the fly, or—as some have said, he was inarticulate (not likely, according to other sources). How do you justify an unjustifiable ambition? Why does it require justification? Who knows?

Roy Smith, while exploring the uncharted Omo River in Ethiopia for National Geographic—a river teeming with deadly hippos, crocs, rapids, parasites and tribes—was asked by an African resident of Addis Ababa, "Why do people like you Americans do things like this?"

Roy only smiled. "I didn't really have an answer," he confided to me later.

Riaan Manser, in his book *Around Africa on my Bicycle*, an account of his 2-year circling of the continent around its often trackless perimeter—an epic ride through unstable, war-torn, corrupt and dangerous countries, made worse by Manser's inexperienced and bull-headed idiosyncrasies—was often asked why he was doing this. For one, he considered himself an "adventurer and explorer". As such, he mused—in the same way, he thought as the old adage, that "someone who asks how much a Maserati costs can't afford it"—that those who question what drives the "adventurer/explorer" to (as he words it) "put it all on the line" simply do not get it.

President John F. Kennedy, while glancingly alluding to Mallory's response, seemed to enlarge upon it when addressing why we—Armstrong, Aldrin…the United States—sought to go to the moon: "Not because it is easy, but because it is hard." And the harder the success, the greater the accomplishment.

Such success often comes with a price. Willie Unsoeld, a member of the first American Everest expedition and a pioneer on its West Ridge (with Thomas Hornbein) lost all of his toes (he later died in an avalanche on a winter ascent of Mt. Rainier). More poignantly, he noted that many of the Everest expedition's members' marriages later fell apart—as did Neil Armstrong's after the moon landing. Harding and Buzz Aldrin, Armstrong's co-mooner, became alcoholics.

Many "adventurers" credit the mystical dimension of extreme pursuits, what some might relate to a sort of vision quest. After Everest, Unsoeld emphasized the spiritual aspects of his endeavors in his public presentations: "You go to nature for an experience of the sacred...to re-establish your contact with the core of things…" Many Himalayan mountaineers return with a fresh appreciation for Tibetan Buddhism.

Closely related are quasi-atavistic explanations for these endeavors. In a March, 2020 *New Yorker* article, Bozeman, Montana, Jungian psychotherapist Tim Tate offers an "inner urge" explanation for why we do what we do: "Athletes have a particular calling we need to address. It isn't a mythology of proving themselves. It's a calling they cannot refuse. They have it on a loudspeaker in their brains. They can't help but do what they do."

Though appealing in its simplicity such an explanation is now mostly discredited because attributing behavior to "inner urges" begs the question and explains nothing. Additionally, the "inner urge" bit, like the ether in 19th century cosmology as an interplanetary medium, is an unnecessary interjection. Still, comparing "They do it because they have an inner urge" and "They do it because they want to" are awfully close concepts.

But as one of our authors has retorted, "No No..."You want to" is enough. No Inner Urge needed. We have such choices…if we didn't, we'd do something else. This simple desire has an ultimate integrity…you have the sublime power to make such decisions. To try to justify this is profanity."

Which leads to a simpler, purer explanation: passion. That is how Dane Jackson, a 26-year-old national kayaking champion from Tennessee, explained his obsession with kayaking Salto del Maule, a 134-foot waterfall located in Valle de Los Condores, a volcanic region of central Chile.

"It's been a dream of mine for years," Jackson said. "I think it's just one of the most photogenic waterfalls I've ever seen. And it's also quite tall."

Verlen Kruger, too, was passionate, though he never used that exact word to describe his motivation. A blue-collar plumber and born-again Christian who never finished high school, he nonetheless managed to become a fighter pilot in WWII and paddled his canoe over 100,000 miles *after* the age of forty-one, crossing North America east-to-west and cruising from the McKenzie's delta on the Arctic Ocean down to Cape Horn... among many, many expeditions. He preferred upstream paddling, being the only person (along with his partner, Steve Landick) to navigate the Colorado River through Grand Canyon *upstream* in a canoe. Considering that some rapids, such as Sockdolager, are presumed to be un-portagable—requiring ascents and descents of hundreds of feet of rock climbing over the Inner Granite Gorge with a fully-loaded boat—the fact that they completed the trip in 21 days, the usual time for a downriver traverse, is beyond belief...made more so because Kruger couldn't swim, eschewed life jackets and didn't even like to get wet.

As Verlen has averred, the fun really only kicked in while paddling upstream because of the special skills required. He loved marathon days in his boat and particularly enjoyed adversity, finding a spiritual dimension to going beyond his expected abilities. When lost for words to describe his motivation, he'd often quote Rudyard Kipling:

> "Something hidden. Go and find it.
> Go and look beyond the ranges—
> Something lost behind the ranges.
> Lost and waiting for you. Go!"

One of the most eccentric individuals to inhabit this territory is George Meegan, unsurprisingly, an Englishman. Low key and requiring no special skills, Meegan's feat is nonetheless ex-

17

traordinary in scope, length, duration and raw determination. Over the course of seven years he walked from Tierra del Fuego to Prudhoe Bay, the length of the western hemisphere—the longest unbroken march of all time. But intent on setting a distance record, Meegan took a roundabout route. After bee lining straight up South and Central America, when he reached Mexico he headed to and up the Gulf of Mexico, then went across Texas and the South, up the East Coast of the US, finally crossing Canada to British Columbia and up the AlCan and the Dalton Highways to Prudhoe Bay—a distance of 19,000 miles.

What really sets Meegan apart was his style: essentially, a homeless vagrant with a shopping cart. Eschewing a rucksack, he put wheels on a frame pack which he dragged behind him, like an elderly person's grocery cart. His clothes, boots, tent and rain poncho were tattered and torn beyond repair. Unconsciously describing himself he wrote: "To live in a rain-lashed area and tolerate a leaky roof…is to raise indolence to new heights." He slept in jail cells, firefighters' redoubts, churches, stock pens, begged for shelter and food and depended on infrequent remittances from friends and family.

Why did he do this? He was asked so often that he had time to put words to his motivation. At one point he wrote, "…I chose to define [it] as the largest work of abstract art ever seen, inscribed by the footsteps of a man in his self-created prison yard, the Western Hemisphere." Yet…at the end of the "walk", at a celebration for him, he thought:

> *The gesture was understandable, but all wrong. The journey was dead, and not yet even buried, and at the gathering I was forced into making small talk with people I didn't know, feeling absolutely terrible, all the while screaming inside, 'Awful! Awful! Let me be alone! Can't you see that something inside me has just died!'*

Our approach to contemplating these questions is to tell the stories of a few individuals in the thick of things and let the reader draw his own conclusion. Just be sure to keep Warren Harding's note to the Park Service front and center…and don't forget the fun.

The first story, "Mr. Quarter-to-Two", explores the curious character and personality of a great pioneer white water kayaker, and the first person to kayak the headwaters of the Amazon River—along with some ancillary characters that find—or fail to find—some sort of redemption. Forget Ralph Waldo Emerson's essay On Self-Reliance; Charles D. Carpenter is the kinetic embodiment of individualism.

In "Layton Kor Agonistes" the authors contrast Layton Kor's approach to life, death and climbing with Tina Cobos' weltanschauung. Kor was America's premier rock climber and first ascentionist in the 1950s and '60s. Tina Cobos' only claim to fame was her 1st Place ranking (in her category) at the 1990 Phoenix Bouldering Contest. The two exchanged climbing stories and philosophies just before facing their mortality on the same day just outside Las Vegas. Though much has been written about Layton, the details of his last days remain unreported—until now.

Mark Davis, the protagonist of our second essay, pitted his wits against the FBI. By many accounts, he tried to blow up the Palo Verde Nuclear Power Plant outside Phoenix, Arizona for Earth First! He and the author attended high school and college together. A few years after graduation, they took over the reins of the Libertarian Party in their county. Both shared concerns over man's environmental husbandry, but parted ways over means. Davis' beliefs drove him to extremes that threatened lives and landed him in federal prison. The informer who secured his conviction remains an enigma.

"Adrift on the Shield" contains a potpourri of curious characters, some exorcising demons, some looking for love and some exploring the limits of the possible. Here the author recounts his on-again, off-again quest to cross from the Pacific to the Atlantic

Ocean north of 60° latitude by kayak—battling bears, unrunable cataracts and deadly weather.

"Buying Gasoline in Ethiopia" is a lesson in navigating the bureaucracy of a brutal Communist dictatorship in order to engage in business: the outdoor adventure business...and a lesson on how to lose money taking raw greenhorns down an unmapped wilderness river where severed human testicles were still valued as trophies of rites of passage by the local tribes. Thick with crocs and hippos during daytime—like cars and pedestrians in a Manhattan rush hour—the Omo River's banks also teemed with unidentified predators at night, just out of range of the campfire's glow, and deadly tropical diseases everywhere all the time.

Take a trip back in time, to when Zimbabwe was known as Rhodesia and white Africans—at least north of South (as it was informally dubbed)—were *rarae aves*. Not so long ago, really. Rusty Baillie, the author of "Learning by Falling", was bred, born and reared there...a white African. Once, a quarter-of-a-million white people (and 3.7 million black ones) lived in Rhodesia/Zimbabwe.

Africa was not the cradle of rock climbing. However, Rusty relates how the sport was independently invented by fifteen-year-old Scouts in colonial Rhodesia (as it undoubtedly was in many places around the world by restless souls seeking transcendent adventures). After having read just a few classics such as Edward Whymper's *Scrambles Amongst the Alps in the Years 1860-1869* in the Prince Edward School library, Rusty and his mates set out to test their mettle on the towering *kopjies*.

Finally, in "Learning by Dying" Rusty recounts his spiritual and philosophical epiphany in the Himalayas as a member of the 1982 Canadian Everest Expedition. Too many climbers died on that attempt, not the least being Rusty himself, who miraculously came back from his grave...with an entirely different perspective on life and its meaning; and with a deeper understanding about what truly matters in this brief repast.

Mr. Quarter-to-Two

By Robert H. Miller

There's some come here
For to see me hung;
And some to buy my fiddle.
But before that I do part with her,
I'll break her through the middle.
—McPherson's Lament

Chuck Carpenter was not famous and he didn't write anything, except letters—and those were nearly illegible—scribbled on recycled notebook scraps with the old writing scratched out, or on used, folded brown paper grocery bags sealed with a strip of duct tape and a stamp. His letters were hard to read. Not only did he ignore the lines on the paper (if there were any), he'd write with whatever was handy: pencil, pen, crayon, Marks-A-Lot, highlighter—he even tried disappearing ink once and sometimes cut-and-pasted already printed prose, reminiscent of a ransom note—often mixing everything together in a combination of cursive and printed stream-of-consciousness non-sequiturs lacking any pretense at introductory foreplay and interspersed with hand-drawn cartoon illustrations. And always, they included numerous annotated clippings.

Sometimes, if he thought a response to his letter might inconvenience you too much—or if he wanted to funnel your response into his agenda—he'd include *your* response to him in a multiple choice or fill-in-the-blanks format accompanied by a self-addressed, stamped return envelope.

When zip codes were introduced, Chuck abjured them as needlessly redundant and verging on the fascist, since, to him, they were a bureaucratic attempt at making place names obsolete. Later, when the post office enforced their use, he fought back by writing the numbers out in long-hand—as one single whole number (e.g., eighty six thousand three hundred and five). Of course, this strategy discarded the first-place zero common on East Coast zip codes as mathematically meaningless. Once he got tired of this exercise, he made his point obtusely by doing what he initially feared—he omitted the town and state from his envelopes. For good measure he'd contract the recipient's name to a pair of initials—for greater anonymity.

His last letter was typical. It started out with a global warming rant, continued to an update about an ongoing legal conundrum, jumped to a harangue about the radioactive contamination of the Puerco River, then detoured to an anti-vaccine conspiracy argument and finally came to an abrupt stop at the progress of his cancer. None of it was good news. He'd lost the use of his left arm; now he was losing the use of his right arm. He closed with, "Other than that, how was the play, Mrs. Lincoln?"

The next day I received a copy of his Advanced Health Care Directives. He'd given me the power to pull his plug—if it came to that. The instructions included the following hand-written addition, hidden within the 20 pages of boilerplate: "If I am diagnosed as pregnant, please obtain another doctor for me."

He had also added the following under "Conditions or Limitations": "Before Bob makes the final decision in these matters he should leave the hospital and go for a beer to relax and let the decision come."

Although a scattered, terse writer, Chuck was a powerful singer. His rich and clear-as-cream-sherry baritone once nearly got us incarcerated. Five of us had packed ourselves, river-running and camping gear into a battered, 1972 Ford F-100 pick-up, and driven down to central Mexico to run the Santa Maria River, a serious and isolated white water epic no one had yet run. On the way back we aimed to re-enter the US at Eagle Pass, Texas. We were not a low profile, trouble-free, border crossing outfit: the truck had mismatched panels with notational graffiti (such as, 'gas tank', 'propane', 'paddles', etc.) inscribed by Chuck —seemingly everywhere and with accompanying arrows—with an indelible marking pen; a homemade camper shell topped with oars, kayaks and a rolled-up army surplus raft; and a disreputable looking crew badly in need of hygiene and new clothes. I urged everyone, particularly Chuck, to clean up his act, behave and cooperate with the authorities.

It was hopeless—confrontation was palpable and inevitable.

After checking ID's and locking eyeballs all around, the U.S. Customs & Immigration agents re-directed us for a dogs-and-all, thorough inspection. It didn't take long to get mired in the mud. As soon as Chuck felt his autonomy had been violated, he looked around, scoping out the situation; took a deep breath, filling his lungs with fresh ammunition and, impervious to all reaction, counter attacked with a double-barreled, full-throated a Capella rendition of *Will Ye No Come Back Again?*, a Jacobite dirge of resistance. Thick in the maw and with no retreat visible, I joined in.

Since we were clean (in the legal sense), after a 3-hour, all-but-body-cavity-search and interrogation, we were allowed back into the US.

A Friend for Life

Charles D. "Chuck" Carpenter, Jr.—assistant welding inspector, reluctant union member, ice sculptor, Colorado River guide, mountaineer, kayaker, explorer, raconteur, contrarian, post-outside-the-box thinker, gold buff and libertarian—died in 2010 at the age of 63 of prostate cancer.

Chuck had been studying Business Management in Pasadena, California when he came across a want ad in the *Sierra Club* magazine soliciting boatmen for Colorado River outfitters. Chuck was hooked. He abandoned his studies, drove to Marble Canyon, Arizona, and hired on with Martin Litton's Grand

Canyon Dories, the only outfitter that attempted to replicate the experience of John Wesley Powell's exploratory 1869 expedition.

But Chuck wasn't allowed to row a dory. Instead, as a novice boatman, he was consigned to rowing the rubber raft that carried all the dunnage the graceful dories couldn't carry. But more to the point, his employer had noticed that Chuck was somehow "different"—liable to alienate paying customers by inappropriate behavior, lack of social graces or, worse, reminding them that if "they were serious about running the Grand Canyon, they wouldn't hire a guide, would pilot their own boat, etc." He didn't last long, but he began to become a character of some repute. When Litton let him go he hired on with Hatch, the Earl Scheib of low-budget Grand Canyon river trips.

Camped at the top of Crystal, one of the Grand Canyon's gnarliest and most intimidating rapids, Chuck caught sight of a rattler that had wandered into camp. Without hesitation, he snatched it up. Unwilling to kill or release it where it could wander back amongst the clients, he decided to relocate it across the river on the opposite bank. A fellow boatman, caught up in the excitement, volunteered to ferry a raft over, just above Crystal's head-drop, while Chuck held the snake by the neck. A third volunteer held a flashlight. Engulfed in the pitch-black night and the realization that a few missed strokes would suck them into perdition, they rowed white-knuckled, guided by the flashlight and the subtle Doppler shifts of Crystal's roar—confusingly amplified by the echoes off the canyon walls. At the opposite shore they set it free.

I first met Chuck in 1969 when, in between river trips, he came down to Prescott, Arizona, to check out Prescott College, a new school with—for that time—a radical approach to teaching. Alongside traditional, academic courses, the college required— and provided—practical experience in one's chosen field. And, instead of football, basketball and baseball, the "sports" program consisted of mountaineering, rock climbing, kayaking and such sorts of individual adventure pursuits. Finally, instead of the usual freshman orientation with humiliating drunken orgies, Prescott College subjected its new students to a three-week Outward Bound-type course meant to instill self-reliance, force introspection under stress, and push the limits of one's capabilities. I'd applied there because it was the only college that didn't require SAT or ACT scores—tests I was temperamentally incapable of enduring.

Chuck's getting-to-know-you routine consisted of a couple of six packs of cheap, warm beer—a ruse, no doubt, to inveigle his new mark to buy cold ones—followed by an outrageously intrusive interrogation. Meanwhile, he himself remained cheerfully inscrutable, displaying an endearingly dry sense of humor tinged with cynicism. In conversation, he favored anecdotes and avoided expository tirades, never arguing or attempting to convince anyone of his point of view. Instead, he'd push his agenda through loaded questions, or aggressive bull-headed silence. Never one to disclose his premises, he nonetheless held on to them tenaciously—like a Jack Russell with a bone.

Chuck at Granite Mt., Arizona

Chuck was tall, strikingly well-formed and slightly lordotic; sported thick Barry Goldwater glasses below a broad, bulbous forehead and had a flat-top haircut offset by a Wilford Brimley mustache. I'd been assigned to show him around. It was late August and school hadn't opened yet but I was busy earning pocket money organizing the camping food and gear for the incoming freshman class Orientation Program. He tagged along and lent a hand. That's when I first glimpsed the real Chuck.

We'd loaded a large rented U-Haul full of equipment for the program and were driving it—with the back door open and myself and two employees standing guard to keep an eye on the load's stability—from warehouse to distribution point, a short distance on campus roads. Chuck volunteered to drive. I told him to drive dead slow. He did; but not five minutes into the drive I noticed him jogging next to me at the back of the 26-foot bed truck.

In a panic, I blurted, "Chuck! Who's driving the truck?" He pretended not to understand the question and laughed so hard he nearly stumbled and fell. Then, still laughing—though now with an added touch of concern—he composed himself and dashed back into the cab.

I didn't know what to think. He was an intriguing character and I was inexplicably drawn to him, but he was uncontrollable and anarchic—not really a team player.

I didn't see him again until the following year when he returned to the college and tried to hire on as an Orientation Program instructor. He was politely turned down but hung around helping out wherever he could to show his initiative. He slept in his VW microbus (the only home he had, I suspected). During that intervening year he'd learned technical rock climbing, and was jumping out of his skin to try out his new skills. Soon he cajoled me into attempting a new route on Thumb Butte, a volcanic plug emblematic of Prescott's skyline.

The climb, for a first ascent, was uneventful until, at the top, we set up our rappel anchors. We'd slung a basalt horn but Chuck wanted redundancy for safety. So he went through the motion of nudging a hippo-sized boulder at the edge of the cliff to test its stability as an additional anchor. To our surprise and alarm, the boulder rolled towards the cliff edge—it was already inches away—onto Chuck's ankle and trapped him there in a bearclaw trap vise grip, forcing him to hug the very rock that was threatening to push him over the cliff so as not to fall 200 feet to the ground. He let out a soul rattling scream, flirted with panic and looked imploringly at me.

Adrenaline-fueled hyper-drive took over. I cobbled together a rescue plan, reassured Chuck, and tied him off in case the teetering rock went over the edge; rappelled down the 200-foot face and ran as fast as I could for the nearest phone, at a house about a quarter-of-a-mile away.

Now, back then, local governments' rescue responsibilities were somewhat fuzzy. Although the sheriff's department included the Yavapai County Mountain Rescue Team and the fire department still rescued cats from trees, both ran seat-of-the-pants operations. As luck would have it, the Mountain Rescue Team was out of town, so my call to the sheriff was forwarded to the fire department.

Knowing full well that they'd be clueless in this situation, I requested a selection of technical ropes, a metal basket Stokes litter and a ten-ton jaw-jack small enough for one man to lug up a cliff. After the call I stepped outside to check on Chuck. Conversing in shouts, I brought him up to date. In between exchanges he'd release his agony in willful screams. God forbid the boulder rolling over and taking him down the cliff.

When the fire fighters showed up most were pot-bellied, middle aged, wore Wellington boots and had no idea how to get themselves up to the top of the cliff. But they did bring all the requested gear, including a physician. While some circled to the back of the butte to take the hiking trail up, the MD and 2 men helped carry the gear up to the base of the cliff. There I bandoleered the two 2-inch manila ropes, clipped the jaw-jack to my climbing harness, stuck 4 wooden wedges in my pockets and climbed the fixed rappel rope hand-over-hand—a feat inconceivable under normal circumstances. Chuck beamed. I secured the boulder with the ropes so it wouldn't roll over him and down the cliff when it was jacked up.

Then, with the delicacy of a sapper disarming a mine, I inserted the jack's jaw next to Chuck's ankle and gently pumped the handle. The hydraulic hose strained. I pumped some more until the jaw barely, just perceptibly lifted the rock. When Chuck pulled out his foot, I stuck the wooden wedges where his foot had been and looked at his ankle. Its distal end along the vertical axis was nearly as flat as a tortilla; but he was free and the boulder was stable. He'd been stuck for 4 hours.

By the time I hauled up the Stokes litter and remaining climbing ropes, a handful of college volunteers and the firemen hiking up the back of the peak had reached us. We set up a vertical cliff evacuation and lowered Chuck in the litter to the waiting doc at the base. Chuck, however, refused the MD's examination figuring he'd take his chances at the hospital and save some money. When the doctor billed him anyway (just for showing up), Chuck refused to pay the bill explaining, "It takes two to make a contract"—and *he* hadn't been a party to any contract. The injury forever gimped his gait but saved him from the Vietnam draft.

From that moment on, I was Chuck's friend for life.

Love & Marriage

During my senior undergraduate year I'd moved off campus and shared a cabin with Hambone—a friend and fellow student—and his sister. When Chuck came to visit, she was there and we introduced them. Now, Chuck is a creative conversationalist, jumping from one subject to another, savoring irony and vocabulary. He's garrulous but guarded, never answering a direct personal question, rubbing his chin as if he had a beard—which he sometimes grows—mulling over suitable responses but always deflecting direct questions with some out-of-the-blue displacement remark. He'd never specify what he'd done or what he was planning. Though not transparent and always guarded, he was at least honest.

A beer or two, engrossing conversation, familiar territory and proper introductions never fail to grease the skids of romance. Chuck and Hambone's sister soon warmed up to each other and Hambone and I were left out of their loop. In due time Chuck upped the ante in a way that still amazes us, drawing on all the sexual revolution's ammunition—humanistic psychology, encounter group techniques, sensitivity training, etc. He drew the conversation around to honesty, social facades and the hollowness of conventional mores declaring that, "People ought to be able to say what they mean regardless of the consequences, and others ought to be able to respond in kind", or some such sophism.

When Hambone's sister took the bait, Chuck dropped the bombshell: "I want to have sex with you." Hambone and I froze, trying to become one with the upholstery. You'd have thought our presence would inhibit them, but no; the sister fixed her eye on him and off they went into her bedroom for the rest of the day.

Still, though Chuck had a certain way with women, he was too much of a crank to connect too often and never had a long-term or live-in relationship; and like an old prospector (a profession he pursued intermittently), never married. While most folk's idea of romance might include champagne, round beds and fruit-flavored lubricants, Chuck's revolved around cheap beer, a 3/8" closed cell ensolite pad, organic p-nut butter and sardine oil.

He'd invited a gal nicknamed Latch on a three-day outing to float Salt River Canyon with him on his military surplus raft—Chuck's idea of a perfect date, except that he invited me along as kayak support. The first day was hot and Latch was a free spir-it—vaguely Mediterranean and Rubenesque, reminiscent of a young Bette Midler with a Greek nose. Off came her bathing suit top, the better to catch the sun's rays. Except that she'd forgotten sunscreen.

"No problem," Chuck told her as he opened up a can of sardines. "Sardine oil is just as good."

Latch didn't question Chuck's wisdom; she was ready to go along for the ride. "Would you rub it on my back?" She asked.

I turned away and paddled ahead. The fetid aroma of sar-dine oil on a half-naked and sweaty, the-hell-with-dignity prospect, with Chuck's hands freely exploring the territory was more than I could stomach at that moment. Something was brewing that I wanted no part of.

That night I slept under the stars…as far away from Chuck and Latch as possible. But the next morning I couldn't help my-self, "Catch any fish?" I asked when Latch was off doing her toi-let. Chuck just snorted and gave me his signature sideways smirk.

Sometimes he'd go to bars to try to hook up. But he was par-ticular. Once, at a local pool and beer joint, we met a couple of loose floosies and teamed up for a game of 8-ball doubles. Prospects were looking good when, at 8 pm sharp, Chuck an-nounced he had to go to his truck to listen to Howard Ruff's gold report. The gal who had her eye on him had figured this was his subtle way of suggesting a joint exit and followed him out. Once inside the truck Chuck turned on his radio and attempted to lis-ten intently while the redhead chattered mindlessly and snuggled up to him. She wasn't interested in Ruff's insights. But Chuck was, and when he missed that day's gold closing price he told her to shut up and get out.

Another time, he was introduced to an attractive off-duty Tongass National Forest rangerette, Ketchikan District, Alaska, at a friend's house. Passing time soon became making time. Since he'd been considering kayaking Alaska's Inside Passage, he asked

her from which direction the prevailing winds blew. She responded that she hadn't noticed. All of a sudden, Chuck visibly lost
interest and left. Puzzled—they'd already locked eyeballs and
were sniffing each other like dogs—I asked why he walked away
from pay dirt.

"She's unobservant," he tersely declared with not a little contempt for her, her competence, the Forest Service, the question,
and even me—for prying.

Real Men

The Last Frontier. Alaska attracts a certain sort of end-of-
the-road misfit, socially inept and vulnerable, outgoing but quick
to take offense, bombastic yet shy and given to disjointed conver-
sational spurts and lapses reminiscent of communication on
time-delayed satellite radios complete with bad reception and
static. All are eccentric to a fault but faultlessly self-reliant—
sometimes perseveratingly so. To a special sort of woman, these
are MEN, *real* men—never mind the smell of dirty socks, sweaty
armpits, soiled sheets, dog, fish and diesel fuel that forms an all-
too-penetrable barrier around them.

In 1973 Chuck packed his van with a month's supply of p-
nut butter and headed for Alaska where he hoped to strike it rich
with a job—any job—on the proposed oil pipeline. Unable to
sign on with the Alyeska Consortium, he joined the commercial
crab fishing fleet for a stint in the frigid waters of the Gulf of
Alaska, arguably the world's most hazardous job, though potentially an extremely profitable one. He survived one very lucrative
season—his skipper had landed a record haul and the crew
shared in the take.

The following year he hired on to the pipeline with its generous pay scale, further inflated by Alaska's premium wage rate, a
consequence of having to import all necessities from the lower
48. In spite of living in a tent out in the bush and clearing taiga

with an axe (he thought a chainsaw unsportsmanlike) like some modern-day Gulag zek, Chuck hungered for some *real* adventure.

By this time Chuck, along with the likes of Rob Lesser and Walt Blackadar— men whose definition of the possible was making the impossible obsolete—had become a world-class kayaker in a sport so new that virtually anyone who sat in a kayak became an instant pioneer.

In the 1950's fiberglass technology had been adapted to the construction of kayaks, a bone or stick frame-and-skin Inuit hunting craft that is more prosthesis than boat. Instead of being occupied, a kayak is more accurately grafted onto the lower limbs of the operator, allowing extreme gymnastic flexibility, including the famous Eskimo Roll, where the kayaker can roll upside down and right himself at will—even without the aid of a paddle. But becoming a mermaid is tough: anyone can sit in a canoe, but the first time in a whitewater kayak lands most people in the water— even when it's dead flat.

At first, fiberglass whitewater kayaks sallied no further than slalom competitions in small European rivers. By the 1960's a few of the new kayaks had found their way west of the Mississippi, where BIG rivers with BIG gradients drained fathoms of snow pack off the Rocky Mountains creating gigantic rapids with waves sometimes exceeding 20 feet in height with crowning, cross-firing cockscombs of 10 feet or more—such as Hermit Rapid on the Colorado River—or cavernous weirs (frothy, bottomless reversals without exit) that can swallow a Greyhound bus —such as the one in Crystal Rapid, also on the Colorado River. Few kayakers attempted such fare, and those that did followed the white-knuckle strategy of avoiding every hydraulic or stationary obstacle.

In the late 1960's US, whitewater kayaks were still about as common as drive-through liquor stores in Utah. Chuck and I had discovered the nimble water striders separately, and shared many of the idiosyncrasies of the self-taught—especially manic obsession and wild speculation, coupled with excessive caution *and* reckless abandon. Neither one of us had mastered the Eskimo roll on our own. Someone—in my case, an English Outward Bound instructor—had to work the moves out for us in a pool.

By the spring of 1970, I'd built one Czech-designed slalom model from scratch, but had totaled two German kayaks in the rapids of Grand Canyon. I was frustrated and ready for a new approach. I'd become so risk averse that I focused on skirting rapids instead of running them. When unavoidable, my only recourse was to "Major Powell" through, windmilling hard and straight, and hoping to God to break through to the other side.

Meanwhile, together and separately, Chuck, Lesser and Blackadar were shattering existing barriers and were going—on purpose—where no one had ever been *on purpose* on Idaho, Alaskan and Canadian rivers. Instead of approaching a rapid as an obstacle course with the obstacles to be avoided at any cost, these water striders saw whitewater as a throbbing stage upon which to choreograph a ballet. They would drop into a rapid sometimes without paddling, backwards or even upside down, and then react, executing incredible and magnificent maneuvers—side surfs, multiple rolls, upright enders, pirouettes, bow-over-stern cartwheels—at whatever the river served up, in hydraulic flows at times exceeding 50,000 cubic feet per second.

Chuck on the Santa Maria River in Mexico

Somewhat surprisingly, Chuck never displayed a competitive streak—always focusing on his own objectives, oblivious to other's concerns or reactions—except when he heard that Walt Blackadar was organizing an expedition to nab the first descent of the Rio Grijalva through Sumidero Canyon in Mexico. So, on the spur of the moment, he recruited two companions and beat Blackadar to the punch.

Apurimac

Flush with Alaska pipeline and fishing funds, Chuck was jonesing for some *real* adventure. In 1975 he was invited to join a kayak expedition led by J. Calvin Giddings down the Apurimac River, *the* true headwaters of the Amazon, and a river so isolated and with a gradient so steep it had never been properly mapped much less navigated by a living human being. The Apurimac is the longest tributary—and hence considered the source—of the Amazon River. It is forbidding due to the extreme ferocity of its cataracts, and also due to the fact that in many places along its course climbing out of its canyon or going back upstream would be impossible. Thus, the discovery by Giddings and his companions of a scenic forty or fifty foot waterfall on the unexplored sections could well have been a death sentence.

J. Calvin Giddings, distinguished professor of chemistry at the University of Utah, president of the American Whitewater Affiliation and leader of the Amazon Headwaters Expedition, counted himself lucky to have Chuck along on the Apurimac. Chuck had just been written up in *Mariah* magazine, precursor to *Outside* magazine, not for his wave-parting exploits, but for his innovative menu on a trip down the Colorado River in Grand Canyon.

Chuck had heard that strapped inner-city senior citizens in New York City were resorting to subsisting on pet food for its value-to-volume efficiency, so he packed a month's supply of Gaines Burgers for the river trip. When they turned out to taste like lard-laced sawdust with just a hint of offal, he tried cooking them. Though still inedible, he nonetheless ate them. To his grumbling teammate, a redhead with a limp whom he'd enlisted during a night of excess at the Red Dog Saloon in Fairbanks, he declared that if she didn't like the way things had turned out, he'd "buy her out!"—never mind the thousand foot walls that made the river their only exit strategy.

Giddings' expedition started out on the wrong foot with one of its strongest members dropping out at the last minute. Out of the five remaining kayakers—one an MD—Chuck was by far the strongest and most skilled. But he didn't take orders well. They survived by the skin of their teeth—and not just because of the river's challenges. The tiny, narrow kayaks were overloaded with a month's supply of food, camping gear and emergency supplies stuffed fore and aft. Chuck described Giddings as a "pompous, micro-managing tight-ass"; but then, that was coming from Chuck, a willful misfit and self-described contrarian. The rest of the team's members—all headstrong personalities—danced to their own loony tunes and coalesced as seamlessly as the philosophers in the Monty Python sketch, The Philosophers' Football Match, on psychedelics. Twenty-two years later and facing his own imminent death, Giddings finally published his account of the expedition in *Demon River Apurimac*, University of Utah Press, 1996.

After the Apurimac, SOBEK, the international whitewater adventure guide, hired Chuck and "Rocket", another hairball kayaker, as kayak safety support for their rafts on an exploratory first descent of the Baker River in Patagonian Chile. Almost immediately after launching, both rafts got sucked into perdition and disappeared, never to be found again, their four boatmen miraculously surviving and making it to shore miles downstream but forced into a long overland survival trek in the southern Andes. Chuck and Rocket soldiered on nabbing the first descent. Not quite content (and since he was in the neighborhood), Chuck then tackled the infamous Terminator section of the Futaleafu River and the second descent of the Bio Bio River.

Once he ran out of money, he returned to Alaska and rejoined the pipeline consortium as a welding inspector's assistant. But Chuck hadn't yet learned to compromise and, when urine tests (to test for drug use) were later required for a range of positions, he refused to participate. Although his principles seriously hindered his prospects for advancement, they didn't dent his ability to make money. Bob Barfoot, a friend and fellow worker, recalls that union scale—during the '80's—for an unskilled laborer, was about $30/hour, with time-and-a-half after 8 and 40 hours and double-time on Sunday. Those were 12-hour days, so on a week they grossed about $420/weekday, $540/Saturday and $720/Sunday. A total week's gross came to about $3,360. A typical Spring/Summer working season of 7 months grossed nearly $100,000. And he had no expenses.

Pipeline workers lived in company "man camps" with all food and living quarters provided—either tents or trailers—and so, didn't get much of a chance to spend money, usually squirreling the loot away for travel or early retirement. What they did spend was usually on beer at bars while recounting bear stories. But Chuck was especially frugal. Barfoot recounts one instance when, nearly out of gas at a closed filling station on the Henderson Highway, it dawned on him that the extra-long hoses—for filling the big rigs along Valdez highways—and lying in big loops, would retain a substantial residue. Sure enough...gasoline. He drained all six into his pickup and drove to another, open station to fill'er up. Chuck only put in a quarter-of-a-tank, which he calculated would last him for another week.

After a few years of $100k earnings, he decided to settle down in Fairbanks and build himself a house. Yet he mostly wintered in Arizona staying at friends' homes (inevitably overstaying his welcome), camping out, overnighting in highway rest areas and such but never paying rent.

The Deliverance Boys

The first time I was exposed to the avant garde, innovative kayaking style practiced by Blackadar and Lesser was with Chuck on the Verde River in full, rampaging flood. In 1976 a series of Pacific storm fronts invaded Arizona and for the following four years laid siege to its watersheds. The Verde, a stream whose normal flow averaged 600 cubic feet per second (cfs), soon ballooned into a 25,000 cfs out-of-control, channel-shifting, trailer park-threatening, cottonwood-uprooting anaconda. As soon as he found out, Chuck showed up at my door with his kayak and Socratic-dialogued me into running it.

For our proposed week-long descent of the Verde River through the Mazatzal wilderness, Chuck and I would paddle kayaks. For our other two companions, Chuck brought along an army surplus raft that was state of the art when the 2nd Marine Division stormed the beaches at Tarawa in 1943. Made from real rubber, it was heavy, floppy, and puncture prone; pockmarked with patches upon patches. To pilot the 350-lb. state-of-the-trash inflatable he'd brought along Haines, a fast-talking Phoenix-area commercial property realtor. Garbed in an excruciatingly brief purple Speedo with a matching, oversized, purple engineer's cap splotched with giant white polka dots, Haines did not immediately impress.

Chuck had met him as a Grand Canyon customer who'd decided he had more in common with Chuck than with the other clients, and so had joined the exiled boatman in the luggage raft. Interminably loquacious, Haine's BS flowed like blank hip-hop verse—some of it undoubtedly true. But his whoppers were so big, and told with such a straight face, he could short-circuit a polygraph just by saying, "Trust me." Though he'd never piloted a whitewater raft, he didn't lack confidence.

To run swamp—that is, help launch the raft, bail it, beach it, secure it, load and unload it, and generally submit unquestioningly to the boatman's bidding—I'd brought along Joyce, a gullible high school football star who was dating my sister. Joyce would later end up wholesaling chicken parts, finding Jesus, and marrying my sister—not all as a result of multiple contusions. That day, at the river's edge assembling our kit, he thought we were all gambling with empty purses. Later he confided that, save for knowing me, he'd have folded his hand right then and there.

On the banks of the Beasley Flats put-in, our adrenaline-fueled banter was only slightly tempered by introductions, handshakes, and the business at hand: assembling the raft, packing gear, and girding for combat. Chuck and I paddled Lettman Mark-series fiberglass slalom kayaks imported from Germany. We wore Bell multi-purpose helmets and kapok Mae West life jackets over half-inch-thick, full-body wet suits so constricting, that every maneuver was like mixing concrete with a hoe.

Except for the occasional floating tree, and Chuck's insistence that we "have fun" dropping into and surfing reversals, our first half-day was uneventful—until we arrived at "The Falls." Not an exceedingly difficult run—it has a steep and narrow, but straight slot at far right—the approach to The Falls is complicated by a gnarly rapid immediately upstream: the "Pre-Falls". Blow the run above, and disaster awaited below.

Scouting both rapids from a respectable distance upstream on the right bank, we discovered that the river, at this water level, had changed. Unable to contain the volume of water in its banks, the Verde had cut a new channel on the right, creating two channels divided by an island. However, that new channel was useless. Clogged with rocks and obstructed by strainers, it was impassable.

To make things worse, there was no way to row the raft left from our scouting vantage point to avoid the new channel, then right for the run through the pre-Falls rapid, and then even farther right to catch a tiny eddy in order to set up for The Falls' slot. So we decided to line and portage along the verges of the new right-hand channel—a task marginally superior to lugging a loaded palanquin over greasy dragon's teeth. It was then that we first saw the Deliverance Boys upstream on the opposite bank.

There were four of them, in two canoes, with cowboy hats—about all we could make out at that distance, but enough to trigger warning alarms. It wasn't just the cowboy hats, or the cheap, horse-collar PFDs around their necks. Or the orange crates filled with tin cans, loose produce, and loaves of white bread. Or even the battered canoes, victims no doubt of some municipal park's rental inventory upgrade. No, it was the high-top Keds and .44 caliber six-shooters holstered high on their belts, Filipino-style, just below the floating rib that bespoke a tale. This river, now flooded to 40-times its normal size, could grind up and make sausage out of this crew.

Shouting, waving, and gesturing for them to stop finally got their attention. They pulled over. Although the opposite bank was steep, it was safe and passable for a carry past both rapids. The right shore—where we were—though gentler, dead-ended in a cliff below The Falls' downstream turbulence and upwellings—a nearly impossible portage.

Wrestling our hippo over the river edge's obstacles, we paid the canoers no more attention. Our plan was to plop the raft into the tiny eddy above The Falls and then run the slot. After helping to line the raft, Chuck and I went back to our kayaks to run the pre-Falls rapid—luckily, without a hitch. We caught the eddy where the raft was parked and decided Chuck would run The Fall's slot first—to provide rescue for the raft in case of a mishap. Haines nearly panicked. This was his first serious run piloting a raft. A courage pep-talk from Chuck steeled him.

Perfect runs all around. Regrouping at the outwash below The Falls, we met up with the canoers as they were completing their portage. We got a good look at them and their outfit—incongruous spic-and-span stuff mixed with navy surplus duffel bags, orange crates, guns and all.

"Nice canoes...where you from? How far you goin'? Have you run this river before?" It was a one-way conversation. Like a dog staring at a ceiling fan, the canoers didn't know what to make of us.

Who were we to question their vision? Not that we were much of an improvement. After all, none of us was any wiser than the proverbial blind men figuring out an elephant. Their approach was just a bit more "traditional" than our avant-garde, seat-of-the-pants approach. We exchanged pleasantries and wished them well.

"Thanks...OK," they mustered. We left it at that and said we hoped to see them downstream—shaking our heads in disbelief.

Not ten minutes later we noticed an apple and an orange floating by. Before we could snag them, an upside-down canoe followed by a cowboy-hatted head gasping for breath appeared, surrounded by all sorts of stuff too numerous to notice individually. The Deliverance Boys had ended their portage prematurely among the upwellings and eddies below The Falls. Turbulent water had grappled one of their canoes.

While Haines and Joyce towed the canoe and a totally-out-of-it hanger-on to shore, Chuck and I gathered as much of the floating gear as we could muster. Back on land, with the other canoe, its occupants, and the fourth canoer—now walking, having reached shore safely—we helped them regroup. They were shaken and stirred but seemed OK. After a decent interval filled with reassuring banter, it was time for us to part. Still—and against Chuck's categorical imperative never to patronize anyone's judgement—we offered advice:

"There's a serious rapid up ahead. The entire river crashes into the right bank creating a tubular wave that bites back on itself, tunnels left and will swallow a boat whole. You can cheat it on the left. Trouble is, the recon is on the right and there's no place to land on the left. If you stop on the right to recon it, you'll never make it left to cheat it."

At Voodoo, the above-mentioned rapid, we stopped to recon on the right. While discussing our strategy, we caught a glimpse of the canoers half-a-mile upstream, approaching left. Totally engrossed in our deliberations, the canoers became a footnote in our minds. It was the last we saw of them.

The 'normal' run was to enter the rapid on the left and paddle like hell leftward fighting the current's draw to the right—an inelegant, desperate thrash full of rocks and flooded trees in shallowing water: the raft's route. At the prospect, Haines shook like a dog shittin' apricot pits. Chuck gave him another courage peptalk and off he went, executing a perfect run.

For the kayaks however, Chuck proposed going right down the middle of the entry tongue where all the flow channeled (without so much as a single paddle stroke), hitting the curler wave dead-on sideways and, just at the point of contact, throwing a paddle brace into its gut and surfing the tunnel to its exit.

We'd talked about such theoretically possible maneuvers; but they required such precision, strength, agility and timing in the midst of such gut-wrenching danger that *I* wasn't going to be the guinea pig. Chuck just said, "Watch me", and off he went, pulling the run with Cirque du Soleil precision. Then it was my turn. What followed wasn't pretty.

With no excuse to back off, full of apprehension and an adrenaline surge that forced me to piss, shit and gag with nausea all at the same time, I dropped into my cockpit, sealed my spray skirt, locked my feet and hips, strapped my helmet, clutched my paddle and pushed the kayak off the bank. With one stroke I was sideways to the current and positioned perfectly parallel to the curler wave at the bottom. All I had to do was wait, keep my position and throw a perfectly aimed, timed and pressured brace into that wave when I hit it. Meanwhile, refraining from paddling in the rapid felt unnatural, counter-intuitive and absolutely wrong.

When I hit the curler my aim and timing were perfect but my commitment vastly underestimated the strength of the wave. It grabbed my paddle and Maytagged me into a giant, combination spin-and-rinse cycle halfway to hell that nearly dislocated my shoulder and dislocated me from my kayak and my paddle. A hundred yards downriver, Chuck helped me to shore and recovered my boat and paddle. "Nice run", was all he said.

It was a perfect time to be on the river. Equinoctial temperatures and torrents of water had transformed the desert into a garden, engorging succulents, and rendering sepia hard pans sensual with velvety green grass shoots. The smell of rain intoxicated and energized. Warm days followed chilly nights so full of stars that they turned the skies into bio-luminescent seas. Convivial campfires, fueled with tamarisk, ironwood, cheap Mexican weed and even cheaper Chianti, rendered us both pensive and eloquent, egging us into ever-more unrestrained mendacity.

Our last night on the river turned particularly festive. Joyce pulled out a bottle of rum to accompany dinner. We'd all brought along our own provisions. While Haines relied on cans of Dinty Moore stew, and I supplied Joyce and myself with dehydrated Mountain House meals, Chuck—who would later gain notoriety in *Mariah* magazine, precursor to *Outside* magazine, for eating dog food on an expedition—hit new lows in culinary creativity with the fewest funds. He victualed himself with a disposable, expanding aluminum foil frying pan of Jiffy-Pop popcorn kernels for his first night out. For the remainder of the days, he subsisted on onions, potatoes, and a can of butter-flavored Crisco, which he'd fry up in the now-empty, thoroughly mangled, Jiffy-Pop fry pan.

And then everything changed. Like the buzz of an approaching mosquito, Chuck suddenly sensed the hum of a helicopter so far away it wasn't visible. "It's coming here," he declared.

"Yeah...right!" we all responded, scanning the skies for a sign. Though helicopters didn't frequent the Mazatzal wilderness, the Mexican weed made anything possible.

To call Chuck paranoid is to call Sisyphus conscientious (or the USS Enterprise a boat, or Balmoral Castle a summer cottage). He eschewed credit cards, relying on cash or gold for all purchases. When asked for ID or personal information by a merchant, he'd grumble "What's wrong with an anonymous cash transaction?" If pressed, he was out of there.

Once, when a grocery store clerk asked if he had a loyalty discount card, he responded with, "Hitler would have loved to keep track of who was buying kosher food." He didn't receive mail at home, a log cabin in Alaska built on skids—so he could move it quickly (just "in case")—relying on friends' PO boxes, with the added security of a separate alias for each address. No public utilities penetrated his cabin.

Chuck's paranoia girdled the globe and once bent back and bit him in the butt. When (much later) he was planning a river trip in Tanzania, the heavily discounted price of a round-the-world airline ticket lured him in. Perhaps target-fixated—like a moth drawn to a fire—he routed himself through Moscow during the Brezhnev era. At the Intourist hotel, he refused to hand over his passport to the then-ubiquitous hotel floor monitors, explaining that it was illegal to surrender an American passport and, anyway, he was only going out for a walk. Before he could further elaborate his "nyet," two beefy men in ill-fitting suits grabbed him by the elbows and escorted him out.

I don't know how long he remained in KGB custody (he wouldn't say), but he left Russia as soon as he was allowed.

In a few minutes the chopper was visible. It was headed straight for our campsite. Chuck's paranoia had turned to prescience and become contagious. What could they possibly want from us? We scrambled to bury the pot and hide the liquor (Joyce was under age), and cover our nakedness (an eccentricity indulged in by all but Joyce). But it wasn't enough to still the fear and angst that by now shook us mercilessly and wouldn't let go. Unable to just sit and wait, we tidied up camp.

The chopper landed on a hill behind us, about 100 feet away. Out jumped a Department of Public Service officer in full storm trooper regalia, and walked over to our kayaks. "Those your canoes?" he asked.

Like a scene out of a Cheech and Chong sketch, Chuck blurted "No" and I said "Yes." The cop looked at us suspiciously. We clarified that they were kayaks, not canoes; but that yes, they were ours.

"But they're green and red," the officer declared, seeking confirmation in an attempt to clarify any misunderstanding.

"Well, not actually," I said, pointing out that my kayak was orange and Chuck's lacked gel-coat, rendering it translucent, albeit vaguely greenish. The cop was losing his patience.

Finally he said they had a report of four overdue canoeists in two canoes, one red and one green. With our communication finally cleared up, the tension eased, and we told him about the Deliverance Boys, where we last saw them, and our assessment of them. He thanked us and left. A bit later, soon after nightfall, we heard the helicopter retracing its flight path and wondered what had transpired.

The following day a much bigger helicopter awoke us at dawn, passing right over on its way upstream. Haines, a National Guard pilot, identified it. Based on the model he speculated that one or more of the Deliverance Boys had gone on to his reckoning.

The Verde River ends its unconstrained run at Horseshoe Reservoir, seven miles of impoundment above Horseshoe Dam. We took turns rowing the raft across the lake and spoke hardly at all. As we neared the take-out, the big chopper passed back over us and landed next to the dam. Meanwhile, a Game and Fish Department skiff approached us. The ranger, ignorant of our part in the unfolding drama, brought us up to date—without details—on the canoers' rescue. He advised us not to approach the goings-on on shore. Ambulances awaited—but with no sirens blaring. We stayed away, busy loading our shuttle vehicle and hesitant to confront the vagaries of fate any closer.

The next day's newspaper carried all the details, many of them garbled, as newspapers are wont to do. But they got the basics right: One canoer had abandoned the trip and walked out to civilization safely, another had broken a leg, and a third had nearly died from exposure. The fourth had drowned. We were not mentioned—a fact that relieved Chuck immensely.

El Niño Blesses the Verde

During the winter of 1979-1980 the Gulf of Alaska turbo-charged the Pacific fronts invading Arizona. A continuous and terrible keening and weeping of the firmaments pummeled the Mogollon Rim. The Verde River surged to over 100,000 cfs and kept rising. Its waters lapped highway bridges, threatening to sweep them out. Roads were closed. Communities evacuated. Trailer parks annihilated, with double-wides floating downstream like icebergs. Niagara, Iguazu, Victoria...none held a candle to the torrent over silted-up Sullivan Dam, at the Verde's source—at the time invisible for the sheer volume and force of the water, itself also nearly invisible for the blinding drisk enveloping everything.

"Let's run the Verde right from its source..." declared Chuck.

"...all the way to its confluence with the Salt River," I finished, adding, "We'll get Kathy (my girlfriend) to run shuttle for us."

"Hmm..." he responded noncommittally—a sign he had something up his sleeve, something he was reluctant to disclose just then.

We immediately began preparations, starting with a shuttle arrangement. I'd just acquired a used, first-generation, roto-molded (aka, "Tupperware") kayak made by Holloform. Virtually indestructible and requiring no emergency repair kit, it was—in that respect—incomparably superior to fiberglass boats.

Chuck, however, stuck to his tried-and-true, thoroughly patched Lettman Mark IV and carried fiberglass resin, accelerator and cloth, along with the tools for repair. We both used one piece, over-sized, then-state-of-the-art, flat, Iliad paddles. We'd have to go light, 'dirt bagging' it—fires for cooking, plastic sheets for shelter, and minimal clothing and gear. Chuck wouldn't even take a sleeping bag, planning to sleep in his wet suit, bundled in all his additional clothing over buried hot coals, an example he insisted I follow (to no avail). And, finally, food: p-nut butter, top-ramen, and Vienna sausages for me; peanut butter, tortillas and canned beans for Chuck—a strategy that, unlike mine, required no cooking pot.

It was when planning how much food to take (based on how long we'd be out) that Chuck revealed his cards. He declared that we were running only to Horseshoe Dam, the Verde's upper, free-flowing section. He had no intention of running on down to Bartlett Dam, much less to the Verde's confluence with the Salt. And he brooked no opposition. Moreover, he was bound and determined to keep me from going beyond Horseshoe Dam, his position vaguely based on the "buddy principle", the idea that, for safety reasons, wilderness outings ought never to be undertaken alone.

Though I've never met anyone as willfully obstinate and subtly manipulative as Chuck, he challenged my premises, and I rather enjoyed matching wits with him. Since Kathy had agreed to pick us up—and since she was *my* girlfriend—I didn't argue about how far we'd go. After all, if he chose to leave at Horseshoe Dam, that was his business—even though Horseshoe Dam was only accessible over a long, traffic-free dirt road, over which he'd have a difficult time hitchhiking out with a kayak.

The Verde River is formed by the junction of Big Chino Wash and Williamson Valley Wash just above Sullivan Dam, but it gets most of its water from Oak Creek, which drains the San Francisco Peaks—at 12,637 feet, Arizona's highest point. It runs free for 125 miles to Horseshoe Dam and then another 45 miles to the Salt River, including 12 miles through Bartlett Reservoir for a total length of 170 miles.

Sullivan Dam, built in 1938 and anchored in 150-foot-deep Sullivan Canyon, has been fully silted up for many years. The canyon is sculpted from irregular columnar basalt—perfectly vertical—and has become a popular northern Arizona rock climbing area accessible only via rappelling—except for one detrital fan 0.1-mile downstream from the dam, the result of a pipeline-crossing excavation.

Although spurning the lower 45 miles of the Verde, Chuck didn't want to miss the initial 0.1-mile of inaccessible river. "Bad form," he quietly averred. So he finagled an assistant into belay duty to help him lower his fully loaded kayak—with two ropes—into the maelstrom below the dam while, at the same time, rappelling down next to the boat, guiding it, and, finally, maneuvering his entry into the cockpit—an impossible feat.

But Chuck was a visionary. He scoped out a tiny cleft on the north bank that, at much lower water levels, would have held an eddy. But under these extreme conditions, it instead impounded an upwelling pillow of recirculating water, surging unpredictably, sometimes up to 3 feet, but at least moving neither upstream nor downstream. Though still 0.05-of-a-mile short of the dam, it was his best bet. As I scrambled down the pipeline easement on the opposite bank I stopped to watch Chuck's dramatic entry.

"Make sure you get a picture of this!" he shouted, posing in mid-air, paddle in one hand, rap line in the other, with a big grin on his face, looking like Slim Pickens headed for perdition in *Dr. Strangelove.*

By the time I was ready to launch, Chuck had sealed himself to his kayak, cut the tethering ropes with the knife he always kept in a hand-sewn pocket on the side of his Mae West life jacket, and ferried over to me to coordinate our strategy.

For the first 1.8 miles, the river drops an astounding 66 feet per mile. We'd heard that not far below the dam lay a major rapid, nicknamed "Little Lava", which drops at the rate of 100 feet per mile. But that name had been given at high-normal water levels of perhaps 5,000-10,000 cfs (measured farther downstream). It was anyone's guess what "Little Lava" might look like at anything over 50,000 cfs (again, measured downstream).

Before launching we'd walked the canyon's rim for a short distance hoping to glimpse the territory ahead, but didn't spot anything of note. With the water running this fast, shoreline eddies were rare as arugula in Arkansas. Once launched on the current, it might be nearly impossible to land. Worse, major rapids tended toward steepness, and dropped so fast that kayak-level scouting meant running blind.

Bob Williams, author of *A Floater's Guide to the Verde River*, describes the Verde's first mile-and-a-half in the following way:

> "...it was inconceivable to me that the Verde's origin canyon could ever be floated at <u>any time</u> in <u>any way</u> above mile 1.3— inconceivable period...! Huge boils; meat grinder holes; angular and sharp boulders unshaven by such waters; squirrelly, confused and horrific currents; trees; nearly impossible scouting and portaging footing; difficult rescue and the 100-feet-per-one-mile drop all made this maelstrom very hazardous territory."

We were in for a special treat. Chuck would lead. I would follow 50 feet behind. We set off.

Sure enough, Little Lava's deafening roar soon enveloped us. Yet the horizon revealed nothing but a broken horizontal line, with not a plume of water or blinding mist visible beyond. It looked like the edge of the world. And, sure enough, there were no eddies to catch.

Chuck disappeared over the lip. I followed. To our enormous relief, there were no sudden, waterfall drops—the rapid descended at an even, albeit steep angle. But it was unexpectedly long and complex, requiring instant reaction and technique, and

brooking no time for strategy, or aiming for position. Miraculously, neither of us rolled or swam.

Once past 2-mile-long Little Lava, the river's gradient eased
to 10-20 feet-per-mile, but its speed didn't. The bullet-train current carried us past Perkinsville in no time. Nevertheless, we
camped early. It had been an exhilarating day.

The following morning we slept in. Chuck, having spent a
miserable winter's night without a sleeping bag, dawdled in bed
(such as it was). But when he finally arose, he dawdled even more
—ambling about, rearranging his pittance of stuff, fiddling with
the fire, and mumbling. By 11am I suggested that we should get
going. But then he declared he had to repair his kayak. He
turned it over and examined—slowly—every inch of his boat,
then proceeded to go through the motions of repairing it.

However, I soon noticed there were no repairs to be made.
Chuck was up to something. Under my insistent interrogation he
finally admitted to willful delay, hoping we'd use up our food and
I'd be forced to cut my trip short at Horseshoe Dam—as he'd
been insisting right from the start. I called his bluff with my own
bluff, and threatened to leave ASAP. By the time I was ready to
launch, he was too.

Chuck's campsite on the Verde River in Arizona

The river had lowered some, but it was still on fast forward. Riding through Clarkdale, the first town of note, we were shocked by the devastation. Along the entire Verde Valley stretch, humble homesteads, single-wide toeholds, and double-wide dreams close to the banks had become nightmares—most probably uninsured for the owners' modest means.

The extremely high water levels had planed most all the rapids, empirically averaging the river's gradient, and obliterating sharp drops. Still, it was hard to imagine "The Falls" and "Pre-Falls", downstream of Beasley Flats, disappearing. Yet that was nearly the case. We ran both without scouting.

Late on our second day out, another storm cell darkened the skies and threatened us with a downpour. So we decided to call it a day at the Verde Hot Springs—an ideal bivouac under the conditions, especially for Chuck who spent most of the night in the hot springs out of the rain. The next morning dawned clear, bright, and cold. Chuck emerged from the stone shelter covering the hot pool complaining that he felt like a prune.

We were making such good time on the super-charged current that by now it was obvious we'd reach Horseshoe Dam by mid-day on the third day, foiling whatever remnants of Chuck's delaying plot he was still holding in reserve.

At the dam's take-out point we both made one last appeal to convince each other of his point of view—again, to no avail. I left him sitting by his kayak, a forlorn figure in the endless Sonoran desert—now blooming in the early spring rains—looking down the road, vigilant for any improbable potential ride, determined to have his way, come what may.

Meanwhile, I was having my own way dragging my Tupperware boat the half-mile around the dam, to re-launch at its base. Turning the dam's corner I was met by an eerie silence that didn't fully register until I was near streambed level. Then it struck me, and I confirmed it: Horseshoe Dam was releasing *no* water.

How could that be? The biggest floods in years and…*no water*? After the trip I checked the Salt River Project (SRP) gauge measurements near the dam's outflow. They reported, I think, 62 cfs—natural leakage from the structure. Apparently, SRP, relying on its meteorological forecasts predicting a dry spell, was maximizing its storage capacity. Downstream Bartlett Reservoir, one of the state's premier outdoor recreation areas, is usually kept full; Horseshoe Reservoir, its homely next-door neighbor, is its spare tank, and it wasn't quite full.

I wasn't about to give up—or drag the loaded boat back uphill and an additional half-mile to the road-head, much less give Chuck some sort of schadenfreude satisfaction. It was only about 7 miles to Bartlett, with intermittent pools, *and* 62 cfs of flow, which—with a little luck, might be enhanced by ephemeral springs, inconsequential enduring run-off, and wishful thinking.

I launched upon a puddle, paddling and knuckling my way forward like a Victorian amputee on a roller-board begging for alms. My fatuous strategy soon paid off. Before long I was paddling happily in continuous water. But the day had taken its toll, my mileage was minimal, and I decided to camp on one of Bartlett's beautiful developed campsites.

The next day, after portaging Bartlett Dam, ditto: no water was being released. With 26 miles left to the Verde's confluence with the Salt River, I went for broke. But this time there was no waiting reservoir downstream, no noticeable dam leakage, and no standing water anywhere. Still, I persevered, dragging the old Holloform in a fruitless search for draft.

It was not to be. The stream bed was dry as bone and the rocky channel resembled a field of skulls. About 9 miles later and late in the day, I saw a house. I'd entered the outer verges of North Scottsdale. Swallowing my pride and girding my meager social skills, I approached the house and asked to use their phone. A couple of hours later Kathy was shuttling me back home to Prescott.

Chuck's attempt at begging a ride out of Horseshoe didn't pay off right away. Without so much as one vehicle passing by, he had to spend the night next to the dirt road. But the following day, after a succession of rides, he made it back to Prescott. When I related my experience to him, all he said was, "Hmm…"

Paranoia Is Not a Vice

Chuck was a thrifty pack rat. On a rafting trip down the Middle Fork of the Salmon, he'd run across an abandoned 1930's homestead with a rusty, 200 lb. cast iron wood burning stove—just the perfect central heating for his new home. So he cajoled his passengers into loading it up, floated it down the river, lovingly packed it into his VW and drove it to Alaska.

Chuck valued his privacy to a degree bordering on paranoia, a condition first noticed by his father when the boy was six-years old (and soundly ridiculed for it). On the other hand, his mother, the daughter of a judge, instilled in him a life-long vigilance for his constitutional rights—especially privacy. Additionally, although instinctively skeptical, Chuck was sympathetic to conspiracy theories—about as far as his capacity for empathy seemed to extend. His home reflected those values: no phone, no electric utility, no TV, no municipal garbage (Chuck *never, ever* discarded anything; he once grabbed an empty foil hot chocolate envelope from the fire declaring that, "it has other uses"; of course, none were named) and no piped water—a necessity he hauled in his pick-up, along with back-up heating oil, eschewing the bills associated with those conveniences. What's more, the house was built on skids, "just in case—so I can move it."

After his cancer had jumped the prostate into his bones and then broken out into other, softer tissues, he was put on radiation and chemotherapy treatments. This required multiple trips to the drugstore for pain medications. During one of our infrequent phone conversations he commented that he'd have to take a personal defense course. Confused, since he'd lost the use of his left arm and was as weak as a clam without a shell, I asked, "Huh?"

"Twenty Benjamins", he replied.

I still didn't get it. So, somewhat impatiently, he explained that thieves case pharmacies in order to mug old people exiting with expensive drugs. Apparently, considering that the street price for Oxycotin/Oxycodone was near $100 per pill, and that he usually carried $2,000 in gold or cash in his pockets, he was worried he'd get robbed. I didn't argue—never mind that no one would know what he was carrying, or that the prescription had been phoned in: Chuck couldn't be too safe. He always spoke in code or sign language when referring to his pain medication in public.

Or have too many aliases. When living out of his van he'd receive mail at my house addressed to Chuck La Queue. Short-sightedly, he at first didn't even tell me about the ruse, and so ended up losing all his mail when I returned it to the Post Office labeled "not at this address." Oddly, Chuck savored his junk mail, carefully reading even the most egregiously useless broad-sheet, discount coupon/ad combos, and candidates' election propaganda especially when addressed to one of his aliases. He was particularly enamored of one prank—lesson, really—for junk mail he disliked. If it included a "No postage necessary if mailed in the United States" envelope, he'd duct tape it to a cin-der block and send it off.

For Chuck, revealing his name was almost worse than under-going a colonoscopy. He was temperamentally incapable of ut-tering his name to a stranger, believing that normal, day-to-day intercourse should proceed anonymously. He'd give taxi drivers the name Chick Carter. Once, when feeling particularly generous at a small get-together, he offered to buy pizza for all. So he called Domino's, placed the order and gave the address. But when the voice at the other end of the line asked for his name Chuck parried the query with, "When will it be ready?"

"Quarter-to-two", answered Domino's, asking for his name again.

"That's it," he responded, "that's my name: Mr. Quarter-to-Two."

Mexico

Chuck's self-reliance was as close to a religion as he ever let on, and he was wont to proselytize—sometimes to extremes. We'd teamed up to climb Picacho del Diablo, Baja California's highest peak at 10,154 feet, a long, difficult and extremely isolated mountain requiring lots of water, technical mountain skills and a rugged vehicle for crossing the Salada del Diablo, a dry lake bed. We piled into my old VW microbus. After two days of dusty, hellish driving the van quit cold turkey on the third morning in the middle of nowhere. I opened the hood, looked under the chassis and walked around the vehicle murmuring to myself.

Now, I'm about as mechanically adept as Lucy Arnaz on an assembly line, so I asked Chuck to take a look and see what he thought—after all, he drove a VW microbus dating back to Hitler's bunker days and maintained it tolerably well. He looked up at the cloudless sky, the rocky road bed, our objective, and then fixed me his 'You know better than that' look, declaring that it was *my* vehicle and I should not only figure out what was wrong with it, but also be ready to fix it.

Needless to say, we argued endlessly while I went through the motions of diagnosing the problem for the remainder of the day...and through the night, until the following day when a rattle-trap Chevy with two Mexican vaqueros happened by and asked, "Que pasa?"

With my Cuban-inflected Spanish I explained the problem. The driver did a quick inspection, took out a roll of bailing wire and a nail file and said "el coile" was shot but he could fix it—which he did—until we could get a new one. Unfortunately, by now our window of opportunity for the climb had closed so we drove to a mechanic in Mexicali, got a new coil and drove on home. Chuck remained silent the entire way. He didn't need to explain himself—for him the ends never justify the means.

I should have learned my lesson, but I didn't. Sometimes—not often—Chuck's self-reliance would morph, like Dr. Jekyll's personality into Mr. Hyde's, and into a selfish sort of communitarianism, but only when testosterone got the best of him and his oxygenated blood drained to his masculine nether regions.

Before that year was out, we packed ropes, tents, ice axes, crampons and gear for a total of 110 lbs. each into giant backpacks to forge our mettle on the test-pieces of the Andes. We'd take a train from Nogales, climb central Mexico's volcanoes—Popocatepetl, Ixtaccihuatl and Orizaba (at 19,000' the highest point in Mexico)—on the way down to South America and then head further south on buses, trains and whatever rides we could muster—low-budget mountaineering at its best. Kathy Corr, a US Olympic Team javelin thrower whom I'd recently met and who had fallen for my line about the 'romance' of mountain climbing, had decided to join our team. She was built like the Hulk with the face of Penelope Cruz and kept crooning Roberta Flack love songs in my ear.

Trouble reared its ugly head right away. Chuck expected Kathy to share her charms with *him*, "after all, we're all in this together", he declared. He was adamant and there was no reasoning with him. But then, on Popocatepetl, Kathy—although competent in every respect—discovered she actually hated mountain climbing; while Chuck, who had sat Popo out due to lack of acclimatization, discovered on Ixta that he just couldn't acclimatize to high altitudes. I ended up climbing Orizaba by myself but by then, Kathy and Chuck were ready to call it quits.

Kathy took a plane home while Chuck and I stuck our thumbs out for Texas. Outside Veracruz we considered ourselves lucky when a rusty panel wagon, like a Black Maria, but pastel green, driven by two bearded gringos looking like meth-crazed

Jack Elams and going to Brownsville, picked us up. It was a ride we should have declined.

Chuck in the back of Bro & Bro's van

"Bro" and "Bro", identical twins, weighed in at about 300 lbs. each, some of it on display between the edge of their filthy, once-white T-shirts and their 2-inch thick leather belts with foot-long bayonets strapped to them. The bed of the panel wagon, where we were privileged to ride, was one giant mattress with soiled bedding, cheap pornography—including a vintage edition of *Hefty Mamas*—and intriguing unidentifiables best left unidentified.

Bro and Bro seemed nice enough until, from some hidden arsenal at his feet, Shotgun Bro started pelting road signs with baseball-sized rocks. In between signs he turned around and confided mischievously, "Target practice." When a Mexican on a burro appeared riding along the road, both Bros shouted, "Target! Target!" and let loose a barrage that made my testicles withdraw into their ischial cavities. Luckily, they missed the man. I'd never seen Chuck intimidated by another human being, much less show fear. We both wanted out but were just as afraid to ask. I was glad the Mexican government hadn't extended Second Amendment rights to American tourists.

Both Bros, by way of explanation I suppose, and perhaps, hoping to find some common ground with us, proceeded to revile Mexicans and, in the same breath, declared it was mealtime; so we stopped at a roadside café. I wasn't hungry. The Bros didn't speak a lick of Spanish and, before they got too far intimidating the waitress, which they were warming up to do, I offered to translate.

It was a welcome time out. In between menu translations and orders I slipped in a quick explanation of the situation to the waitress, as she was becoming visibly uncomfortable. When it came, the Bros inhaled their food and left without paying. Chuck and I picked up the tab. The Bros ridiculed us for our gullibility and hustled us into the wagon.

Finally, just before the border, Chuck said he was carrying contraband. Would the Bros let us out so we could walk across and not imperil their border crossing? They let us out, thanked us for our thoughtfulness and promised to be friends for life. We never saw them again. Chuck and I split company; he thinking a better hitching strategy was to go north on a major road, then west; myself, taking my chances on rural roads along the border directly to El Paso.

Dancing Outside the Box

As a rock climber, Chuck was never on the cutting edge, but his style was world class. The ultimate ideal in rock climbing, man vs. a rock face, is to pit oneself against the challenge with as few aids as possible. John Bachar, the not-long-ago deceased master of the sport who died free-soloing, climbed the big walls of Yosemite without a rope, at degrees of difficulty akin to climbing sheet rock on the edges of glued-on dimes—with only his shoes, shorts, gymnastic chalk and *cojones* to match his skill, confidence and ego. Chuck, while seldom eschewing the rope, went him one better—he'd climb naked whenever the opportunity presented itself.

Chuck climbing outside the box in Mexico

He was always physically uninhibited, dancing while talking, scissoring arms and legs, stretching limbs or standing one-legged like a Dinka, with a foot nestled in the crook of his knee—perhaps a physical manifestation of his dancing around direct questions, but definitely an indication of an intense love affair with life. He once arrived in Arizona during springtime wrapped in Alaskan winter gear, stepped out of the taxi (no tip, of course), stripped down to his shorts and lay down, limbs splayed on the warm concrete driveway declaring, "Ahrrg… Spring!" He lingered out there so long the neighbors called the cops.

Chuck wasn't quite housebroken, a trait that mixed badly with his exuberance. The first time he came into my mother's house he was determined to make a good impression, but the full measure of himself got the best of him, and like a chimp with a new best friend, he exploded into the living room grinning, looked at everyone and everything at the same time, caught sight of the overhead light fixture, lunged for it and chinned himself up. Chuck, chandelier, wires and sheetrock all came down.

Later—much later—after a tenuous *modus vivendi* had been established and we all felt comfortable with Chuck as a house guest—as comfortable as one could be living with Bigfoot—Chuck got hungry and decided to heat up a can of beans. Conscious of minimizing his impact he decided not to unnecessarily dirty a pan, so he placed the open can of beans with the lid still attached, like Boxcar Willie on a rail-side bivouac, upon the coil burner of the electric range. He turned the dial on high and went off to do some Chuck thing.

Now, cans don't make good cooking pots—no room to stir or margin for bubbling, boiling viscous mixtures—and the glop soon overflowed onto the red-hot coils, burning, smoking and filling the house with the stench of burnt beans and creating a mess only a disaster response team could scour. That was just too much for my mom; shaking her head she apologetically banished Chuck from her house.

No Bounds

Chuck didn't so much hate the government; rather, he treated it as a plague—something to be quarantined from his life. But he did actually hate the National Park Service, an agency that, to Chuck, needlessly over-regulated adventurous pursuits in the National Parks. Kayaking the Colorado River through Grand Canyon National Park requires a permit, compliance with 20+ pages of rules and regulations (including containerizing and carrying out the contents of every bowel movement, something that elicited the comment, "Anyone who focuses on shit..." shaking his head deploringly) and a thorough inspection by a ranger at the launch ramp.

To Chuck this was an opportunity to practice his debating skills and explore the dialectics of citizen-to-government relations. He'd interpret every rule in novel ways and push every possible semantic envelope. His reputation was such that rangers would flee from him, calling in their supervisors for the inspection of Charles D. Carpenter.

In later years National Park Service management policy gravitated toward treating the parks as wilderness, limiting the number of visitors. Private permits to kayak Grand Canyon might take 10 years or more to acquire (but, in what many consider a gross injustice, one can pay an outfitter thousands of dollars to float in a giant rubber raft anytime they want). So Chuck took to running the river in the dead of winter, when permits were easier to get—no one wants to whitewater kayak in freezing temperatures—still, the restriction rankled. This, coupled with Yosemite National Park's closure of 2 out of 6 valley campgrounds, seriously impairing visitors' access, brought forth the declaration that, "They're frigging *AMUSEMENT PARKS*, not wilderness areas!"

Chuck recognized no authority. He'd match wits with any person, entity or situation, always trying to suss out the underlying schema. We once teamed up to build a spec log cabin on some isolated rural acreage in hopes of doubling our investment. Since he'd already built himself a house in Alaska, I figured he knew his stuff. We worked well together—more or less—closing in the outside shell until I had to leave for a spell to take care of distant business. His task, while I was away, was to frame the inside walls. Skeptical of his seat-of-the-pants approach to building, I left him a construction manual for reference, in case he needed to verify procedures.

When I got back, all the walls were framed—haphazardly, with no regard for blocking, bracing, doors, sheetrock, electrical wiring or plumbing. So I gently asked whether he'd consulted the manual. "What's to know? Any idiot can frame a wall," he responded. After pointing out all the deficiencies and explaining why his framing wouldn't work, he agreed to take down the walls and re-erect them properly—under my supervision and at his cost.

Homesteading on the Cheap

Around 1980 Chuck bought 40 acres of bare land an hour's drive from my house and about half that distance from the nearest town in northern Arizona. Many Alaskans had developed a pattern of working summers in the north and wintering in the lower 48, and I was heartened that Chuck finally seemed to be following a familiar trend. The house he built there, however, was anything but common.

It was built suspended on four telephone poles struck in the ground in a square pattern about 16 ft. on each side. The floor was cantilevered beyond the poles and supported eight walls of equal size, creating an octagon about 30 ft. in diameter approximately 6 ft. up off the ground. Since the telephone poles penetrated through the interior of the house and were treated with stinky, noxious chemicals, Chuck wrapped them in plastic with duct tape, his favorite solution to any problem (closely followed by bungee cords, blue tarps and WD-40). The house's only door was industrial-strength steel with 2 dead bolts. It had only one window with a top-hinged steel storm shutter operated from inside the house. There was no insulation anywhere and the walls, floor and ceiling lacked sheetrock or any sort of finish. Its one interior wall provided partial privacy around the toilet—which was flushed with a bucket of water. A shower curtain provided full privacy.

His homestead had a well, which was hooked up to plumbing, but never actually worked, hence, the bucket of water. Since, as in his Fairbanks home, Chuck wasn't hooked up to the electric public utility, he depended for running water on a bicycle he'd attached to the well pump. But because the bicycle was second-hand, rusty and in need of serious maintenance, it never pumped water—something Chuck ended up hauling in 5-gallon containers.

Chuck's 8-sided house had a 4-sided conical roof. He asked me and Steve, another friend, for help roofing it with asphalt shingles, which we agreed to after he promised us dinner and all the beer we could drink. After a hot day roofing in the Arizona sun we were looking forward to a few cold beers and a first-class dinner. But when Chuck proudly pulled out a case of warm Old Milwaukee, a #10 can of Rosarita refried beans and 2 dozen tortillas, Steve and I threatened to pull the shingles and insisted he at least take us out to the nearest café—which he graciously did.

Contrary to the common trend, Chuck ended up working winters in Prudhoe Bay, Alaska, where temperatures regularly plunge to -30°, and framing houses in Phoenix, Arizona during summers when temperatures normally exceed 110°. "To do otherwise", he quietly averred, "would be un-Alaskan".

Art & Gold

Chuck's artistic pursuits—besides his singing—were, on the one hand, as eccentric as his writing and, on the other hand, quintessentially Alaskan. A gifted photographer, he'd always carry a 35 mm camera on his adventures. After leading a three-month expedition that included a descent down an isolated river through the Selous Game Reserve in Tanzania, he put on a slide show for a small audience back in the US. For over an hour he projected stunning photos of exotic flowers, strange insects and close-ups of tree bark and fungi—all without narration, context or chronological order; and without a single photo of his teammates, the government appointed (and required) guide, the river, the raft, the rapids, the kayaks, the natives or the landscape.

Photography wasn't Chuck's only artistic talent. Back in Alaska, he teamed up with two Russians who either couldn't or wouldn't speak English (when they spoke at all—which was seldom), but whose capacity for work and vodka, often together, was phenomenal and usually indulged in at random and without warning, for the annual Alaska Ice Carving competition. The contest takes place every April, includes a variety of categories including 'realistic' and 'abstract', and requires a delicate hand with a chain saw. Sculptures range in size from about a Smart car to a bus, all carved from locally harvested, exceptionally clear ice blocks about a cubic yard in volume. Chuck's team took first place one year. Check out icealaska.com, for his *Dance of the Shaman*, 2006, and a more detailed description of a truly ephemeral art form.

I don't know what he did with the prize money; it probably wasn't much anyway. He had no bank account or credit cards, yet he was by no means a man of no means. He always carried cash and Kruggerands, offering to pay for his purchases with either. Chuck would always cash his pipeline paychecks at the Alaska bank upon which they were drawn so as to avoid any middlemen. Sometimes uncashed checks would pile up in his Fairbanks P.O. box and, if he ran short of funds—no matter where he was—he'd think nothing of flying up to Alaska to cash some checks. Bob Barfoot recalls Chuck rummaging through his pockets once looking for ready cash and pulling out a roll of uncashed $3,300 payroll checks so big they barely fit in his very large hand. Chuck thumbed through the massive roll and pulled out the smallest check ($1,500) to cash—beer money. For transactions at a distance he'd use money orders.

Chuck's 401k was Kruggerands. He did all his trading at a small Scottsdale bullion dealer who didn't ask many questions. When the cancer impaired his mobility and he needed help getting around, he'd resort to elaborate ruses to keep his companions in the dark about his comings and goings. But his secret gold stash wasn't his only ace-in-the-hole. At the height of the real estate bubble his 40 acres in Arizona was worth well over a million dollars. He was visibly uncomfortable when I jokingly called him Mr. M, behavior he'd also exhibit around census takers, inside government offices or when accosted by overly inquisitive, overly friendly strangers. I was flabbergasted when I found out he not only had an attorney but that, by pure coincidence, I'd attended high school with him.

Chuck's lawyer was a piece of work. Logjam (his real alias) lived on a houseboat on the Tanana River in Fairbanks. His oversized head had a manic or apoplectic grin—depending on your point of view—permanently plastered on a shrewish face framed by Brezhnev eye brows, the whole tempered by an unctuously apologetic and solicitous manner. He was expelled from high school for being a bully and lacking all respect for authority. He once sailed around the world solo but hit rough seas on the homeward stretch near Hawaii and sank. Somehow, he made it to Oahu, bought a fixer-upper and asked Chuck to help him sail it home. I never found out the details of that voyage—privacy issues (on both sides), I suppose.

One or Two Fingers

"When was your last STD test?" Terry asked Chuck.

Thrown off guard—he didn't know what an STD was—Chuck mumbled something about incomprehensible acronyms.

"Sexually transmitted disease, Chuck! If you want to get laid you'd better get a test," Terry matter-of-factly informed him.

Years previously, Chuck and Terry had been an item—an item that was never to endure. Yet they kept in touch. In 2007 Chuck was invited on a Grand Canyon river trip. An Alaskan river guide friend's Grand Canyon private permit application had finally came through. He needed a crew. Uncharacteristic nostalgia impelled Chuck to invite Terry; while reluctance and apprehension at butting heads with Chuck kept her from immediately accepting. After contentious negotiations—no WWII surplus rafts—they sealed the deal. That's when Terry brought up the STDs.

The river trip did not go well. The usual suspects—Chuck's anarchy, his total insensitivity to mixing crew members of wildly differing temperaments (or, conversely, of mixing them on purpose for his own entertainment), or just the alignment of the stars every time Chuck was involved in an adventure—did not materially play a part. Instead, it was the permit holder's tyrannical temperament that alienated nearly all the dozen or so participants. Partway down the 300-mile trip, everyone except the permit holder, his wife, kids and Chuck abandoned the trip and hitchhiked out. They'd had enough of the tension and bickering.

On the trip Terry and Chuck had gotten on well. But during the course of the outing she'd noticed that he'd get up much too often to urinate even for a 60-year-old man. Yet, more seriously, his urination was oddly irregular and out of sync with his urges. Terry advised him to get checked out.

Chuck had already sensed something was wrong, but had ignored it. Once someone else noticed, it all of a sudden became real. Back in town he drove to the nearest hospital emergency room. Outside, he paced back and forth for hours unable to entrust himself into someone else's hands and unwilling to cross a threshold that would probably change his life forever.

When Chuck was finally diagnosed with prostate cancer it was already well advanced and terminal. He'd avoided doctors and insurance all his life figuring it was all a crapshoot anyway. Back when he'd turned 50 I'd asked him kiddingly whether he'd gotten "one or two fingers". He smirked wryly.

The doctors told him that he had two years left. I suggested he sell his Arizona property so he could pay his medical bills and enjoy some sort of retirement, but by then not only was the Great Recession well on its way, but his innate obstacles prevented him from taking any meaningful steps (of course, no one knew about the gold—and he pretended he didn't either). He distrusted realtors and lawyers (except for Logjam) and just couldn't bring himself to pay them any sort of commission, while a sale might have generated capital gains taxes and he hated paying taxes; so he was always looking for a private trade or some sort of under-the-radar deal, but could never bring himself to take out a want ad—that would have been too much of a breach of his privacy. And he couldn't bring himself to let the property go at a fire-sale price.

What's more, the one realtor that looked at the property suggested bulldozing the house and implied that all the dead batteries, rolls of 90 lb. tar-impregnated, construction felt paper, second-hand concrete blocks, junked cars, 55-gal drums filled with who-knows-what, Hanta virus-harboring out-shacks, piles of firewood and other priceless stuff might constitute an environmental hazard *even if removed*. And, in spite of the TARP (Troubled Asset Relief Program), banks weren't lending on raw land (his 8-sided shack wasn't considered habitable).

No Regrets

In a way it was understandable. Deathbed conversions are overrated. People who change their lives when faced with death are repudiating how they lived. People who don't are already living life "as if today is their last day". Chuck was Chuck to the very end and was even conscious of setting a good example for his nephew—his closest (and only) living blood relative—on how to face death.

Still, Chuck did experience one minor and one major change during his fight with cancer: he got a cell phone and he hooked up with Alison, an Alaskan woman who'd had a crush on him for 15 years. Why he resisted her charms for so long is a mystery. Perhaps the terminal diagnosis concentrated his perception.

Alison was perfect. She loved him as he was, and made sure he didn't die alone, unsung or uncared for. When I finally met her, I took him aside and asked, "Can you still get it up?"

He beamed and interlaced his fingers back and forth with glee, exulting, "Yes!"

But he remained uncompromising. Chuck declined to meet Alison's mother decrying, "What's next?" alarmed that the meeting might somehow ensnare him into a web of unforeseen ties, commitments and even an expectation of marriage—to Chuck as foreign and useless a concept as deodorant.

Males of many species, when building their nests, incorporate features designed to attract a mate. Not Chuck. When Alison first saw his Alaska cabin she said "it made his Arizona stilt-home look like Gaudi's Sagrada Familia." As his condition deteriorated, she invited him to move in with her—an offer he didn't refuse.

Death was never a stranger to us. We were experienced actuaries at assessing our own risks and dangers in whatever hairball enterprise we came up with. Chuck mentally minimized most risks believing he'd die in a car accident or some other unheralded tragedy. Dying doing what you loved was just an unlikely joke in poor taste. But he always declared that I should "pull the plug" if he was ever reduced to a condition that didn't allow him to enjoy his life. I was skeptical, knowing how much Chuck loved his existence. With almost any degree of life there is always some pleasure, especially if one harbors a sunny disposition.

Months of chemotherapy and blood transfusions didn't dampen his spirits. He reveled in cocking a snook at doctors and death. He enrolled for singing lessons—sharpening an already sharp talent and one of the few creative outlets still left him. Alison recalls that he'd take CD's of Irish music into the hospital waiting rooms, quietly replace the 'soothing' muzak with lively reels and jigs—and even dance. Pretty soon the other patients were all chatting about their early days and sharing stories instead of staring at their shoelaces.

Six months before his death, confined to a wheelchair he could barely propel with his weakened arms and reduced to (in his mind) dire financial straits, Chuck decided to hitchhike from Alaska to Arizona. Everyone told him it was a crazy idea and tried to talk him out of it. Chuck countered that hitchhiking in a wheelchair was actually an advantage: drivers would feel sorry for him and pick him up.

At the last minute he was stopped by a bout of pneumonia. After antibiotics took care of the infection, the cancer spread to his jaw bone. Never one to give up, he decided to fly to Mexico, shop for a cheap surgeon and get the lesion excised. In Cabo San Lucas his prospects were so bleak Mexican doctors refused to operate. So he flew to Phoenix to bid a last farewell to his Arizona property and friends.

At the Phoenix airport terminal he suffered a minor fall at the sidewalk curb that ultimately landed him in the hospital for a series of palliative blood transfusions. Alison immediately flew down from Fairbanks. The emergency room doc was ruthless. Cutting to the chase, she asked him where he wanted to die: Arizona or Alaska.

Now, Chuck was never one to sacrifice the present for an uncertain future—he lived permanently in the here and now, relishing means and process over ends and objectives. Put on the spot, he temporized and then blurted, "Alaska", although he was determined to somehow make it up to his northern Arizona spread. When Alison insisted on returning to Fairbanks as soon as possible, Chuck fixed her in the eye and drew a line in the sand, "If that doesn't fit your plans, you can return to Alaska," without a trace of rancor.

Chuck's penultimate discharge from the hospital was classic Chuck. Attempting to recoup the expenses of Mr. Carpenter's hospitalization from the Social Security Administration, a hospital representative tried to get Chuck's Social Security information. Before saying anything, Chuck called his lawyer. After an hour on the phone with Logjam, he declined to participate. Minutes later, wheelchair-bound in front of the elevator, he was asked for his signature authorizing the release of his medical records to *himself*. After much deliberative and argumentative back and forth, he reluctantly signed—even though *he* had made the request.

In spite of his secret gold stash, Chuck played the health system as if death was not a factor, weighing the costs and benefits of getting something for free, revealing his privacy, leaving a legacy for his nephew and Alison, and even—as some have suggested not totally in jest—taking it with him.

A macabre game of musical beds then ensued. Hoping for an opportunity to see his northern Arizona homestead once more, Chuck began shuttling among friends' homes, hospice services in tow, oblivious to his fast deteriorating condition, biding his time between storms waiting for a break in the weather that never came. Finally, totally spent, failing fast and resigned to never returning to Arizona, he flew back to Alaska on short notice.

His final goodbye to me included a knuckle bump celebrating that he'd outlived his original prognosis of 2 years by 9 months and that he'd lived life on his own terms.

After his death, at the memorial service, Alison declared that, "It had been a privilege to care for him."

Epilogue

Months after Chuck's death, his testamentary lawyer, a man with two first names—we'll call him Michael Thomas—came to Arizona to collect Chuck's fungible assets. Thomas was our guest during his stay in Prescott. Keeping his client confidentiality about details, he nonetheless disclosed that Chuck had bank safety deposit boxes scattered throughout the western US. He'd come to collect the contents of Chuck's bank boxes in Phoenix, Prescott and Chino Valley.

The following evening after performing his duties, Thomas returned to our home for dinner with a carpetbag he could barely lift. He allowed us to heft it but declined to open it. Without actually disclosing its contents he, in a very roundabout way, let us know that the proportion of silver to gold was slightly higher. I estimated the weight at about 50 pounds.

"How are you going to get that back to Alaska?" I asked.

"Carry-on," he responded without a trace of concern, as if he'd done this before.

With many claims against it, mostly from hospitals and doctors, Chuck's estate took years to settle. Tina, my wife, whose affection for him had grown over the years, was the beneficiary of an old, western-themed quilt.

There's a little bit of Chuck Carpenter in all of us—literally—especially now that his many friends have scattered his ashes to the four winds throughout the West and beyond.

Chuck a week after being diagnosed with cancer expressing his disdain for cell phones

From Ayn Rand to... Hayduke Lives!

By Robert H. Miller

The woods are lovely, dark and deep.
But I have promises to keep,
and miles to go before I sleep.
—Robert Frost

When faced with a complex and dangerous rapid, river runners will scale the river's banks and scrutinize the cataract for possible routes through it. If a route isn't obvious, they'll resort to throwing pieces of driftwood above its headfall in order to determine where the main current—or subsidiary currents—take the logs. This exercise reveals the path (or paths) of least resistance—usually the ones with the most volume of water—and the one that a fully-laden boat can take with the least effort. Often, separate pieces of wood, in spite of beginning in the same spot, end up floating down wildly different routes and ending up at disparate destinations.

Human beings sometimes resemble the logs. Starting from similar premises, two individuals faced with a difficult philosophical conundrum, can take wildly diverging trajectories to a solution...

* * * *

On May 14, 1986, three of the four sets of power lines leading to the Palo Verde nuclear power plant 25 miles outside of Phoenix, Arizona, shorted. Inside the control room, technicians scrambled to ensure that the backup generator would kick in.

Preliminary investigation revealed sabotage. The perpetrators—there were at least three—had climbed more than 100 feet up the high-voltage power transmission towers, tied 40 feet of hemp cord to a medium-gauge chain, tossed it over the lines—probably by tying a rock at one end—and hoisted the chain up to connect the wires. The chain liquefied, spraying white-hot metal everywhere. The saboteurs dove for cover and then drove off into the night in a rattle-trap Toyota Land Cruiser.

The *Los Angeles Times* reported that:

> *"The raid on the remote power lines followed a string of acts of vandalism and unexplained incidents at the $9.3-billion plant... and came at a time when the Palo Verde owners faced a punitive fine of $100,000 over alleged security shortcomings in the facility's most vital areas—shortcomings the Nuclear Regulatory Commission (NRC) had refused to publish for fear of compromising security further."*

Following this incident, the NRC did, however, notify all 101 nuclear plant operators across the nation to be on the alert for similar strikes.

Now, pairing the words "nuclear reactor" with "sabotage" on the front page of newspapers and on the morning news just a month after the Chernobyl disaster was not a good idea. Phoenix was immediately downwind of Palo Verde. Chernobyl had spread radiation all over Europe. Phoenix nearly panicked. And it had been only a few years since the accident at the Three Mile Island nuclear reactor had put the country on edge with visions of melting and exploding nuclear reactors, thousands dying, and radioactivity spreading far and wide rendering vast areas uninhabitable and forever poisoned. Yet the devil/angel was in the details, details not everyone paid attention to, and whose dots could be connected in various ways.

For starters, the sabotage occurred 30 miles from the nuclear facility while both Unit 1 and Unit 2 reactors were idle; one for scheduled maintenance, the other in between initial operation tests. And had all four transmission lines to the plant been knocked out of service, the plant would have been shut down and power cut off to a wide area.

Myron Scott of the Coalition for Responsible Energy Education, a Tempe-based consumer and environmental group, opined, "I would assume whoever did it knew what was going on at the plant. Neither unit was operating, and the fourth line was not cut. It's like somebody, or some group of people, is trying to send a negative message without creating a safety hazard."

When word of the sabotage reached the FBI offices in Phoenix, FBI headquarters in Washington, DC ordered an investigation opened immediately. It was to be code named THERMCON.

Assorted low-tech attacks continued throughout the next year, but the FBI had few leads. Until October 5, 1987, when someone with a propane torch burned through several of the metal pylons supporting the chair lift towers at the Fairfield Snow Bowl ski area atop the San Francisco Peaks outside Flagstaff, Arizona. The Peaks, the highest point in Arizona and visible from over 100 miles, are sacred to the Navajo and Hopi Indian tribes living just to the northeast. An obscure organization acronymed EMETIC claimed public credit.

The Evan Mecham Eco-Terrorist International Conspiracy (EMETIC) was sardonically named after the sitting Republican governor of Arizona. No doubt it was dreamed up by Mark Davis, EMETIC's Brainiac. I know: he and I had been buddies in our early years in high school. After college, we ran the Yavapai County Libertarian Party; he as chair, I as treasurer. Mark was sharp and had an even sharper sense of irony. When I first heard of his involvement in these events, I wasn't surprised— Mark was capable of almost anything.

Mark's partner in crime was Peggy Millet, the half-sister of feminist author, Kate Millet and a member of Earth First! The rest of EMETIC's members consisted of a constantly fluctuating cast of curious characters. They were preparing to take their political activism to, as they say, the next level.

For the FBI, something in the *modus operandi*, some piece of evidence—or intuition—connected the two incidents—the ski area and the nuclear power plant.

The Road to Galt's Gulch...

Libertarians of a certain age, when reflecting on their political odyssey, usually invoke Ayn Rand as the source of their epiphany—in spite of the fact that Rand herself repudiated the libertarian movement and labeled her philosophy Objectivism. Most libertarians weren't persuaded: they continued the one-way love fest, though many were beginning to feel embarrassed by the dogmatism, stubborn intransigence, absence of warmth or empathy, and cultishness of her aptly-nicknamed "collective".

Gagging on Objectivist correctness, Jerome Tuccille, a former *Wall Street Journal* writer and libertarian child of the Goldwater campaign, hastened the split between Rand and many of her erstwhile followers with the publication of his 1971 memoir, *It Usually Begins with Ayn Rand*, in which he lampooned Objectivists as zombie sycophants. Nevertheless, Rand remains the most influential libertarian of the twentieth century, though less and less so as more varied paths to right- *and* left-wing libertarianism open.

Libertarians are radicals. Randian libertarians have especially radical expectations of the world. Relying on a philosophy so internally consistent that its dots nearly connect themselves, they continue to proselytize, believing that exposure to self-evident tenets will result in massive conversions. Next to the Bible, Rand's philosophical novel *Atlas Shrugged* remains one of the best-ever-selling books in English. But while the Bible continues to make converts, particularly of the fundamentalist sort, Rand's oeuvre is not nearly as successful.

Evolutionary psychologists hypothesize, on a smidgen of evidence from the Human Genome Project and other sources, that both religious inclination and political persuasion have genetic bases: that the apples don't fall far from the tree. Perhaps.

My father, founding CFO of what would later become AIG, admired Lyndon Johnson's Great Society—its attempt at eradicating poverty. My mother had favored Richard Nixon over John Kennedy—despite the fact that she was a Catholic. Before she died, she'd become a staunch Reagan supporter, in spite of the fact that she was opposed to the death penalty. Though both had read *Atlas Shrugged* and Rand's other major novel, *The Fountainhead*, neither perceived them as particularly political. Their politically schizoid children became, in turn: a conservative turned Obama-backer with vague New Age inclinations (oldest son); a seeker settling into religious-right Republicanism (oldest daughter); a liberal attorney who later found Christ, Fundamentalism and conservatism (youngest daughter); and a left-right flirter slouching into moderate libertarianism and radical atheism (myself).

I place libertarians smack dab in the middle of the left-right continuum (as does the "world's smallest political quiz")—and there *is* some truth to that. It seems that unless chaos theory is resorted to, political hegiras are often unpredictable and the motives behind them inscrutable.

At first, Ayn Rand didn't charm.

Recently graduated from college, I'd joined a group of 14 friends who proposed to kayak the 600-mile length of Mexico's Baja Peninsula—at the time, a nearly preposterous undertaking considering that back in 1972, kayaking, as a sport—much less *sea* kayaking—didn't really exist in the US, and Baja's infrastructure consisted of widely dispersed fishing villages connected by 4-wheel-drive tracks. We resorted to ordering kayaks from Germany, carrying our own essentials, and fishing for protein.

It was almost more than we could handle. Averaging, at first, only 10 miles per day due to winds, contrary currents, swell and some of the highest tides in the world, most of the group abandoned the expedition at Santa Rosalia, Baja's midway mining town. Still, four of us decided to forge on. Those who departed left us whatever we could use to aid our success. Except for Tek. He insisted that we pay—if not market price, at least *something*, for his dry noodles, stale crackers, p-nut butter, GI ration chocolate bars, rusty lures and battered reading material. I stared at him incredulously and asked, "Why?"

Now, on any long expedition, reading material is essential. While I had taken John Steinbeck's *Log of the Sea of Cortez*, Tek had taken *Atlas Shrugged*. "Because it's my stuff and I don't owe it to you," he responded, adding that I'd understand once I'd read the book, which he ended up giving to me. I paid him a token price for his offerings but used the book's pages as fire starters after reading the back-cover blurb. Not only was his arrogance insufferable, but that title seemed a pretentious conceit, with the book's catch-phrase, "Who is John Galt?" (touted as cutting-edge slang somewhere—I don't remember where), as catchy and pithy as a bad English-speaking foreigner's attempt at neologizing—which is exactly what it was.

...Runs through Havana

The strongest formative influences on my political development occurred around puberty. I grew up in Havana, Cuba, the son of a well-to-do, *noblese oblige* capitalist entrepreneur who'd married his Cuban secretary. Not only had he established Cuba's AIG (American International Group) branch, but he introduced Volkswagen to the island and opened Cuba's first paper products factory.

In 1960, a year-and-a-half after Castro's revolution, my family was forced to abandon everything, pack one suitcase each and flee Cuba. All of our property was expropriated. Unsure of their next move, our parents placed us children in boarding schools along the Mississippi Gulf Coast where we perfected our English and got dropped—unwittingly and unknowingly—into the vortex of the American Civil Rights movement, an upheaval we couldn't fathom, having come from a country with little to no racial prejudice.

By the time I entered high school, my political consciousness was being forged by the Vietnam draft and the presidential campaign of 1964. The Jesuit high school I attended in Phoenix, Arizona, stressed critical thinking and public involvement, going so far as to hold mock Goldwater-Johnson debates for the entire student body. English classes included up-to-date reports and discussions of the goings-on in San Francisco's Haight-Ashbury, interspersed—at one time—with an in-depth study of Emerson's "On Self Reliance," a curious albeit insightful juxtaposition. I rooted for Barry, an unpretentious straight-shooter, with a solid grasp of the issues. But it wasn't just his political values that attracted me. When I heard he'd mooned a censorious group that objected to the carousing at one of his campaign parties, he became my hero.

My friend John Clarkson and I decided to get involved. He joined YAF (Young Americans for Freedom) and introduced me to the John Birch Society's nearby American Opinion Bookstore, which enabled me to buy and read *None Dare Call it Treason*. John was sharp as a scimitar, a whiz at Latin and classical Greek and unbeatable in debate, with a vocabulary that rivaled William F. Buckley's. Together we joined the Model UN, a national high school mock UN project, where we hoped to be assigned to represent some second-tier heavy-hitter country—like France or Canada. Instead we were assigned Ghana. Knowing nothing about Ghana—and just a tad disappointed—we decided to meet with President Kennedy's ex-ambassador to that country, William P. Mahoney, who happened to live in Phoenix. Ambassador Mahoney was kind enough to grant us an interview just days before the conclave. True to form—and with John's command of parliamentary procedure—we brought little Ghana to the forefront by tabling some outrageously radical proposal in the General Assembly. That really stirred things up.

By now I'd put together a presentation on the Cuban Revolution that I shared with some of the older students around the Phoenix metro area's elementary schools. They were a big hit. Instead of regular class, a school assembly for a show-and-tell by a kid one or two years older than the audience, and one who had lived through war and revolution always managed to spellbind. With John's entrée to the Birch Society, he and I took the presentation on the road to society chapters as far away as Montana. Again, our age—this time a young kid presenting to adults the refugee experience—never failed to fascinate.

John and I ended up at different colleges, where we both broadened our horizons: me, in northern Arizona where I discovered girls, drugs, outdoor adventure sports such as alpinism and kayaking, and acquired a knowledge base that instilled confidence in my developing opinions; John at the University of Virginia, where he discovered boys, the law, and the power of big government to set certain injustices right. At first, John was up to his old tricks. He and several right-wing buddies planned a takeover and subversion of the U of V branch of the SDS (Students for a Democratic Society), a firebrand, radical left-wing organization that, by 1969, was already falling apart. As he recounts,

> *"Our strategy was to have some of "our people" attend and cause a disruption and dissention. I, then, would emerge as the voice of reason. The "disruptors", as the plan called, made impassioned speeches, attacked me viciously (of course, we all reconnoitered later for a few beers to celebrate our triumph), and then called for a massive walk-out. Many people followed them. Of course, that meant that the people left in the room would be easily convinced to elect me as their leader. (Others of my "planning committee" remained to make and second the nomination.) From a tactical perspective, it was very successful. The local newspaper ran an*

article about "Young Turk John Clarkson." After that, I did nothing. I never attended another SDS meeting. The joy was in formulating and executing our plan. We had no intention of going further."

While at the University of Virginia, John (with his gay, black roommate) discovered his tastes ran counter to the norm. Appalled at the social treatment his new friend was subjected to, John came to the conclusion that it was only through the Federal government's efforts that racial bigotry would ever begin to be eradicated in as short a time as it ultimately, mostly, was. So he pursued law, a skill that, by the time he passed the bar, he used to advocate gay rights. Today he describes himself as an anti-establishmentarian.

But back to high school. I first met Mark Davis, the once and future eco-warrior, on our very first day there. We'd both been placed—as incoming freshmen—in homeroom 1-C, not the brightest class, but at least not with the juvies and idiots in 1-E.

The first order of business—according to our homeroom prefect—was to elect a class president. No one knew anyone else; we were all shy and insecure, unsure how to act in "high school", clueless as to what was expected of us and terrified of screwing up. The vote was taken strictly on first impressions and the gift of gab. For some reason I can't recall, I ran and won. It was my first foray into politics. I remember noticing Mark because he had what looked like a flesh watch on his wrist and a sliced nostril, a Mensur scar from a tussle with a dog—deformities that drew me to him. Mark was freckle faced, wore black-rimmed glasses and explained that the ping-pong ball-sized appendage on his wrist was tissue that had been removed from elsewhere on his body and temporarily set on the wrist for later use to repair his nostril. None the wiser about such things, I believed him. Mark and I hit it off: he a misfit, me an aspiring big-man-on-campus.

Mark's family was a little strange. His mom wasn't warm (to me, anyway) and his two sisters stayed away from me. I never met his father or his brother. Mark had grown up the son of an oil man, bumping around places like Indonesia and Libya. He was precocious and idealistic from the start, with a sharp mind and boundless energy. He had raged in one direction or another since he was a pre-teen growing up in Phoenix, his hidebound father ineffectively attempting to corral the boy's energies with beatings.

We'd found what we thought was a discarded B-52 fuel tank and decided to convert it into an outrigger canoe—the perfect undertaking for two hyperactive teens uncomfortable with just hanging out. The project was a big deal for a couple of 15-year-olds; it took most of the year. But we worked well together, and by the time I got my driver's license, we had successfully launched the canoe on nearby Lake Pleasant. After that we drifted apart, no doubt due to his expulsion from Brophy for some infraction I was never privy to and his move to California.

By the time Mark turned sixteen, he'd been in and out of so much trouble that he was put in the California Youth Authority's Los Angeles rehab center for unruly kids. Years later Mark reflected on his first incarceration: "There was a lot of fighting, rapes, attempted rapes. I'm this screwed-up, basically naïve, suburban white kid, and this is right after the Watts riots. I came out of there pretty crazy, pretty wild." Swearing never to be taken advantage of, he turned to weight lifting, self-defense and extreme endurance.

I, on the other hand, was a model student. Already president of my class—both as a freshman and sophomore—decided to run for the Student Body Council, first for treasurer, then later for president. My libertarian inclinations were already evident in my platform. I reasoned that since Student Body funds belonged to the students, my job was to maximize revenues and then return them to the students. The assembled student body had never heard such radical, logical populism before. I could barely get through my speech for all the hollering and clapping. Meanwhile, the faculty members standing on the verges grinned nervously, wondering what their democracy had wrought. I won overwhelmingly. My opponent, Dick Mahoney (son of Ambassador to Ghana Mahoney), who was later to become Arizona's Secretary of State and a Democratic candidate for Governor, never stood a chance.

Center rear, Mark Davis; far left, John Clarkson; next to Davis, front right, author.

I kept my promise. To maximize Student Body revenues, I got the administration to fire the snacks-and-refreshments purveyor for varsity football games and, with a small crew of volunteers working out of the back of a pick-up truck outfitted with counters, ice chests and a till, took over the concession. The money poured in. Unable to convince the administration to issue rebate checks for each and every student at the end of the year, I decided to throw a big party with the funds. Between prom and graduation celebrations, I got Linda Rondstadt and the Stone Poneys—who'd just released their hit single "Different Drum"—to put on a dance-concert for the combined student bodies of our own Brophy Prep and our twin neighbor girls' school, Xavier High.

A Different Drum

In college I was still torn between Right and Left: on the one hand, debating the merits of Nixon's Vietnam peace plan with fellow Prescott College students Tom and Randy Udall, scions of the Stewart and Morris Udall political dynasty (Tom would later become one of the US Senators from New Mexico); and on the other hand, convincing prospective conservative donors such as the Adolph Coors Trust and nascent Goldwater Institute (*not* today's Goldwater Institute) that the small, private, liberal arts "hippie" college I was attending was worth supporting. I'd been hand-picked for this PR fund-raising job by the college's president as an example of the caliber of student the college was training for "tomorrow's" leadership role in society—in spite of my Mohawk hair-do, sometimes flamboyant dress, VW van pimp-mobile and, of course, my outspokenness.

The outdoor adventure sports Prescott College offered as an alternative to the more traditional football, baseball and basketball at other colleges, instilled self-reliance and initiative. They also imbued a passion for the natural environment and its wild places that, over the years, has only grown stronger. But it was the academic pursuits that were truly formative intellectually, especially anthropology. Not your garden variety, Samoan-kinship-and-Arunta-fertility dance studies, but "processual archaeology", at the time a new, cutting-edge approach to history that attempted to explain the nature and fabric of civilization.

While traditional archaeology collected potsherds, studied changes in art motifs and concentrated on dating and categorizing sites and cultures, processual archaeology studied human adaptation—mostly technological—to changing environmental conditions and increasing population densities. Its corollary in cultural anthropology is known as the "ecological" approach (without the ideological baggage that term carries in common parlance).

The specific question that gripped me was, "Why did the people who would become the American Indians, initially a homogenous population at the time of the Bering Straits crossing, develop high civilizations in the Andes and Mexican Highlands but remain hunters and gatherers or incipient agriculturalists in the Great Basin and Amazon rain forests?" Today the synthesis this approach yields to the study of humanity is probably best—albeit only partially—exemplified by Jared Diamond's *Guns, Germs and Steel* and its sequel *Collapse*, and given more scholarly exposition in the works of Karl Wittfogel, Leslie White, Gordon Willey, Marshall Sahlins and Elman Service, among others.

One elementary conclusion from the "New Archaeology" was the correlation that government power and control increases as population densities thicken and civilization becomes more technologically complex. However, correlation is not cause and effect—much less destiny—and, though the association of the two makes intuitive sense at some level, to this incipient libertarian the challenge was to analyze and discover just how much government denser and more complex societies actually required.

The School of Hard Knocks

Meanwhile, Mark Davis' life had taken quite the different turn. I'd heard that he'd landed at "24th & Van Buren", Phoenicians' euphemistic name for Arizona's hospital for the criminally insane. Mark was strong-willed, somewhat of a loner, contentious and violent but he wasn't crazy.

An *Arizona Republic* October 17, 1967 article headlined *LSD User, Committed to Hospital* reported that "Maricopa County Juvenile Court Judge Thomas Tang ordered the commitment after he learned that [Davis] was denied admission to a California rehabilitation center because he is 'teetering on the brink of psychosis.'"

"The youth, in hearings on an incorrigibility charge," the article continues, "said he had used marijuana since the summer after his grade school graduation…that he has taken 174 LSD 'trips" [and] has had mescaline, STP, psilocybin, DMT, hashish…and…heroin."

"Records show that [Davis] tests in the upper 10 per cent IQ…he reads at the Ph.D. level." Two psychiatrists, after examining Mark said he "has temporary impairment of orientation, judgement and emotional control. His intellectual processes are impaired." They attributed this to his "excessive and continued use of LSD," reversible with time, good nutrition and treatment.

Mark was able to convince Judge Tang of his aversion to institutionalization stating, "If I'm put in an institution where the situation is intolerable, I'll suicide. I'm getting sick of being locked up." Judge Tang took steps to mitigate his judgement, commenting that Davis was unusual because of his high intellectual capacity, and took the time to explain to Mark his condition in detail according to the reports of the psychiatrists.

I had to visit him.

Sitting cross-legged on the ground across from him in the heavily, thrice-fenced outdoor commons, I asked him what landed him there.

He said he'd killed someone.

I was speechless. Wide eyed. Open jawed. Aghast. Incredulous. My mind somersaulted digesting what he'd just said. The newspaper article did not even allude to this.

Though extremely intense, Mark was no murderer. He'd been a minor at the time of the incident. Now he was in the nut house. Who knows exactly what he meant by "I killed someone"? He could have meant anything from murder to accident, to he just felt responsible for someone's death to…who knows? I didn't question him further, fearing that covert eavesdropping might pick up our conversation, and I didn't want to blow his cover—if there was one. But I also didn't want to set off emotions neither one of us wanted to entertain just then. I assumed it had all been an unfortunate accident and that he'd feigned insanity to ease his plight. If anyone could fool a bevy of psychiatrists, Mark Davis, with his sharp intellect and determination, could. I wished him well and promised to visit again, but never got around to it.

After his release from 24th & Van Buren, Mark poured his energy into saving lives. Perhaps it was remorse or, just as likely—Mark was, after all, a good person—he needed a positive framework into which to channel his difficult-to-control fanatic vehemence. In 1969—at the age of 19—he co-founded Terros, an extremely successful—albeit, at the time, controversial, both for its unconventional methods *and* staff—crisis intervention program in Phoenix. Mark poured himself into it and took a hands-on approach, applying lessons he'd learned in his own life. He's particularly proud of talking a man out of a very public attempt at suicide, for which he received a citation from the mayor. (Today Terros is a multi-million dollar Healthcare organization providing primary care, substance use and mental health disorder treatment, recovery, crisis, and prevention services.)

True to his vow never to be bullied again, Mark took up body building and martial arts, which he combined with a new spirituality that included those pursuits: he became a Sikh...and he acquired a Harley. Mark Davis was the poster boy for nuclear fusion—a dream of unlimited energy containment perceived but unrealized, especially now that he looked like the Terminator. To release his pent-up energy and even relax, Mark took to riding his Harley through Phoenix in the evening and late into the night.

He rode trolling for rednecks that didn't like his long hair, beard and turban, so he could teach them tolerance. One time he stopped at a red light next to a pick-up whose riders were looking for rough fun. They riled and ridiculed him, picking the wrong fun hog. At the next red light Mark jumped off his Harley grappling and swinging a 4-foot length of chain capable of mooring an aircraft carrier. While the fun seekers froze to the upholstery, Mark turned their windshield to silica dust. Neither party exchanged insurance information.

Back to the Land

After graduate school I became a Mother Earth News-subscribing, back-to-the-land homesteader on an isolated parcel of rural Arizona land where I built my own energy-efficient home (powered by a wind generator), raised cattle, and grew a garden and orchard. I earned money doing archaeological environmental impact studies, building homes and doing some outdoor guiding. My wife made cowboy shirts and managed the local commercial truck garden. It was then that I discovered the Libertarian Party, through Karl Hess's seminal article, "The Death of Politics", Roger McBride's *A New Dawn for America* and one of David Nolan's local screeds. My wife and I both joined and decided to become politically active.

Our nearest municipality, Chino Valley, had just hired its first town manager, deciding that its exponential growth was just too much complexity for its traditional mayor-and-council government. Academically trained professional town managers often have a statist bent. Our newly-hired statuesque blonde bureaucrat (with hair tickling the dimples on the backside of her knees), prided herself on her ability to extract state and federal funds through her skill at writing grant applications. Nonetheless, she was young and hip, and found us kindred souls. She hired us to write a pamphlet guide to local government for local citizens, a task we tackled with a libertarian bent. Additionally, she sponsored an Economic Development Committee to attract businesses to Chino Valley. I joined, though as something of a Trojan horse. Our little town wanted a supermarket, such as a Safeway, to locate nearby while I—not averse to the new facility—was afraid our committee members would sell their souls by imposing liens on the taxpayers (such as tax breaks for the chain), engage in imminent domain abuse, issuing industrial revenue bonds or resorting to any number of other unfair competitive practices.

Nineteen-eighty-two was a threshold year for the Arizona Libertarian Party. The popular five-term Republican Congressman, Sam Steiger, an outspokenly colorful character, declared his candidacy for governor as a Libertarian. Sam was a rancher, journalist, and Korean War hero who had twice represented Prescott in the state Senate. He was plainspoken in the Goldwater mold, had a contagious smile and an outrageous sense of humor. His very public debate with his new party over military conscription and subsequent flip-flop actually helped him; it indicated that he was amenable to reasoned argument and not afraid to admit he was wrong.

When I first met him, at the offices of the *The Prescott Sun*, the newspaper he published (and for which my wife worked), he was wearing a Stetson and cowboy boots, and was chomping on a big, lit cigar. He shook my hand, twisted his head back—as if to get a better perspective to look me over—and baited me with repartee.

"I'm all for the little guy," he declared, pausing dramatically. "There goes one now!" he blurted in mock surprise, pointing at the floor, and stomping on the spot with an exaggerated goose step.

Sam wasn't popular with the intelligentsia. He was once stopped by a traffic cop and the verbatim transcript of the exchange was published as a full-page article in Prescott's other newspaper, *The Prescott Courier*. To every polite request from the officer, Sam responded with a "Fuck off" or some other expletive-laden insult or an accusation of harassment. Neither a reason for, nor a conclusion to, the traffic stop was mentioned—absolutely no explanation other than the implication that Sam Steiger was not a fit citizen. Oddly too, the article was accompanied by a large, close-up picture of Sam's face—apparently snapped from the passenger side—sardonically yet patiently putting up with the ordeal.

But he was an active citizen. When the Prescott City Council erased a mid-block crosswalk connecting the courthouse with the bars on Whiskey Row in downtown Prescott, because a state highway ran concurrent along that street, the citizenry raised holy hell. Sam took the matter into his own hands and personally repainted the white lines. He was arrested and charged with criminal damage and disorderly conduct. At the trial, he defended himself by arguing that "it wasn't criminal damage, it was historic preservation". The jury acquitted him after deliberating for 25 minutes.

In 1982 Sam ran for governor under the Libertarian Party label. He lost his bid but garnered over 5% of the vote, crossing the magic threshold that gave the Libertarian Party ballot access. It was a sweet defeat. Years later, in 1999, he was elected mayor of Prescott.

Guru Nanak, Mao Zee Dong, Milton Friedman & Edward Abbey

Ballot access electrified Arizona's Libertarians. State and county chapters organized. Precinct committeemen were appointed, elected or volunteered. I attended my first Yavapai County Libertarian Party meeting—an intense mixture of misfits, cranks, anarchists, hippies, dropouts and nerds from both left and right, kitted up extremely informally (if not outrageously)—all united by instinct, intellect and outside-the-box thinking.

There, at the meeting, I ran into Mark Davis—the last person I thought I'd run into. He recognized me and gave me a warm hug. He was big—solid and powerful (an amazing Charles Atlas-like transformation)—with long and thick, unruly strawberry-blonde hair; but still freckled with his distinctive nostril slit, a scar from a tussle with a dog when he was a kid. We caught up.

The raging Sikh had experienced another Pauline conversion exactly when or how, I don't know. But he'd fallen in love, gotten married and sired two daughters. With a family to support, he needed a trade—forget working for "the man." Mark became a master craftsman, building high-end, lacquered, exotic-wood, shoji-screened cabinets for rich clients in, among other places, Santa Barbara, California. He called his business The First Noble Truth Woodwork.

While there, he'd taken to some sort of Maoist revolutionary ideology. Surprised, I asked him if he hadn't had a bit of a conflict between his political views and his commissions. He responded that he was volatile, his thinking was always evolving, and that his convictions followed his conscience. But now, he was a Libertarian—and he was raring to act.

We discussed political philosophy. Mark's libertarianism burned with the faith of the newly converted—it gravitated toward anarchy. Mine, tempered by experience, was more moderate. He ran down the list of government functions that could be privatized or eliminated. Mark being Mark (and now a Libertarian, a species whose propensity to cavil is only exceeded by Marxist theoreticians and Orthodox rabbis), pounced on my uncertainty to eliminate the police force, asking, "What crimes have the police ever prevented?" Mark could go from convivial to confrontational in the flash of a rhetorical comment—eyes popping out, spit flying, face too close for comfort. But I'd grown up with him, liked him, and could calm him by tactfully pointing out that my opinions were provisional, while subtly reinforcing my affection for him.

Luckily, the party chairman called the meeting to order. He announced that he was stepping down. He'd taken a political preference test and discovered that he was more conservative than libertarian. The honorable course, he believed, was to resign. The Yavapai County Libertarian Party chair was open. With only a moment's hesitation, Mark grabbed the baton and volunteered me for treasurer adding that my clean-cut good looks, conventional attire, and calm demeanor where a necessary face for the party. It was a done deal: he became chairman and I became treasurer.

After re-connecting with him at the Libertarian Party meeting, we started to hang out together. Mark loved to take long runs in the mountains near Prescott. At sunrise, he'd run barefoot two-and-a-half miles and up 2,000 feet to 7,000-foot Granite Mountain Pass and back, cutting a maniacal figure as he hurtled over rocks, prickly pear cactus and blazing decomposed granite. I accompanied him once—with shoes. For us, being far from the beaten track, up on a mountain, down on a river, out in the desert or out at sea was a meditation, a challenge, and a love affair all rolled into one. At his cabinet shop, he had a 'heavy bag', which bore the brunt of his kickboxing workouts or his frustrations, demons that could materialize unpredictably at any time.

Libertarian Party meetings under the Davis-Miller leadership were a complete flop. After a few ill-attended party meetings where no one but me, Mark, and the new party secretary (of whom I retain no memory) showed up, even we lost interest. We drifted our separate ways: me, to teach at an Outward Bound-type school in Colorado; Mark, to apply his boundless energy in new, more radical directions.

When local author Edward Abbey published *The Monkey-wrench Gang* in 1975, it became an instant cult classic—the *Atlas Shrugged* of the environmental movement. The novel revolves around the unlikely alliance of four wilderness lovers who wage a war of low-tech sabotage—"monkeywrenching," as they called it —against mineral exploitation and development of all stripes. The group is composed of Seldom Seen Smith, a beer-drinking "jack Mormon"; Dr. Sarvis, a rich, angry surgeon; Bonnie Abzug, his (of course) gorgeous nurse; and an end-of-the-roader Vietnam vet named George Washington Hayduke. While "Who is John Galt?" became the catchphrase of Rand's followers, "Hayduke Lives!", appeared on bumper stickers, T-shirts and graffiti—an expression of solidarity with monkeywrenching.

Monkeywrenchers proliferated—not least in Prescott. At our local college, a small group of activists fired up a chain saw and, in the wee hours of the morning, cut down a new billboard just outside of town. But the novel's impact was national. As Dean Kuipers recounts in *Spin*,

> "In April 1980, Dave Forman and four other radical environmentalists took a hiking trip in the Pinacate Desert. They had all read about Hayduke and the Monkeywrench Gang, so as they sat in a dark, rural bar in San Luis, Mexico, they weren't surprised to find themselves creating an organization that would advocate widespread "ecotage"—property damage used to free wilderness areas from the blight of mining, foresting and commercial development. They named the group Earth First! (EF!) after the premise of biocentrism that John Muir and Aldo Leopold had put forth: Every species on earth has an equal right to exist, the planet is not meant to be exploited, and measures must be taken to assure this. By 1989, Earth First! had a network of over 50 "bureaus" worldwide guided by project organizers rather than a main office. Edward Abbey's fiction has become reality".

Five years later (1985), Foreman published (both as editor and partial author) Earth First!'s field manual, *Ecodefense: A Field Guide to Monkeywrenching*—a how-to book that details everything from foiling coyote traps to spiking trees to decommissioning heavy construction equipment to downing power lines.

Sometime between 1983 and 1986, the demons of perfectibility demanded another dose of commitment. Mark Davis dedicated himself to a new cause: saving the earth. He'd later say he was willing to die to prevent the rape of Mother Earth, yet—oddly—was unwilling to join Earth First! formally. Not only was he not much of a joiner; he viscerally disliked Dave Foreman thinking him a poseur. Later on though, he'd accept operational funds from him. Mark and the small group of Prescott-area activists that had coalesced for monkeywrenching operations dubbed themselves the Evan Mecham Eco-Terrorist International Conspiracy (EMETIC), deriving the name from the later-to-be-impeached, car-dealership-owning, hyper-conservative, piccanniny-invoking Mormon Arizona governor.

Mark's first foray into "ecoterrorism" was an almost laughable solo affair, except that he was never caught. In 1987 "The Ranch at Prescott," a new residential subdivision opened its doors for business. Its logo was a golden horse-head bust whose pretentiousness represented the arrogance of needless growth made artificially attractive. It infuriated him. In the middle of the night Mark climbed the pediment and painted the horse head pink. Though there were no repercussions, Mark Davis had now broken the psychological ice into criminality for a higher cause. But that wasn't the only change in his life.

Mark had recently divorced. Whether his notched-up intensity was a cause or a result—or a mixture of both—is anyone's guess. He prided himself on being able to "get into people's heads" and fancied himself a guru, though not one that sought acclaim or a following. Instead, he took to lecturing individuals on their road and purpose in life, even offering to guide them on acid trips out in the desert to help them find meaning and become "warriors."

As soon as he walked into a room, his presence dominated—his overwhelming physicality, his burning personality, his self-assured arrogance, arrogance that brooked no opposition. The very intensity of his being filled all the psychic space around him. One friend described his visits as an infusion of over-the-top energy that afterward—after he'd left—melted into a puddle of vomit on the floor that now required cleaning up.

Meanwhile, my environmental consciousness was fine tuning itself. Though I had no patience for Abbey and couldn't get past the first chapter of *The Monkeywrench Gang*, one contrarian point he made struck a chord—and he made it in a very Randian manner. In a scene from Ayn Rand's *Atlas Shrugged*, Dagny Taggart, a railroad magnate and the novel's heroine, is driving through endless, pristine forest. She's terminally bored—until she spots a billboard. Her eyes light up, her lips curl into a smile, all her senses come alive, and she comments on the contrast between nature's randomness and the billboard, an icon of the creative and purposeful effort of an individual.

Abbey, on the other hand, has one of his characters driving across a stunning Monument Valley-like landscape drinking beer and tossing the empties out the window—a monkeywrencher littering. His point is that compared to industrial magnitude pollution, which kills people and animals, empty cans along a roadway are not only harmless, they provide income for homeless scavengers. It got me to thinking about the difference between environmental aesthetics and environmental fundamentals, such as those with public health consequences, like air pollution.

As a sometime small-time land speculator, subdivider, and home builder, I faced a few decisions that helped focus my libertarian environmentalism—particularly in regard to zoning. At first I favored underground utilities, and was instrumental in getting the county to institute a zoning ban on mobile and modular homes—both of these on aesthetic grounds—in my neighborhood. But when I received a cost estimate for underground utilities versus power poles for one project, I quickly changed my mind: the aesthetics were just not worth the price. The huge difference reflected a much greater expenditure of energy, time and manpower. Aesthetics would have substantially increased the price of the finished product, thereby making it less affordable to more people. In my mind, the additional energy expenditure alone cancelled any green aesthetic concerns.

One evening at my girlfriend Sheila's home, her dad took to complaining about his difficulties trying to obtain a permit to develop a mobile home subdivision next to one of Prescott's most beautiful lakes. I could hardly believe my ears. He was such a kind man, dedicated to his wheelchair-bound wife. And he'd lovingly—and to great expense—restored an old Victorian home in the center of town. How could he be a trailer park slum lord? I asked him: Didn't he care about the quality of life in our town?

"Poor people have to live somewhere," he responded philosophically, adding, "And they shouldn't be zoned out of beautiful areas." It was a perspective I'd never considered. He added that the subdivision would not be the typical cheek-by-jowl mobile home park, but would have decent-sized lots with many trees.

Another day a neighbor dropped by, worked up into a lather. He informed me that the state was planning to register all our wells with an eye, ultimately, to meter them, measure our water usage and even *charge us for the water from our own wells.* My first reaction was outrage. But then the calmer strains of research took over. First, an overview of water policy, in libertarian author Terry L. Anderson's *Water Crisis: Ending the Policy Drought.* Then, a reading of the pending legislation.

The long and short of it was that some critical Arizona aquifers were being depleted at an unsustainable rate. And Chino Valley was smack dab in the middle of one of these. As Anderson had clearly pointed out, aquifer extraction is a "tragedy of the commons" phenomenon. His mitigating proposals were right in line with Milton Friedman's solutions, and, to my surprise, so was Arizona's new law. The new AMA (Active Management Area) designations were meant to monitor water extraction, granting first-come-first-served rights to users in, as it seemed to me, an equitable solution to our home-grown tragedy of the commons. John Maynard Keynes, the English economist, once said, "When the facts change, I change my mind. What do you do?" I changed my mind about this particular government intrusion.

But it was zoning, after one contentious, standing-room-only, public meeting of the zoning board that really rattled me. One of my new neighbors (who had bought a 10-acre parcel from me) approached me one day requesting support for a zoning variance he was seeking. He was an elderly man of modest means, living out his dream of retiring to a wooded, rural homestead. He proposed to install a mobile home on his lot and live in it while building a log cabin around it to enclose it, thereby saving time, money and interior finishing materials. Even though, when the project was completed, there would have been no trace of a trailer; its invisible existence was still, technically, in violation of the zoning restrictions against mobile homes I'd previously supported. Hence the need for a variance.

I agreed to support him.

His petition polarized the neighborhood. Ideological lines were drawn and factions formed, mostly by those whose visceral hate of mobile homes was an integral part of their identity. Neighbors who had previously been on friendly terms now avoided each other. I breasted my cards: antagonizing people did not yield beneficial results. Since I'd sold some of the lots and helped establish the zoning restrictions, most assumed I was against the variance.

At the zoning board meeting the room was packed, the tension was thick and the tumult intimidating—particularly for the elderly petitioner and his wife. Visibly shunned by most attendees, they were so nervous he stared straight ahead, stoic and impassive, clutching his notebook of prepared comments, while his wife stood beside him, cheeks wet with uncontrollable tears.

My heart went out to them. I approached them, shook their hands, encouraged them, and sat with them. The meeting was called to order. For most of us, it was our first zoning hearing, so the chairman explained the procedure. First, the petitioners would present their request, along with the reasons for the variance they sought. Afterward, members of the public could offer arguments for or against the proposed variance.

Watching that man kowtow to the zoning board up on its elevated dais with the factious audience murmuring hostile comments gave me a glimpse of what 'struggle sessions' in Mao's China during the Cultural Revolution must have been like. Though already familiar with the political, philosophical and economic arguments against zoning I now became viscerally opposed to the concept.

After the old man presented his case and a dozen antis retorted, I spoke in his favor, surprising myself with such an eloquent supporting argument that the local newspaper quoted me and carried my photo.

All to no avail. The couple's petition was rejected. I walked them out to their car. It was the least I could do.

Platyrrhines vs. Catarrhines

When EMETIC took credit for torching the pylons at the Arizona Snow Bowl ski area on October 5, 1987, their communiques opened up the first leads to the Palo Verde attack and the small-scale monkeywrenching that had continued throughout 1986-87.

Investigators went into overdrive. But it wasn't until nine months later that the FBI got its first big break. Ron Frazier, one of the Prescott area eco-activists, turned coat and became an FBI informant. He'd driven Mark Davis to a Phoenix welding supply store to purchase a torch, regulator and hoses on September 29, 1987—only one week before the Arizona Snow Bowl torching.

Unstable and jilted by his ex-lover, Ilse Asplund—who'd then become Davis' lover—he rationalized that he was protecting Ilse and her kids from the dangerous Davis. Mark could be arrogant and condescending and was oblivious to jealousy—traits that did not endear him to Frazier, a drug-addled stoner of modest intellect, once described as being a few neurons short of a full nervous system.

At the Vern Lewis welding supply store, the manager identified Mark Davis from a photo lineup as the man who had purchased the torching equipment. Mark's nose scar, his red Medusa locks and rock-solid physique made him unforgettable.

Suspecting that EMETIC was somehow linked to—or a front for—Earth First!, the FBI assigned an undercover operative, Michael Fain, to infiltrate the group.

Over the course of a year-and-a-half Fain, using the alias Mike Tait and the persona of a PTSD'd Vietnam vet, finagled himself into the group by attending an Earth First! rendezvous.

Who Fain really was, other than a spic-and-span, be-suited, regulation no-facial-hair FBI Special Agent, is not part of the public record. He must at least have been in the armed forces and known how to frame a house. But his performance as a wanna-be Earth Firster "just beginning to open up to the environment" was Oscar-worthy. To avoid being traced, he said he was a self-employed carpenter. He grew a bushy blond beard and donned a flannel shirt, faded jeans and boots. To dilute an overly macho image, Fain/Tait adopted a guileless and emotionally needy, child-like enthusiasm tinged with a slow-on-the-uptake bearing—perfect for tugging on the heartstrings of Peg Millet, Mark's accomplice.

Peg was an Earth First! activist, a self-described "redneck woman for wilderness," and close confidant of Mark Davis'. She was a stout, good looking 35 year-old woman who had grown up breaking and riding horses—even running a stable in Norway for a couple of years. After a stint as a firefighter with the National Forest Service, she got a sweetheart deal living in the old historic Palace Station, an 1870's stagecoach stop, high up in the Bradshaw Mountains in the Prescott National Forest. For now she was a part-time counselor at the local Planned Parenthood clinic.

On Labor Day, 1988, Fain/Tait, Millet and a few other activists, hit the site of the proposed Mt. Graham observatory near Tucson—this time for a public demonstration that included planting seedlings on the old Forest Service road that was to be tarmacked for the telescope's access. Decked out in forest critter costumes they linked arms, pledged their bodies to the mountain and chanted: "No scopes! Save Mount Graham!" in front of a handful of media representatives and other notables. On the drive down, out of sight of the media people, Fain/Tait suggested they pull out the survey markers lining the proposed access road to the observatory—which they did, slowly zig-zagging back and forth across the dirt road, reaching out of the pick-up truck's windows, snatching bunting flags and stakes. Some would say, later, that Fain/Tait was an agent provocateur.

Before the month was out, they struck again.

One of Peggy Millet's *bete noires* were the Hermit, Pine Nut and Canyon uranium mines on both the North and South Rims of the Grand Canyon. These mines disgorged thousands of tons of earth with radioactive tailings and released a fine uranium dust into the winds—all on the border of national park land. With the North and South Rim mines being separated by a five-hour drive, any attack on both required a greater degree of co-ordination and synchronization than EMETIC had ever under-taken before—just the sort of challenge Mark Davis thrived on.

At first, Mark had big plans, "I'm gonna blow the Canyon Mine and knock over the head frame," he told Frazier, adding that he wanted to get his hands on dynamite.

Frazier then implied that he knew where to get dynamite. Trouble was, Davis had no money for dynamite. "I'd rather steal it," he said, "But not from anybody, not from a human. I'd rather steal it from a corporation...If I steal, I want to steal from a crook, a corporation. I'm real rigid about that...If worse comes to worst, we could just steal it [from anyone] and send him the money."

Mark was also especially concerned with safety. At one point during the planning process he told Frazier, "I want to see it go down," seemingly unconcerned with the details of an immediate escape.

"You want to see it?" exclaimed Frazier, puzzled.

"I want to see it go down because I want to make sure no-body walks out of that trailer. If somebody walks out of that trailer, I'm going to yell at them. And tell them to get back inside, there's about to be an explosion," explained Mark.

"Yeah?" answered Frazier, catching on to Davis' logic.

"'Cause I don't want anyone to get hurt," Mark added.

Frazier agreed, "Right."

With the stakes about to be raised, it seemed to Mark a good time to lecture the somewhat dodgy Frazier on how to keep from getting caught (a pointless exercise with a co-conspirator-turned-informant):

> *"What I do is I clean my house out of everything after I do a strike, before I do a strike. No dope. You know, no Earth First! journals. Nothing. You don't have to do it if you don't want to. Just telling you what I do…And then I don't talk about it on the phone or nothing for a couple of months. Unless we fuck up, and I haven't ever fucked up, or leave some clue that would point to Prescott, they literally have the entire western United States to look at for who did it. Usually cops aren't really very smart. The only way they ever catch anybody, generally speaking, is if someone talks."*

As it turned out, no dynamite was employed. Mark's creativity went into hyper drive. At the South Rim Canyon Mine Mark later related, "…we cut a bunch [28] of poles about three-quarters of the way through…[then] I got on the ground with a hacksaw and cut the [last] one [#29]… That fell over. The whole thing fell over and the lines shorted…those lights they have out there flared…it looked like an atomic bomb explosion. Like this huge flare of light."

With two informants in EMETIC, the FBI had known about the uranium mine strike but declined to act because Dave Foreman wasn't involved. They considered the founder of Earth First! *the* ultimate kingpin of all the sabotage operations and they wanted to nab him red-handed, or at least with incriminating evidence. What they did not know was that a simultaneous attack happened at an Energy Fuels nuclear facility on the North Rim —a testament either to their informants' incompetence, or the planning expertise of Mark Davis, who didn't yet trust Fain/Tait. The events were front page news for days.

A month later, on October 25, 1988, EMETIC hit the Fairfield Snow Bowl again, this time felling one of the chair lift's main supports. EMETIC was getting bold. After the operation it sent communiqués to every radio and television station in Northern Arizona, warning the resort concessionaires to stop developing the San Francisco Peaks. Still, the FBI declined to intervene hoping to somehow implicate Foreman.

Last Stand at Alamo Lake

In order to further inveigle himself into Earth First! circles—and find its connection to EMETIC—Fain/Tait took to dropping by the *EF! Journal* offices in Tucson and shooting the breeze, where he soon became a familiar face. No one gave him a second look. Yet Mark Davis was the one person whose trust Fain/Tait failed to gain. "He's a deep plant," Mark told Peg Millet. Mark didn't even consider himself a member of Earth First! he was so averse to organizations and groups.

It wasn't until March 1989, after Millet claimed to have "checked out" Fain/Tait by involving him in several acts of ecotage, that Davis became a bit receptive to the newcomer. When the FBI plant took to joining Mark on his barefoot runs up Granite Mountain—also barefoot—and his kickboxing workouts on the heavy bag, Mark finally warmed to him. The man who preferred to work alone, who had almost no close friends (other than Millet and Asplund), and trusted virtually no one, now had what some considered an equal partner.

Later that month Davis and Millet included Fain/Tait in the big plans they were developing, plans to do things that would stun the nation: cutting down the transmission lines leading from the Palo Verde (Arizona) and Diablo Canyon (San Luis Obispo, California) nuke plants, and the lines leading to the Rocky Flats atomic weapons facility near Denver. But the group believed they needed a practice run—and money.

The practice run target was a transmission tower that supplied electricity to the Central Arizona Project's (CAP) water-lift station near Alamo Lake by Wenden, Arizona. The CAP diverted Colorado River water to irrigate central Arizona. EMETIC's beef with the CAP was that in some years all the Colorado River's water was diverted to agriculture, with not a drop reaching the Gulf of California—in effect, killing the delta's delicate ecology. The icing on the cake for this operation was the nearly literal rendition of Edward Abbey's script where the monkeywrenchers battle to keep the Colorado River flowing free.

Fain/Tait vehemently opposed the plan. For one, sabotaging a pump station for an agricultural canal just didn't have the impact that attacking a nuclear power plant might stir; impact whose consequences would translate into long prison sentences and the loss of any public sympathy for the ecoterrorists. But more fundamentally, the FBI needed evidence of Earth First!'s direct involvement. So Fain/Tait suggested approaching Dave Foreman for a donation to the CAP caper. Fain/Tait later testified that he saw Foreman hand over $580 in cash to Davis so he could buy supplies.

But that bit of evidence wasn't airtight. Mark turned the $580 over to Frazier who then, as the *New Times'* Michael Lacey reported, "Took a powder." Fain/Tait needed firmer evidence. On May 13, he went to Tucson where the Earth First! office was holding a fund-raising garage sale. Foreman gave him another $100 for Prescott operations. The money wasn't much, but it was the smoking gun the FBI wanted to bust Earth First! along with EMETIC. It didn't cross the infiltrator's mind that he, the FBI, being the conduit for the money, implicated him as an instigator. Still, they waited so as to catch the perps in the act and add to the indictments.

The commando team for the CAP hit was composed of Mark Davis, Fain/Tait, Peg Millet and Dr. Marc A. Baker, an ill-tempered Prescott botanist who specialized in cholla cactus, and whose idea of leaving "no trace" included tying—with bailing wire—18 inch by 10 inch rectangular plywood boards to the soles of his boots to avoid leaving footprints. Millet, on the other hand, wrapped her boots with duct tape.

On May 30, 1989, with Mark as the ringleader bearing the torch—literally—they prepared to strike. All four had crammed into Fain/Tait's Chevy pickup. They parked half-a-mile away from CAP Pole 40-1, a tower that marked a curve in the power lines. Once its legs were cut, the tension of the cables would pull the whole run down.

Impatiently they awaited nightfall, absolute darkness. Davis and Baker, the two claustrophobes, fidgeted. When they piled out of the cab Davis gathered his gas tanks, torch and regulator and assembled them. While he and Baker headed for the tower, Fain/Tait and Millet disappeared into the darkness going in opposite directions, ostensibly as bracketed lookouts.

But so was the FBI ready to strike—with a full SWAT team of more than 50 agents (some on horses), H&K MP-5 sub-machine guns, helicopters with night-vision capability, and even bloodhounds. As soon as Mark cut halfway through the first tower leg, Desert Storm erupted. Baker tried to run but stumbled over his plywood flats. Davis, with his welder's visor, was blinded clueless. He just stood flat-footed, vaguely aware of the guns now pointed at him.

Peg Millet, a big woman, managed to elude capture, running into the desert. She reached Highway 60 and hitchhiked back to Prescott, over 60 miles away. Not even the bloodhounds released to track her succeeded in finding her. She was apprehended the next day at the Planned Parenthood Clinic, where she showed up as if nothing had happened. Ilse Asplund, Davis' girlfriend, and Dave Forman were also arrested after the fact.

The EMETIC Monkey Trial

Over two dozen Earth First! affiliates in Washington, Montana, Colorado and Arizona were subpoenaed, questioned or searched for tie-ins to the group. The EMETIC five were held without bail. The FBI believed they were preventing a "China Syndrome", a nuke meltdown scenario in California, Arizona and Colorado.

From his cell in the Maricopa County jail Mark Davis issued a statement:

> *"We have brutally, brutally assaulted each other and the planet. We have misused the gift of sentience. Once your eyes open up and you see it, the shame is intense and terrible. We're about at the end of the human strain. Unless humans begin to show some of the beauty they were born with, and can actually manifest, our little biological experiment here is ended."*

At the three-month long trial Gerry Spence, the celebrity attorney—fresh from the Karen Silkwood and Randy Weaver (he of the standoff at Ruby Ridge, Idaho) cases—headed the defense team representing Forman.

The prosecution's case was overstated and fell apart slowly. Informant Frazier was quickly shown to not only be an unreliable witness but also to have aided—shades of entrapment—Davis in obtaining welding equipment and instructing him on its use. Fain/Tait was accidentally recorded admitting to another agent that Foreman was harmless, while the $100 contribution the author meant to give EMETIC for undisclosed activities had been handed over at Fain/Tait's instigation. And it was Fain/Tait's truck that was used in the CAP caper—more entrapment upon entrapment.

But Fain/Tait's enthusiasm for the bust hadn't stopped there. When Davis wanted to topple the CAP tower for practice, it was Fain/Tait that tried to convince him to hit the Palo Verde nuclear plant instead. And when Mark mused to him that he was thinking of giving up monkeywrenching, it was Fain/Tait who urged him not to give up the fight.

In a plea bargain, four pleaded guilty to one charge, about $5,200 worth of damage to the Snow Bowl ski lift. Forman, who funded part of the operations, got probation, a $250 fine and was forced to foreswear monkeywrenching. It was the end of Earth First!'s first incarnation. Dr. Baker served six months, while Asplund served one; each was fined $2,000. Millet was sentenced to 3 years and restitution of $19,821. Davis got 6 years and restitution of $19,821.

At the sentencing hearing, the prosecutor wanted Davis to be remanded to jail immediately and to serve time without parole. But Davis had his say:

> *"I have stood in front of men with guns and stopped them from beating women. I have stopped robberies. I have gone up a tower and pulled a man away from a 50,000 volt line. I don't want my species to die. I don't want my kids to die. We are in the process of suicide. It's all legal, but it's suicide."*

Judge Broomfield was taken with Davis' grandiloquence and gave him 17 days to report to prison. Furthermore, he gave Davis a sentence that would allow for parole at any time during his jail term.

In September 1991, four days before Mark reported to serve his time, the *Los Angeles Times* provided him with an editorial sounding board:

> *"An intelligent conservative knows some deep truths, including the illusory nature of free lunches and the inadvisability of taking irreversible actions without understanding the consequences. Our behavior is neither intelligent nor conservative...Growth by its very nature means an increase in the speed and efficiency of environmental destruction. Anyone who says aloud that infinite growth on a finite planet is impossible is ridiculed. Denial has*

become official policy...If what I and my three colleagues did has no effect other than to further damage an already tattered social contract, then I apologize. That was not the point. I acknowledge the necessity of courts and laws, and accept my prison term. But I am not sorry."

In the late '90's I ran into Mark at a local hardware store in Prescott. He'd served four years of his six-year sentence at the minimum security prison in Boron, California. A severe claustrophobe, he had found the incarceration nearly unbearable—he'd lost 40 pounds in the two months of jail following his arrest—as he had found the separation from his two little daughters. Whatever his faults, Mark was a devoted and loving father.

In some respects he was the same old Mark. With fire burning in his eyes he announced the latest outrage against our local environment. The County Board of Supervisors in conjunction with the Arizona Highway Department was planning to build a ring road around the city of Prescott to reduce anticipated traffic congestion in the town by improving it outside.

"What are we going to do to stop it, Bob?"

* * * *

At Brophy Prep's Class of 1968 50th reunion in 2018, Mark Davis did not show up. I wasn't surprised. For one, he hadn't graduated from Brophy. But more ominously, alum Mike Collier, a Flagstaff MD better known for his books on geology with stunning aerial photography, told me that he was under the impression that Mark had committed suicide sometime around 2010. As of this writing I am still trying to verify that.

Adrift on the Shield

By Robert H. Miller

My love is like a red, red rose...
Multi-petaled and prickly.

I hired Fiona—sight unseen—out of necessity. Les, the bartender at Hanratty's—a pub not unlike TV's Cheers—had convinced a dozen of the regulars that a weekend float down Arizona's Salt River Canyon was just what they needed to infuse life into their humdrum 9-to-5 lives. A Viet Nam vet who'd spent too many days at the Battle of Hue City, Les and I ran an on-again, off-again, fly-by-night commercial river rafting operation. I planned on kayaking, both for my own and the customers' entertainment, but also as a safety measure—a kayak's flexibility is indispensable in reconnaissance and rescues.

I needed an oarsman to run my raft full of bar flies. Fiona had come highly recommended...by her own account, touting her experience running commercial rafts down rivers in Georgia and the Carolinas. She looked like Tinker Bell but was built like Abe Lincoln with long blonde hair and a Richard Nixon nose. I liked her right away.

But when she saw the 18' Avon with a rowing frame and oar locks that she was to captain, she confessed that her experience was limited to commanding smaller paddle rafts. "No worries," I reassured her, "The navigation principles are the same and oars allow for greater maneuverability."

That bit of helpful information registered about as well as badly translated Korean in an electronics instruction manual. Fiona just stared at me impassively.

She missed her run on the very first rapid and broached on a rocky shoal. I got up next to the raft, got out of my kayak, loaded it on the raft and shoved the boat off the rocks. Poor Fiona was mortified. The passengers—already three sheets to the wind—didn't mind. It was all part of the adventure. That night at camp she stayed up late by the campfire and drank too much tequila. After I'd retired and fallen asleep, she sidled up to my sleeping bag and passed out after a bout of puking.

On the following day we faced Salt River Canyon's 100-foot-long Quartzite Falls, a Class V+ rapid at nearly all water levels except when it ups its own ante and becomes Class VI, the most difficult of all rapids—a veritable death trap. A small cobble beach and narrow cliff-side trail on river-right permit landing and a difficult portage. The reconnaissance of serious rapids always builds up stress and adrenaline, usually requiring relief through urination. Really bad rapids call for a total elimination of the bowels, and sometimes even the stomach.

"It's unrunable," declared Les.

"I know," I murmured in a daze. Quartzite Falls is formed by an erosion-resistant quartz dike slicing the channel. The right bank hosts a rock slide that further constricts the river. The left bank is a sheer, albeit low cliff. The crux and terminus of the rapid is an eight-foot falls into a weir of recirculating water with no exit. Twenty feet downstream the water is slack, neither flowing up- nor downstream. On a previous run, at a trickle the water volume, a thin serpent's tongue of current overshot the weir creating an easy pour-over next to the cliff. This time, at 3,600 cubic feet per second, there was no exit. Still, I reasoned—more wishful thinking than objective reasoning—that if there were a way through, it had to be there, on the left next to the cliff.

John Wesley Powell boated the Grand Canyon to explore and map new terrain. Most modern river runners pursue rivers for recreation and to maintain a sense of adventure in their lives. I was just curious. I needed to look up the definition of Class VI water in this fluvial dictionary.

But what if I didn't make it? What was Plan B? A river runner's belay is potential rescuers with throw lines on both banks at the foot of a rapid. This time, due to the configuration of the banks, there was no belay. I was hesitant to depend on a novice paddle-raft crew overwhelmed by a ropes-and-pitons portage around a rapid whose roar and morphology impeded their ability to focus on further complexity.

If I couldn't successfully gain enough momentum to jump the falls, clear the froth and gain purchase for the paddle just downstream of the weir, I'd bail out. Forget Eskimo rolling. In a recirculating hole without an outwash, rolling would have been a desperate Sisyphean joke. The weather and water were warm, the wall on the left, by where I planned the run, looked climbable. That was Plan B: bail out and climb the cliff.

Plan C was rank speculation postulated around campfires by minds made creative through intoxicants and hubris. What to do when a hole doesn't let go? Remove the flotation device, dive deep, and grab the downstream current at the bottom of the river. I hoped I needn't resort to this for it required more blind faith than this agnostic was willing to muster.

On the way back to the boat after the recon the roar of the falls overwhelmed my brain's internal dialogue. Anxiety blurred the memorization of signposts—rocks, waves and holes that marked the course of my run—for the precious little time in the rapid is for execution not orientation. Fiona, Les and the crew members of the two rafts totally vanished from my consciousness.

Bail the boat, top off the float bags, secure loose gear. Look up at my first channel marker again; don sprayskirt, adjusting it low, beneath the ribcage so as not to pop it off. Off with the sunglasses and hat; on with the helmet and life-jacket—overtightening both and then having to loosen them so as not to constrict breathing. Relax—don't hyperventilate. Adjust the foot braces one notch tighter: graft the boat onto the lower limbs. Take another look at the entry, another pee. Wet cowling and sprayskirt to ensure adhesion. Stretch the arms and rotate the torso. Push the kayak to the water's edge, slip into the cockpit and lock feet, hips, butt and back.

Slicing into the current with an upstream eddy exit, I pivoted to face the slot. Right away I knew I'd never make it. Rocks, holes and zones of funny water impeded my line. The first drop, about five feet, yielded no surprises. In the relatively slack water below, I fine-tuned the orientation and location of the kayak and immediately dug the blades and pumped the paddle shaft to gather momentum for the jump. It was hopeless.

The high-volume Hollowform kayak hit the weir like a fat drunk plopping on a waterbed. The backwash punched the bow up while the falls buried the stern and, like a Murphy bed slamming back into a wall, the boat rose fully erect and slammed me backwards and upside-down into the falls. Somehow I struggled out of the cockpit without thought to paddle or boat. Water rushed into the boat with such force that the split float bags in the bow popped out. The kayak stood vertically like a dagger in the heart of the cataract, one end full of water, the other bobbing in the air. And there it seemed content to settle indefinitely. Pressed up close and contiguous were the paddle, two float bags and a desperate kayaker fervently reviewing the details of Plan B.

The cliff wall was so near yet I was totally out of control, utterly overwhelmed by the maelstrom of asphyxiating froth. Though grimly trying to retain a clear mind, my brain reviewed all the women I had ever loved and regretted the ones I'd missed.

It was the kayak that saved me. At first I found out I could use it to hoist up and grab a breath. Then it provided me with a potential exit ticket. The kayak had achieved such perfect equilibrium that I was able to place the soles of my feet against the deck, coil my legs like a spring and with a powerful lateral and downstream thrust grab a knob of quartz protruding from the wall.

I clung there catching my breath and savoring the security like an infant on a mother's breast. Though in retrospect I know that overhanging cliff at the base of the falls is a formidable climb, pure adrenalin turned it into a ladder with big rungs. Up I went.

On the ledge above I took stock of the situation. Below, the boat stood nearly still, pulsating up and down with the water's energy, while the paddle danced madly about like a conductor's baton during the climax to some outrageously dissonant symphony. One float bag had disappeared, the other remained pinned into the weir like a clove of garlic punched deep in the fat of a roast. On the opposite bank my companions stood transfixed but unable to help me, their eyes boring through my chest. They were no further along with their portage than when I'd left them.

"Let's get the hell out of here!" I yelled with a disembodied voice that startled me. Yet I still had to retrieve my boat.

Climbing back down a bit, I waited until the paddle flung itself within hand's reach, grabbed it and tossed it up on the shelf. Then, using a long, hooked branch scrounged from the ledge above, I leaned out over the most overhanging portion of the wall and snatched the painter loop on the kayak's tip, tilting the boat until I could slip my fingers through the cord. Carefully and deliberately I pulled it downstream to a low point on the bank and pulled it up. There I emptied it, got in and ferried across the river to rejoin the others.

"Are you OK?" Surrealism laced reality: sounds took on a hollow, distant timbre, my companions' gazes revealed a quantum gap of shared experience. I was stared at with awe.

"Yeah." No one asked for elaboration. I needed time to sort my feelings. The mind collates data at its own pace with little regard for somatic activity. They spent another hour hauling boxes and rafts around the falls.

Living beings use shock to deal with trauma and, sometimes, amnesia to cope with shock. Still, that small blue float bag still trapped in the falls as we floated downriver was indelibly seared into my brain. I'm agnostic because I wish to see things as they really are—Quartzite Falls recalibrated my judgement one notch closer to reality.

For a visual experience of what the Quartzite Falls keeper hole does to a large raft, visit www.youtube.com/watch? v=ib34-4fGXjg to view this short video. The water level here is 2,600 cfs; my run was at 3,600 cfs.

In May of 1993 two experienced California rafters attempted to run Quartzite Falls. Both drowned. They weren't the first. Later that year "Taz" Stoner and seven accomplices decided to dynamite a hole in the quartz dyke on the lower falls that created the keeper hole. After two failed attempts they used a 68-pound dynamite blast that finally burst a hole in the dike. The falls are now Class III and have been renamed Quartzite Falls Rapid.

Stoner and his cohorts were convicted in Federal Court the following year of destruction of federal property. A 2017 account of Quartzite Falls Rapid reports that extreme floods through Salt River Canyon since the 1994 vandalism have obliterated any landing beaches above the falls precluding any reconnaissance of the rapid. Had Stoner not blown a hole through the dyke, the Salt River Canyon's entire middle gorge would now be unrunable due to the Falls' unportageability since the floods.

Skid Marks & Fridge Magnets

On the drive back to Phoenix and during dinner at a Mexican restaurant in Globe no one mentioned the incident at Quartzite Falls. Thankfully, no one asked "how I felt." However, I did invite Fiona on a rock climbing date the following weekend. She batted her eyelashes and accepted.

Fiona was an attractive bundle of contradictions: a track sprinter who smoked, a rock climber who didn't lead, a classical cellist partial to bagpipes and bluegrass, a newspaper reporter who didn't drink coffee. These—and other—contradictions endeared and repelled at the same time.

She had a reputation for being the most dogged reporter at her big city newspaper. Her soft Southern drawl disarmed and drew out her targets. She was particularly adept at putting her interviewees—once she'd gained their confidence—unexpectedly on the spot, often completely discombobulating them and having them reveal bits they never intended to. As a detective following clues, she was unsurpassed. Yet, outside of work, she exhibited little curiosity and woefully lacked a broad knowledge base. When she was promoted to head of the real estate department at her paper, her father remarked, "What do *you* know about real estate, Fiona?" She didn't seem to take the rhetorical question as a put-down—especially coming from her father. The quip was true, it wasn't meant disparagingly and they loved each other. Yet she knew next to nothing about real estate.

Kayaking, rock climbing and writing drew us closer. Fiona could pop out copy as fast as she could type—she was Jerry Lee Lewis on a riff at her keyboard. Typical of her profession though, she waited until the last minute of a deadline to produce. She'd bang away late into the night fueled by endless Pepsis and Salems. Her logical, publishable pieces needed little or no editing.

At the time I met her, I'd just returned from a harrowing trip down the Omo River in Ethiopia. My partner and our crew had avoided having our testicles lobbed off as coming-of-age trophies by one of the local tribes, and I was struggling to write an account of the trip, on spec, for a magazine. As it turned out, my first published piece. I agonized to eke out one paragraph a day. Fiona was endlessly encouraging, to the point of praising my finished product as better than her stuff. Of course, I disagreed.

Our first night together didn't go well. We were both shy and over expectant. Fantasies of sweet seduction through slow, heightened anticipation were dashed when she shut off all the lights, disrobed out of sight, hid under the covers and announced that she didn't want me to see her naked—even though this night was her idea. And then, during her frantic ice-breaking foreplay, she vomited on me.

I'd always been a fan of sex therapist Dr. Ruth Westheimer's insight that "if you have a rocky relationship, the rocks are under the mattress," meaning that behind troublesome relationships there is a lack of effective intimate communication. And, by implication, the inverse is implied: unsatisfying sex is indicative of a bad relationship. In spite of Fiona's and my disastrous first night together, we were both devoted to making a go of a union rich in possibilities.

Amid the rock climbing, kayaking and eccentricities, we fell in love.

Though Fiona couldn't row a raft, she was a good kayaker. The problem, however, was that her boat was at her ex-boyfriend's house. For some reason she was hesitant to claim it, and was coy about their breakup, so I offered to accompany her to get it. After retrieving it—without any drama—we headed for the middle run on the Verde River, a Class III/IV—medium to moderately difficult—jaunt. On the drive over she spilled the beans.

"News", as she'd nicknamed her ex, worked at a competing newspaper. Their relationship was punctuated by practical jokes, jokes that had become progressively more edgy. One of Fiona's household chores was to do the weekly laundry. She had taken to inspecting News' underwear for skid marks, circling the stains with a marking pen, and draping the briefs on the living room furniture with adjoining little signs and arrows declaring, "Ha, ha!", "Gross!", "Really?!" and other ridiculing editorial remarks. The last time she'd done that, company had arrived unexpectedly and seen the display. That ended the romance.

At the Verde's Beasley Flats put-in, we met DB, who was going to join us. Years later he was to pioneer many first descents down impossibly steep rivers in the Andes. But today he was just a nervous novice with a bellyful of butterflies.

Halfway through the first day we stopped to recon The Falls, the gnarliest rapid on this section of river. A successful descent of The Falls required a successful run of the pre-Falls, a Class III rock garden immediately before The Falls; and then a perfect alignment to thread a narrow tongue at the far right of The Falls.

We beached our boats just above the pre-Falls and walked the length of both rapids making mental notes of obstacles to avoid, and landmarks that signaled bear right or bear left—a reconnaissance that elicited little anticipatory stress, much less nausea; only the usual urination. Now out in the field, little modesty is practiced when pissing: everyone's concentration is focused on the throbbing of the whitewater and the planning of one's route through it.

As DB was intently studying the rapid, he casually pulled out his member and began relieving himself. Fiona sneaked up on him with her camera and snapped a close-up photo of his penis. Poor DB. He was completely taken aback between the shock of the invasion of his personal space, an unwillingness to cut off his stream mid-stream and his attempt to pivot away from this crazy woman. Fiona explained that she had a collection of penis photos she'd taken pinned up on her refrigerator. DB's would be added to it. A good sport, he just shook his head, "Whatever."

Now that she'd hooked up with me, Fiona wanted to up her kayaking game. After a few more milk runs down other desert rivers I suggested running Westwater Canyon on the Colorado River—*in flood*. She was game. At normal water levels of 3,000 cubic feet/second (CFS) the 33-mile run is a full day's paddle with a handful of Class III/IV drops. But at 30,000 CFS, the water rises 20 to 30 feet up the walls of the canyon, inundating all the beaches. All the rapids disappear: they merge into one continuous 18-mile rapid with no eddies, a run—without mishaps—easily completed in a white-knuckle 2-3 hours.

We were a team of three, including David S., a firefighter and paramedic. When Fiona saw the brown, frothy water careening by with uprooted cottonwood trees steamrollering past the put-in, she was wracked by all three distresses, including vomiting. But she was still game. With the water zipping by so fast, we held each other's boats to launch, with a camper volunteering to hold mine, the last to launch.

It was hard to believe that dreaded Skull Rapid—and the Room of Doom, its recirculating maelstrom on the right—didn't exist at this water level. We tried to keep a lookout for it, Dave S. and I having run Westwater many times before. But the water was so intense, our eyes were glued to it and each other; we had little opportunity to look at the canyon walls for orientation.

Suddenly Fiona dumped and her Eskimo roll failed. David and I, like orcas herding a hurt calf, rushed to surround and nudge her and her boat close to shore so as to catch the first opportunity to land. We floated at warp speed for what seemed miles, missing two tiny rocky pediments. Finally we caught a third beachlet by shoving Fiona and her boat ashore, but it caused David to dump. He rolled up instantly.

By now we'd nearly reached the end of the 18-mile critical stretch, so David and I waited for Fiona at a comfortable spit. She was none the worse for the wear—a real trooper.

We'd only been together for three months when the opportunity to kayak the Noatak River on Alaska's North Slope and climb Mt. Igigkpak, at the river's source—at 8,510 feet—the tallest mountain in the Gates of the Arctic National Park, came due. The trip had been in the works long before I'd met Fiona. I could see in her eyes the lust for Arctic adventure, but it was too much too soon. A request for a leave of absence from work would have been impolitic at this time.

My double kayak, tent and mess partner was Terry R., a hot blonde with possible designs on me. Fiona was certain I wouldn't be able to resist her charms, and resigned herself to that possibility. At our bon voyage party Fiona presented me with a T-shirt that announced on the front, "My friends call me...", while on the back the sentence was finished with, "Pencil dick." It was a subtle albeit humorous warning to Terry, a woman who didn't give a damn.

The Alaska Airlines flight to Kotzebue was empty save for our five expedition members. At the Kotzebue airport immediately upon landing, we negotiated for a bush plane to shuttle us as high upstream the river as possible.

From the float plane's landing on a wide, flat section of the river, Terry, myself and Les, our shell-shocked Viet Nam vet friend and river running buddy, hiked two-days over tundra puddles and tussocks to the base of Mt. Igigpak. Meanwhile, our two other kayakers waited patiently for our return filling their time by kitting up the collapsible boats we'd brought for the trip. Les carried a .45 caliber pistol for bear defense while Terry and I holstered capsicum spray. The climb, on the third day, was cut short due to white-out conditions near the summit. After a two-day hike back, we launched on the river—at 3 am (no nighttime here) to the wailing of nearby wolves.

As it turned out, I was besotted with Fiona and remained true. Some evenings Terry and I would don bug shirts and head nets and dance on the tundra to tunes from a Sony Walkman streamed through double earplugs—about as romantic as we got. Three-quarters of the way through the trip, Terry switched tents to where the prospects for romance were better. Back home, Fiona, certain of my infidelity, hedged her bets. She remained only partially true: the woman had an uncertain perception of men that was difficult to dispel.

The Yukon

We never meant to stitch together the Bering Sea on the Pacific with Hudson's Bay on the Atlantic. Crossing Canada and Alaska north of 60° by kayak was never in the cards. The Rocky Mountains—the Logan, Selwyn, Bonnet Plume and a seemingly endless number of sub-ranges—slice up the Yukon border to the Arctic Ocean dividing the region into two vast watersheds: Alaska and the Yukon on the west; the great Canadian Shield to the east.

As the bush plane flies, the distance from Norton Sound on the Bering Sea to Chesterfield Inlet in Hudson's Bay is over 2,100 miles. But as the salmon—or arctic char—swims, the distance is much greater. The Yukon River alone is 1,980 miles long.

Fiona was able to sell her paper on a sabbatical: kayaking the Yukon River would broaden her horizons and freshen her perspective, making her a better reporter. But she was still short of funds for the trip. Her suggestion to me was to "do the trip for charity" in order to raise money. She was unprepared for my reaction.

"That's a scam," I said, "I won't have any part of that. It's dishonest to pay for our trip from donations meant for something else. And anyway, if someone wants to contribute to a charity, they can do so directly. What does kayaking the Yukon have anything to do with, say, cancer research? Floating the Yukon is no big deal; a lot of people have done it. Hell, it's even been biked in mid-winter back during the Nome gold rush."

As a conventional newspaper reporter, Fiona didn't understand my point of view. But she accepted it. "How about seeking sponsorship?" she suggested.

"Who's going to want to pay for a gumba trip anyone can do?" I said, adding condescendingly, "Go for it."

Fiona's efforts paid off. Hormel contributed two crates of canned meats, not all of it Spam. After that success, I suggested she approach L'Oreal, Fiona's favorite cosmetics company. She was skeptical. Make-up and adventure expeditions didn't mix. I responded that its very originality might entice the company. With more women alpinists and extreme sport enthusiasts, they'd be ahead of the curve. By the following year, Lynn Hill would become the first person to free climb The Nose on El Capitan in Yosemite, considered the hardest rock climb in the world at the time. It wasn't long after that she was advertising wristwatches on magazine back covers.

L'Oreal bit—but not in any way that deferred our expedition expenses. They sent Fiona a small box of assorted cosmetics along with a very complementary letter congratulating her for originality and wishing us well.

The Yukon River flows out of Atlin Lake in British Co-lumbia, courses north through the Yukon Territory and turns west across Alaska, touching the Arctic Circle at Fort Yukon. There are 20 communities along its entire course, but only seven of them have road access. And out of the four bridges across the river, three are in the Yukon. The only one in Alaska, the Alaska Pipeline bridge just north of Fairbanks, was built to carry the pipeline across the river and is the conduit for the Dalton High-way, the pipeline's maintenance road.

On the 5-day drive up to Atlin Lake, we got to know each other's quirks and habits close up. Fiona hated Mexican food—and most ethnic cuisines (I loved it, all of it); she was given to mini-tantrums of inconvenience when the world didn't conform to her expectations (which she instantly got over); not, mind you, angst over world hunger or man's inhumanity to man, but rather over misplaced car keys, running out of mascara or a run in her nylons—wonderful entertainment for an otherwise deadpan man. Fiona's politics were vaguely utilitarian, without a dollop of ideology. She didn't vote, thinking it interfered with her objectivi-ty as a reporter. But her most eccentric quirk was her 'bugger ball'. To pass the time while driving Fiona took to picking her nose. Whatever came out she'd wipe on her dashboard—always on the same spot. This nasal detritus could accumulate into a little ball the size of a tiny marble, about which time it would dry out, fall off and she'd start a new one.

Les on the Yukon

Les, our Viet vet Marine buddy, joined us on the trip. Of Norwegian stock, he was oddly proud of his brachycephaly: a skull broader than its length. His craft of choice was a Coleman canoe he'd modified with oar locks so he could row, paddle or even use a kayak paddle athwart. We all adhered to a modified Marine strategy: each of us traveled completely self-contained in case we got separated, each carrying food, a stove, shelter and maps along with our personal gear. At first Fiona was a bit skeptical of this approach, inferring that I was putting a certain distance in our budding romance. But when we ran into a father-son duo in Dawson aged 80 and 60 who adhered to the same philosophy for the same reasons, she was convinced. Unfortunately, she had zero map reading skills; a deficiency we worked on during the voyage.

Les was a good map reader. He had seen two tours of duty in Vietnam as a Marine Forward Observer. Just prior to and during an infantry assault, a Forward Observer, armed with map and radio, advances as close as possible to the enemy, often on his belly. With little chance to stand up and survey the territory (sometimes heavily forested and featureless) and always under threat of discovery, he pinpoints enemy troop locations and transmits the coordinates back to the artillery. The artillery then "softens" the position. Before GPS (Global Positioning Satellites) and modern computers to aim the ordnance, this system was prone to error. Les' life and that of his fellow advancing troops depended on the accuracy of his map reading (after all, the distance between opposing factions during an assault narrows to nil). Les could pinpoint any location, anywhere, with the most rudimentary map and intuitive sensibilities forged under fire. He had such confidence in his map reading skills (and he was so cheap—a full set of 1:250,000 scale maps of the river costing a tiny fortune) that he depended on a gas station highway map for navigating the Yukon River.

After Viet Nam Les retreated to a tree house on the big island of Hawaii and grew pot. Other vets had settled there also, escaping civilization and seeking comfort in the jungle. Most were shell-shocked to some degree. It infuriated Les that PTSD was not being adequately treated in the Veterans Administration system. He took it upon himself to read every bit of research on PTSD and became an expert on it. Then he organized the Hawaii vets into the Hawaiian Veterans Association and was elected president. After a concerted letter-writing campaign to Congress and the VA, and a full-court media press including interviews on *20/20* and *Inside Edition*, Les was asked to meet with Senator Daniel Akaka of Hawaii and Congressman Pete Peterson of Florida, a Viet Nam vet, POW and later US Ambassador to Viet Nam. Les' campaign paid off in spades, but after his time in the limelight he preferred to be left alone.

SS Klondike

Yukon River barge

No one would call a float down the Yukon a wilderness trip. Yet it is; punctuated by pockets of civilization—aboriginal, modern, military and remnants of the past. Abandoned villages, cabins, cemeteries, sternwheelers, giant sluice boxes; native reserves and subsistence fish wheels; DEW line outposts and the Alaska pipeline; non-native, end-of-the-road communities filled with left- and right-wing dreamers, trappers, pot farmers, fishermen, bureaucrats and all manner of misfits, all self-reliant in attitude if not in fact—separated by tracks of true wilderness replete with wildlife: black and brown bear, moose, muskrat, wolverine, muskoxen, wolf, coyote, beaver, river otter, lynx, porcupine, fox, marten, mink and nearly all varieties of salmon but especially mosquitoes and black flies so thick they swarm on you like bees on a beekeeper's bonnet.

Approaching Whitehorse, the Yukon Territory's capital, the restored sternwheeler *SS Klondike* stood majestically moored at the river's edge, open for tours. During the Klondike gold rush and until the completion of the Al-Can Highway, Yukon River steam boats were the only means of summer transportation. Some have been abandoned along the shores, ghostly hulks along uninhabited and inaccessible-by-road stretches of river, visited only by canoers and kayakers, their eeriness punctuated by modern government signs proclaiming them national historical treasures. The *SS Evelyn* ran between Whitehorse and St. Michael on the Bering Sea, a journey that must have taken forever. Its rotting carapace precipitously askew was a hazard to explore. We were surprised there were no warning signs. Today, along the Alaskan portion of the river, tugboats pushing giant container barges supply the road-less settlements along the river in summer, bringing heavy construction machinery, vehicles, pre-fab housing and anything else too big to fly in, while trucks ply the frozen surface in winter.

Best of all were the turn-of-the-20th century ghost towns—Hootalinqua, Big Salmon, Fortymile, Dyea and others. At protected heritage site Fort Selkirk lay the hulk of a Model-T, brought in by sternwheeler. Stewart River, an old layover for Klondikers, had been maintained by its ageing owners, but they'd recently retired to an old age home. One young, lone Quebecois, the caretaker, offered us a cabin for $10. Dawson, the last Yukon River town in Canada, has preserved much of its Victorian charm.

The Alaska border was marked by a 100 foot-wide clear-cut swath of forest, a seemingly pointless exercise in full employment for the locals. There was no border control until the village of Eagle, Alaska's first territorial capital. Back then it boasted a population of 1,700. Today only 86 people live there year-round.

We were required to report to the one-man Customs and Immigration office there. Fiona looked forward to activating her reporter's juices.

Our arrival in Eagle coincided with a recent Alaska policy legalizing marijuana, coupled with a U.S. Federal policy of zero tolerance on drugs. Fiona was a pot head; not just a 'pot head', but a 24/7 toker of the strongest strains. Every morning after a Salem and a Pepsi, 3-4 bong hits prepared her for work. She'd come home at noon—ostensibly for lunch (which often consisted of a fast-food cheeseburger, her favorite, albeit one she could never finish)—suck a few more bong hits, and settle in front of the TV for *General Hospital* or *All My Children*, her favorite soap operas. Then…back to work, perhaps interviewing the state governor or a CEO of a big company; the cannabis seemingly having no effect on her performance. For this Yukon trip she'd had to go cold turkey, the consequences of which I inevitably shared.

Many of Eagle's residents also enjoyed pot, growing their own during the almost 24-hour sunlight of the far north. Occasional federal raids weren't a problem. Someone—who knows?—always alerted the residents. They'd load their potted pot plants on skiffs and hide them mid-river on the fronting island's foliage until the bust was over.

We showed up at the Customs office, a small historic building outfitted in period regalia and announced our presence. The officer, bearded and wearing old-fashioned braces, listened politely, asked if we were US citizens and wished us a good trip.

"You're not going to check our boats?" asked Fiona. The man just looked at her, as if trying to figure out what she was getting at.

"I thought you had a zero tolerance policy in effect," she added. "What if we have contraband?"

"Do you?" he asked.

"No," Fiona answered, "but I'm just saying..."

"Get out of here while you're ahead," he finished with, what seemed to me, a mischievous grin on his face, as if this was the most fun he'd had in ages.

Between Eagle and Circle, Alaska's northernmost town connected to the continental road grid, the river begins to braid, a prelude to the Yukon Flats, a vast area of wetlands, forest, bog, and low-lying ground with about 40,000 small lakes and streams. Nine major rivers, including the Porcupine—the old route and portage from the Mackenzie River—and Chandalar Rivers join the Yukon along this stretch, vastly increasing its flow. The braiding is so extensive and the terrain so flat, a boater can easily lose track of his location.

Fiona had scored some dope in Eagle. She was busting out of her skin with energy, eyes all aglow, ready to make her boat dance. Earlier on the trip, after we discovered that we each had different paddling rhythms and speeds, we'd agreed to paddle at our own pace for an hour and then wait for whichever one of us lagged—usually Fiona—so as not to cramp our separate styles.

When she hit the water at Eagle Fiona took off like a NASCAR racer at trials. Try as I might, I couldn't catch up to her. After a couple of hours I worried myself into a frenzy thinking that she might miss Circle, located on an extremely braided part of the river, get completely lost and we'd never see each other again. She had no maps.

But there she was, at the boat ramp in Circle, waiting patiently for me. I blew my top. Had she forgotten our protocol? Did she not realize the consequences if she missed Circle? No anger is more righteous than that which boils over the safety concerns of a loved one—even when directed at the loved one (or so goes the rationalization). I insisted that we stay together through the Yukon Flats. We made up.

Les didn't always travel with us. He sought solitude in the vast northern wilderness, the better to tame his inner demons. We began referring to him as an "end of the roader" because he envied the lifestyles and people who lived on the verges of civilization.

Approaching Fort Yukon, eight miles north of the Arctic Circle, temperatures hit 90° and the skies filled with smoke. Fort Yukon has the distinction of registering both the highest (100°) and lowest (-78°) temperatures ever recorded in Alaska. It lies at the junction of the Yukon-Porcupine Rivers confluence and was a major nexus during the fur trade era. A short but difficult portage from the Mackenzie River up the Rat River and over the divide to the Bell and Porcupine Rivers allowed traders to navigate mostly downstream from Great Slave Lake to the Bering Sea.

Fiona craved a cheeseburger and Pepsi, the $25 price notwithstanding, at the only café in town. The scuttlebutt there was that bored native firefighters had purposely ignited the blazes creating the smoky skies in order to earn some extra money. No structures were threatened and a 'let it burn' policy hadn't yet reached the area.

With the combined flows of all the rivers converging on the Yukon—and our ethic of paddling hard—we were easily covering 60 miles a day. Past the native settlements of Beaver and Stevens Village we ran into Kristen, a lone kayaker floating midriver in the water next to her boat to cool off. She was extraordinary in every way.

Later, when Kristen stopped for lunch, I got a good look at her. Quiet and verbally shy, her eyes were pools of mystery, revealing little. Pouty, everted lips shielded oversized and bunny-toothed incisors that hinted of prognathy. She had a perfectly rounded, dolichocephalic skull with a high forehead. A hint of lanugo caressed her cheeks. Only 24, she was becomingly steatopigyous with a strong upper torso to match. She was quite compelling in an untraditional sense.

If you, dear reader, think the previous description a bit overwrought, it only reflects my own reaction upon encountering this

Freya of the Yukon. Fiona told me not to stare and paddled away huffily, withholding conversation for the rest of the morning.

Kristen was barefooted, unkempt, and underdressed, with a shotgun slung from her shoulder. She was impervious to the sun, the mosquitoes and black flies, but at least was vigilant for bears. An assayer by trade, she hailed from Dawson, Yukon Territory, and was traveling light—no stove, no brand-name gear—cadging salmon from the fish wheelers. With few words exchanged, we parted company.

Alaska Pipeline

At some point Les and Kristen had run into each other, passed the time of day and discussed map skills. We all rendezvoused to camp on the north shore by the cleared area below the Alaska Pipeline bridge. Les brought out his special bottle of Barbancourt Rhum. Before long, Kristen was sidling up to Les with more than a cocktail in mind.

But then, down the scarp, a clean-cut, red-headed man in a white shirt ambled in. He was carrying two six-packs of Budweiser and packing a side arm. He introduced himself as the pipeline's security guard and added that he never got company. We were special and the beer was on him.

Yukon River camp at the base of the Alaska pipeline.
L to R: Pipeline guard, Kristen, author, Les.

Before long Kristen's charms were aimed at the security guard. Not that Les was less of a find, but the security guard was only available tonight. Les was available downriver. Was Kristen so cynical?

As we found out later, Kristen was kayaking the Yukon to find a *real* man. She was an apparition I imagined few Alaskan backwoodsmen could resist and she was obsessively focused on her quest—no single man got away from her. She was literally testing every available male on her route, fishermen first. Kristen and the guard spent the night together in her laboratory…er, tent.

Poor Les. His confidence and social graces—not to mention his dating skills—were already in the ICU from his PTSD. Kristen's behavior was inexplicable—even to a bartender. When we awoke the next morning he'd already decamped and was long gone. Fiona, Kristen and I launched at the same time and soon caught up with Les. After greeting him, Fiona and I discreetly paddled away giving Kristen a chance to work her magic.

She tried engaging Les about map reading—as he recounted later. But he shut her down; he was too hurt. We watched as she paddled off around one of the many interminable bends in the river.

When we last heard of her—she was a minor legend by then—she'd taken up with a fisherman, trapper and jack-of-all-trades living at the edge of the small waterfront community of Ruby.

When we passed by Ruby, there she was, beaming, standing on shore with her new beau—not too improbably, since life along the Yukon is lived next to the river—a very hairy, bearded, stocky young man with fire in his eyes, dressed in an orange jump suit. We all waved in recognition.

Floating by the Ramparts of the Yukon, impressive grey eroding bluffs on river left, we kept an eye out for mammoth tusks. We'd been told of recent finds there, especially after break-up, when ice flows scour the bluffs and unearth old bones.

We ate well. The King Salmon were running and we benefitted from a loophole in Alaskan law. While commercial fishing licenses were pricey, "subsistence" fishing was widely allowed. It was defined as fishing for one's own consumption. To protect the resource, both types of fishing are well regulated. Subsistence fishermen were prohibited from selling their catch. Most used fish wheels, an ingenious water wheel contraption with wire baskets that sweep up fish swimming upstream and dumps them in a repository. We'd offer to buy a salmon when we passed one that its owner was harvesting. Invariably, he'd give us a fat King—a fish that probably retailed for $100.

We carried plastic bags for these so as not to contaminate the boats with fish smell; we didn't want bears sniffing around camp while we slept. We'd also gut and clean the fish miles before making camp and usually boiled the meat with ramen noodles.

A day's float downstream of Tanana we passed a lonely homestead where an elderly native—or so we thought—woman waved us in. She was Filipino. Her husband, a lonesome Alaskan back-to-the-lander, had tired of living alone. Through a company that arranged foreign marriages he'd corresponded with her and made, what seemed to her, an attractive offer. Sight unseen she traveled to his outfit and married him. They had two sons, but she hated the life.

Yukon River fish wheel

Her man had recently died and one son had left for better prospects. She and the remaining son had a modest fish smoking operation. They gave us a gallon Zip-lock baggie full of "candy," the local name for alder-smoked salmon. We asked why she didn't go back to Manila. "My son, he love this life," she said, adding, "he never been to Philippines; he don't speak Tagalog. We stay here." On our return to Arizona I went to a Filipino grocery store in Phoenix and had the proprietor ship a box full of Filipino specialties to her.

Drying salmon

We lost Les in Galena. He'd had enough of the Yukon and figured that in the Air Force Base town he'd be able to fly out to Anchorage or Fairbanks. When word got around that a marine canoeing the Yukon was looking for a ride out, a resident marine officer sought him out. Les was wary. He hated marine officers that hadn't seen action or risen through the ranks.

Back in Viet Nam, his commanding operational officer had gotten so many grunts killed with uninformed and inexperienced decisions—decisions that brooked no criticism—that Les was determined to put a stop to it: he was going to frag him. He swore that not one more marine was going to die due to that man's stupidity. Packing a side arm he steeled himself for the deed, knowing full well the consequences. He planned on calmly explaining what he was about to do to the officer, both to be fair to him and to allay his own conscience.

Les knocked on the officer's door. "Enter," came the response. But when he walked in, someone other than Les' target sat at the desk. The original officer had been replaced. The new officer however, was aware of the circumstances—the bad decisions, the complaints, the possible repercussions—hence, the replacement. Assessing Les' state of mind, he greeted him cordially, put him at ease and asked for his side arm, which Les placed on the desk. Les could sense that the new officer was well aware of his intentions, though neither said anything. After a few more minutes of sympathetic conversation the new officer told Les that he deserved a break and issued him a 3-week R&R in Japan. It was just what Les needed.

The marine officer in Galena immediately intuited Les' hesitation; the divide between battlefield and desk COs was well known. It soon became apparent to Les that this man had seen action. They discussed battlefield experiences. Les warmed up to him. He got a flight out to Anchorage.

Fiona and I cranked out the miles, paddling target-fixated now that the end was near. We paddled 10-hour days and stopped taking rest days—an unwise move. Twenty-five miles out of Holy Cross, after nosing onto a sandy beach for lunch, I herniated two lumbar spinal discs (as I was later to be diagnosed) jerking the loaded kayak up the slope. I was paralyzed with pain. Fiona erected the tent and I crawled in, hoping a half-day's rest would improve me. But after two days of immobility I experienced zero improvement. Fiona was getting impatient and anxious.

On the third night, lying absolutely naked on top of our sleeping bags, the shotgun between us, Fiona leaned over and whispered, "There's someone outside the tent". It was a sweltering and, this being the northern latitudes, not very dark night. The no-see-um-netting zipper had given up the ghost, so the ripstop door was closed, blocking any possible breeze.

"See who it is," I smart-assed back. With the door closed, there was no way to see out. Then I heard what sounded like the grunt of a pig right next to the fabric of the tent wall. Fiona was terrified (it was on her side). My back was so bad I was in the land of lumbago and Percocet. Suddenly our guest thumped the ground loudly and repeatedly, not 18 inches from poor Fiona. And then he did it again. It had the same rhythm as a gorilla beating his chest. We cringed quietly. After what seemed like ages, the presence left. When we finally gathered the courage to go out, there, right next to Fiona's side, were the paw prints of a huge mama grizzly, as clear as only damp sand can preserve. About 20 feet away were the prints of two cubs.

Inside a small dome tent a shotgun is useless; it requires too much of a turning radius within a very confined space. And pepper spray is a mixed defense: deployment inside the tent affects the human as intensely as the bear. Fiona had had enough. The following morning she set off for Russian Mission, about 25 miles away, to get me a rescue.

Oh, the indignities of helplessness! Fiona returned hours later on a skiff piloted by a giant Yupik native. I crawled to the boat and was helped in. Fiona and the native loaded up my boat and gear into the launch. After a grueling ride we arrived in Russian

Mission, an Eskimo village founded in 1842 as a Russian fur trading outpost. The onion-domed Orthodox Church stood above all the other buildings. Fiona had arranged for a room at the only hostel, a modest little rectangular hut with 3-4 rooms owned by a Yupik and used by the infrequent visitors to the village—mostly medical, government or research personnel. I had to crawl one block—a couple of hundred feet—to my bed. It seemed that the whole town watched.

After a week of further misery with little improvement—I could at least walk bent over now—we decided to fly to Anchorage and seek medical help. Wilbur's Family Airlines serviced Russian Mission on a bi-weekly schedule with prop planes capable of carrying about six passengers. The pilot himself issued tickets and loaded baggage. A few passengers disembarked from our prospective flight, while Fiona and I were the only outgoing passengers. It was a very convivial, cozy atmosphere in the cabin. Fiona sat next to the pilot, on a seat with auxiliary controls.

Taking flight out of Russian Mission; author bent over on far right

After a while in the air, the pilot announced that he was in the Guinness Book of World Records. He pulled out a dog-eared copy opened to his entry and handed it to Fiona who shared the story with me. His claim to fame rested on the length of time he'd survived atop Mt. Rainier huddled next to the volcano's steam vent after crashing his plane on the mountain. Though he perceived his feat as an act to be proud of, Fiona and I focused on the fact that we were in the hands of a pilot who had crashed on the one obstacle in completely flat terrain. Had it been a case of target-fixation? Where the one thing one is trying to avoid one inexplicably hits? We were not reassured.

After another short while the pilot began rocking side-to-side from one butt cheek to another, as if he had ants in his pants. He announced that he had to urinate something fierce. Would Fiona hold the controls steady while he knelt on his seat, sidled up to his window and relieved himself out the window?

Fiona would have none of it. Piloting a commercial airliner? She had never piloted anything more complex than a clutch-operated car. What really flabbergasted us was the pilot's inability to follow the number one flying protocol—no, not the safety check list: relieving himself before a long flight. Fiona and I had both taken that precaution.

We told him that we used zip-lock baggies to relieve ourselves while paddling far from shore; that we could give him a baggy so he didn't need to leave the controls. He liked the idea, but he was shy; insisting that Fiona still take the controls while he traipsed to the back of the plane where Fiona couldn't look at his penis. When Fiona said she'd seen enough penises to spike a railroad and promised not to look, I couldn't help laughing, hoping she didn't pull out her camera.

Try as we might the pilot insisted on going to the back of the plane. Having taken flying lessons, I reassured Fiona that holding the steering wheel steady and doing nothing untoward was very easy. When the pilot returned to his controls he cracked open his window and dumped the piss, baggy and all, out.

In Anchorage we immediately took a flight to Whitehorse and then a taxi to Atlin Lake to retrieve our truck. We then drove back to Anchorage. All the traveling and sitting didn't seem to worsen my back. Perhaps the passage of time and activity were beneficial.

How to pick an MD? Looking through the Yellow Pages I spotted what then must have been a novel specialty: Sports Medicine. Perfect! I called the one listing and was agreed to be seen that very day. Up on the doc's walls were signed photos of Susan Butcher, four-time winner of the Iditarod race, and her dog team, and a plaque naming him the official doctor of Alaska's Olympic athletes. I'd hit pay dirt. He explained that I'd herniated the 3rd and 5th lumbar discs; that recovery required time, rest and anti-inflammatory medication, but I wasn't completely limited in my activity—except of course by my tolerance for pain—and that maintenance required a regimen of specific stretches, exercises and self-administered chiropractic movements that I should perform regularly.

After a few more days in Anchorage we flew back to Russian Mission, thankfully with a different pilot, and resumed our Yukon quest—but at a much reduced pace, with many stretching breaks.

At Andreanovsky we decided to call it quits. It was the last village before the Yukon's huge delta. The primary reason was Mark Air Express' cargo planes, which offered to ship our hard-shelled kayaks back to Anchorage for a price based on weight irrespective of size. We pulled in at the first likely pier that seemed close to the airfield. A white clapboard house stood adjacent (or was it an aluminum-clad double-wide shipped up the Yukon on a barge? Memory is a fickle friend). Fiona knocked on the door to ask permission for the use of the pier to exit the river and organize our gear for departure.

When the owner saw our kayaks he invited us in for refreshments and snacks. He and his wife wanted to hear about our trip. They were seasonal fish buyers from Seattle, coming up to Andreanovsky for the August salmon run. During the conversation, out of a side door emerged a bearded man in a gray jumpsuit, their "brew master," with a plate of teriyaki-marinated and smoked salmon strips.

To call those salmon strips "snacks" was to call Balmoral a "country cottage" or the *USS Enterprise* a "boat". While Fiona politely held herself back and nibbled a few in between appropriate intervals of time, I couldn't keep them out of my mouth. When our hostess exited to the back to get more, Fiona admonished me not to be such a pig. "I have never tasted anything this good," I said, adding "To hold myself back is not only dishonest; it's an insult to a creation so exceptional. These folks know what they have here. To pretend it's just a snack is an insult."

My assessment was vindicated when we heard a float plane land on the river and sidle up to the pier. We all walked outside. Two Asian men in suits exited the Cessna. One had a black briefcase handcuffed to his wrist. Fiona and I made ourselves scarce, going off to pack our gear for the next day's flight.

Later that evening, after the Cessna had departed, the Seattle couple elaborated. Their "candy" was a big hit in Japan. These buyers flew over to buy their entire product—no price was mentioned to us—for cash. Perhaps two dozen crates were boarded onto the Cessna. The Seattle couple's operation was low on volume but high in income. Earlier on they had recounted the obstacles in buying perfect and fresh Kings; that they had to examine each fish; that their fishermen suppliers varied considerably in dependability; that their brew master was indispensable and their formula priceless. They offered us a room in which to spread our sleeping bags.

Our return flight to Anchorage and drive back to the Lower 48 went without a hitch. Fiona and I returned to work refreshed and with an invigorated perspective on life. Life was good.

The Thelon

Now that we'd explored the west slope of the Rockies above 60° to the Pacific, we wondered what the east slope was like. Only one river seemed to fit the bill and be analogous to the Yukon; one that flowed continuously from the edge of the Rockies to the Atlantic Ocean. And it was the largest river flowing into Hudson Bay: the Thelon River (plus, it rhymes with Yukon). But unlike the Yukon, the Thelon is "as remote as you're likely to encounter on the Northwest Territories," according to the Canada Resources River Profile. There are no communities along its entire length or anywhere near, except at the end.

There once were, but their story was not encouraging. The Ihalmiut, Caribou or Inland Eskimo, numbered about 7,000 in 1886. Their subsistence centered on hunting the barren ground caribou, supplemented by musk ox and fishing. But by 1950 only 30 remained. Disease—both human and canine—and overhunting, with guns, once they acquired them, radically reduced their population. By 1949 starvation among the remaining Ihalmiut was so extreme that the Canadian government stepped in and forcibly relocated the survivors. Today their descendants live along Hudson Bay in Whale Cove, Rankin Inlet and Baker Lake, the terminus for our proposed Thelon kayaking voyage.

White men in that country fared little better. A handful of explorers and mappers traipsed through the area on dog sled and canoe in the 1890s. One, Joseph Tyrrell of the Geographical Survey of Canada, experienced such severe weather in August that he was forced to abandon his canoe and proceed on foot, a nearly impossible feat due to the impenetrable marshes, bogs, streams, rivers and more lakes and ponds than stars on a moonless night.

In 1908 four Royal Northwest Mounted Police in two 18-foot Peterborough canoes paddled and sailed from Fort Resolution on Great Slave Lake to Chesterfield Inlet on Hudson Bay, a distance of over 1,200 miles, to reconnoiter their newly-assigned fief.

Not many followed. By 1930 only a handful of trappers had penetrated the area. The three most famous, John Hornby, Edgar Christian and Harold Adlard, died of starvation after wintering on the Thelon in 1927. Like Scott and Oates of the Antarctic, their memory is recorded in the diaries they kept right up to their death. Their cabin, in ruins, still stands—what little is left of it.

And few followed them—a handful of missionaries and government functionaries; some trappers and the occasional RCN-WMP patrol. With concern that the most extensive herds of musk oxen in Canada might face future extinction, the Thelon Game Sanctuary was created in 1927. Billy Hoare, a Department of the Interior, N.W.T. Bureau, was assigned to go up, take a look at the resource and count musk oxen.

Recreational (if one can call it that) river running on the Thelon, never very extensive, began in the 1960s. Prime Minister Pierre Trudeau, an avid outdoorsman and conservationist, no doubt helped the trend with his descents of northern rivers such as the Nahanni. Most voyagers experienced epics. Pamela and Eric Morse describe in their diary a 9-day blow of gale force winds:

Pinned down by strong winds near east base of big peninsula on Aberdeen Lake. Cannot make rendezvous at foot of Schultz Lake. Prepared to abandon our canoes unless wind allows us to proceed.

"It would be unwise to assume…that the journey will be an easy one. In this part of the North, there is a good chance that you'll experience the four seasons in a single day". So continues the Canada Resources River Profile. We'd run into such hyperbolic descriptions before—after all, government warnings tend to err on the side of safety—so we took the two sentence admonition with one grain of salt. Anyway, canoes were not for us. Single collapsible—no hard-shells on bush planes—kayaks presented much less windage profile than high-sitting canoes. And in terms of expedition harmony, we'd nicknamed canoes "divorce" boats.

"The Thelon is the quintessential 'wilderness'." So begins David F. Pelly, a connoisseur of Canadian understatement, in *Thelon: A River Sanctuary*. A glance at the Great Canadian Shield, the land between Great Bear and Great Slave Lakes and the Atlantic Ocean, on a map reveals a flat plain composed of half land, half water. It resembles a giant parking lot after a heavy rain: hundreds of puddles connected by confused, dendritic flows so difficult to make sense of that even the source of the Thelon is disputed. Is it Whitefish or Lynx Lake?

The Great Canadian Shield

The Great Canadian Shield is the largest expanse of the oldest rock in the world, the bedrock forming the craton of the North American continent. It is composed of Precambrian igneous and metamorphic rock with little soil formation atop but lots of incongruous white sand. Except for a few isolated copses there are almost no trees. What little relief exists consists of bedrock outcrops too tough for the ice to grate down; eskers—remnants of the glacial scouring of the last ice age—and pingos—hills resembling a giant wart. These form on permafrost, and are analogous to the bumps that form on ice cubes from the expansion of water as it freezes.

But it is a starkly beautiful, austere land whose antiquity and isolation bore right into one's soul. A vast and clear sky whose air nearly stings the nostrils with its pure intensity; vistas so immense that the Inuit erected inuksuits—giant cairns shaped like men atop distant high points—to bolster the resolve and lift the spirits of lonely travelers and mark the route of traditional trails. Dark rock, white sand, a blue sky dotted with cotton puffs, and green ground cover—sometimes only mosses and lichen—dazzle the eyes: a stark palate of fiercely contrasting colors. It is not a place for the faint-hearted.

Fiona on the Thelon

Only three vestiges of civilization (and a fourth one, which we had no inkling of and proved a lifesaver later) intrude along its 560-mile length: A seldom-used seasonal cabin used by trappers, surveyors and explorers; an unmanned weather station, and the remains of Cosmos 954, a nuclear powered sputnik that had crashed next to the river in 1978.

Fiona obtained another sabbatical from work and we left Arizona on the 4th of July for Yellowknife, capital of the Northwest Territories. The end-of-the road city is located on bare granite along the north shore of Great Slave Lake and is only accessible via two ferry crossings, one over the Mackenzie River, the other over the Camsell River.

The float plane pilot who contemplated taking us to Lynx Lake, the Thelon's source, looked at us as if we were kids armed with toy hammers and saws who'd declared we were about to build a house. Where was our voyageur canoe? How long were we going to take? Did we have enough food? A stove? Had we logged a float plan with the RCMP? Did we have a gun? Maps? A radio? Like a bartender serving a drunk one more drink, he didn't want to be the chauffeur responsible for delivering us to disaster.

Yes, we had logged a float plan with the RCMP. And after answering the rest of his questions, allaying his fears and showing him my Canadian-designed Feathercraft kayak, he agreed to take us.

It took three-and-a-half hours to reach Lynx Lake, out by the eastern extremity of Great Slave Lake. Following the Canada Resources River Profile advice, to "ask the pilot to do a fly-over of the point where the lake meets the river." We did. It is an extremely complex geography.

He landed us by a pristine white sand beach adjacent to extensive rock outcrops and bonsai evergreens—a wilderness Japanese garden. Instantly, as soon as he flew away, the sensation of total severance was absolute. Other than that, everything was perfect.

Except for one cloud in an otherwise empty sky. It was dark and menacing, and had no acolytes—a giant sci-fi apparition, a Star Destroyer of the north that hid an entire universe of evil within its dark mass. Surface and internal lightning bolts randomly punctuated its slow progress...towards us. Though it only took up less than ten percent of the sky, its dominance grew more ominous as it approached.

We gave it little thought as we went about setting up camp and kitting up the kayaks. Strange that it was the only cloud in the sky. By the time we hit the sacks that cloud was almost directly over us and covered a substantial portion of the sky. Its internal electrical activity continued unabated with thunder now distantly audible, yet the horizon—all 360 degrees—remained clear and cloudless. Not the slightest breeze stirred. I'd never experienced any meteorological phenomena quite so eerie.

Suddenly, in the middle of the dusky night, the cloud, its lightning and thunder—now blinding and deafening—settled directly over our tent. Yet it unleashed no wind or rain. And then the finger of God reached out and touched us. A blinding ball of fire and light, like a celestial bowling ball, flashed immediately next to the tent sending a throbbing current of reality distortion deep into our bones. It was not like a psychedelic experience: this was all too real. We locked onto each other automatically, sobbing in terror.

And then it was over. The cloud moved on...or dissipated... or who knows. I looked outside half expecting to see, if not a burning bush, at least charred ground. Nothing. Fiona was still crying, disconsolate. We held each other all night.

The morning was beautiful and cloudless, yet we couldn't dispel the unsettling hangover of the previous night's ominous introduction to the Shield as we set out on the lake to find the outflow of the Thelon. We felt snug and safe in our sealed kayaks.

Reconning the Elk River waterfalls

The first forty-five miles of the river were swift, with many Class I to III rapids—challenging in a canoe, but cake in kayaks. Feeling vulnerable, however, we scouted all those we couldn't clearly see all the way through. Four miles before the junction with the Elk River, a spectacular set of waterfalls preceded by a gnarly rapid stopped us cold. Our Canada Department of Energy, Mines and Resources Map indicated a 1.2-mile portage river right. It was still early in the morning of our third day out.

The portage would require many carries. We decided to break them up into relays and, for the first relay, began stockpiling gear atop the escarpment that defined the river channel's gorge. We would then do a second relay and negotiate the steep final descent down to the put-in eddy. I tired of lugging the damn shotgun on every single carry (there were many). After doing the penultimate trip down to the river, we trudged back up for one more load. Suddenly, I turned to Fiona, "Look!" I screamed in a whisper.

Where the bear appeared...

There, only about 20 yards above us (it was nearly a 45-degree slope…well, maybe only 30°), stood a grizzly bear, enthroned amongst the blueberry bushes—it was August and the harvest was ripe—with a foot-long purple drool swinging from its mouth, legs splayed like the Colossus of Rhodes atop my too-tired-to-carry shotgun. We backed away slowly just as every bear-warning pamphlet advises ("Never turn your back to a bear!"), and decided to execute a very wide and slow end-run around the spot. It didn't give chase. We were hoping that, by the time we circled around, he'd have moved on.

On our second (and much delayed) approach, this time arriving in a different spot—against all odds—he surprised us again. Fiona panicked and ran.

The bear charged. I was right in his path.

It wasn't a malicious charge, nor did it seem premeditated. It was instinctive, automatic. Instead of my life flashing before my eyes, all the potential lovers I

had ever known but never consummated ran through my mind (as in my previous near-death experience in Quartzite Falls). At the same time, my brain reviewed all the possible effective strategies I could now call upon in a split second. Warrior mode took over. I put on a terrifying face, waved my arms, screamed, and counter charged up the steep slope.

The bear stopped, turned around and ran off upstream. We watched as it plunged into the water just above the falls, swimming desperately for the north shore as the fast water drew it inexorably closer to the falls. It barely made it to safety.

My response was not supposed to be a good strategy with a charging grizzly. In extremis, it's an option for dealing with a black bear. If a grizzly charges, at best it's a bluff; it'll stop short of you or run past you. Make not a sound, cower, give up, and assume the fetal position to protect your vitals. At worst, he'll thump and scratch you—no small thing. Just don't resist. But two factors determined my unconventional response. The first was my intuition that its charge wasn't defensive or offensive—simply instinctive. The other was the realization that if that bear started barreling downhill on such a steep declivity, it would have too much inertia to stop short of me or veer away.

I was torn between relief at my deliverance on the one hand, and anger and contempt at Fiona for her cowardice and her lack of resolve that triggered the bear's charge on the other. But I kept my counsel...and an eye on the bear on the opposite shore.

As we headed downstream that bear paralleled us along the shore. Was it running away? Or was it stalking us? Who knows... but we had lots of daylight left and the river offered a much faster avenue for us than the bays and peninsulas that bear had to navigate around on land. We soon lost track of it, but then it would reappear over a hill...and do so again. We paddled continuously until 9 pm, long after we'd lost sight of it for good.

Before bed I vented my spleen on Fiona. She didn't attempt to defend her actions and was suitably contrite. But the consequences of her behavior might have been so grave that it tore out a big chunk of my estimation for her. We slept fitfully that night, not only for fear of the bear reappearing but also because of the discord between us.

Inukshuk on the Thelon

After the falls the river left the comparative relief upstream and entered low arctic tundra, a terrain graced with visibility far and wide. We spotted our first tuk-tuk, Inuit for caribou, swimming across the river. It didn't seem too concerned at our presence. And our first Inuksuit. It was built out of megaliths chosen for their symmetry and suitability. It was impossible to imagine them being transported (also unlikely that they were all originally right at that spot), or erected in a land without trees, with no means for rolling them into place or building any sort of mechanical advantage contraption to hoist the stones up into the beautiful apparition that announced, "Take heart, man has been here."

The weather remained clear and beautiful. Caribou became more common...as well as boulders shifted from their lairs by bears looking for grubs. Giant sand hills peppered with compact evergreens gave this arctic landscape a surreal effect. Hugging the shore we turned a bend and saw what had to be the largest grizzly in creation. It was nestled in the low ground cover, sitting on its haunches, its back turned to us, but its shoulder hump indicated an immensity beyond belief. We were perhaps 100 feet away from it. We stopped paddling: not a sound emanated from our direction. Let sleeping bears lie.

Musk ox

And then it got up and turned toward us. To our immense relief it turned out to be a musk ox, the first one we'd ever seen

—as prehistoric a creature as we'd ever laid eyes on, like a Lascaux cave painting come alive. It had a reassuring bovine placidity...one we didn't wish to test.

We'd heard about the day-long portage around Thelon Canyon. Technically a Class III rapid, it was very long, not well shored and—at this water level—boasted 6-8-foot reversing waves located willy-nilly along its length and peppered with weir holes. We couldn't afford to dump there. The Canada Resources River Profile indicated a portage river-right, but we found a suitable alternative on river-left. The break from paddling was welcomed...except for lugging the shotgun on every turnaround. We didn't rush it: one camp at the take out, another at the put-in; in between, carrying boats and gear across the plateau at the canyon's top.

Warden's Grove

Soon after the canyon we entered the Thelon Wildlife Sanctuary. A day didn't pass without encountering herds of musk oxen, caribou, and even solitary moose, or being attacked by swarms of black flies and mosquitoes—actually, a good sign: calm, pleasant weather. Six miles past the Thelon's junction with the Hanbury River, we stopped at Warden's Grove. The old log cabins, located behind a stand of spruce, were a welcoming diversion. Snowshoes and traps hung outside; inside, a stove, hovered over by a make-shift clothesline, dominated the center.

Fiona found a caribou rack she mounted on her deck. It would remain her figurehead mascot for the remainder of the voyage. Nearby the remains of the 1954 Russian Sputnik, Cosmos 954, could be spotted glinting in the sun. Nuclear-powered, we didn't walk up to inspect. No point in adding radiation poisoning to the Thelon's natural hazards.

Camp near Beverly Lake

Soon the trees—what few spindly specimens remained—completely disappeared. The 200 miles from Thelon Canyon to Beverly Lake went by without a hitch: a few easy rapids, some picturesque bluffs, unconcerned wildlife—no bears—flower-filled tundra and relaxing camping. Just before the lake Environment Canada's weather station appeared. The 16-foot by 8-foot aluminum siding-clad box was completely weatherproof, and secured firmly to its foundation. It had no windows but its one door was unlocked, a courtesy of the far north. Inside was a desk, a bunk, some victuals and instrumentation. We lunched inside away from the bugs.

The Canada Resources River Profile ends at Beverly Lake, implying that no one in their right mind would continue. It strongly suggests canoers end their Thelon River cruise here with a pre-arranged float plane pick-up on the river just before the big lake. Extreme winds can buffet Beverly, Aberdeen and Schultz Lakes, the last large bodies of water before Chesterfield Inlet on Hudson Bay, preventing any progress in a boat. And if the gales kick up, they can keep a plane from landing, so it behooves paddlers to be prepared to wait them out—often for a very long time. My parsimony and purist streak rejected the flight pick-up option, figuring kayaks could paddle through some pretty heavy blows that a float plane would avoid, especially when the winds kick up heavy waves.

Twenty-mile-long Beverly Lake was a study in tranquility. Fiona even sat on the deck of her very tubby Folbot for a change of pace while paddling. After a short stretch of river, 60-mile-long Aberdeen Lake opened up. Only 150 miles remained to our destination, the village of Baker Lake on Chesterfield Inlet. After lunch however, a head wind picked up. I love head winds; they're invigorating, while the miles advanced are the reward for real effort—a very satisfying sensation. Fiona, on the other hand, struggled, so we camped early.

Up here permafrost is only four inches below the surface; that is, if the impenetrable obstacle below ground isn't bedrock. There are no trees, bushes or grass, only very small, craggy dispersed ground cover, no more than 3-4 inches tall, with twisted little trunks no more than half-an-inch in diameter and growing well away from the water where the summer ice break-up can't scrub it away. Securing a tent to the ground requires ingenuity, starting with piles of rock. The only way to attach tent lanyards to rock piles is with "deadmen," strategically placed horizontal stakes cunningly burrowed inside the rock piles.

That night the wind freshened. When I heard the kayaks roll over I got out and repositioned them on the windward side of the tent parallel to the wind, added some rocks for ballast and tied their bowlines to the tent. Sleep evaded us. Even though everything was secure, we were on the *qui vive*, as heavy winds are wont to cause.

At dawn it began to rain. The sky was black as night. I had a funny feeling conditions were going to deteriorate further so I set out to find the largest boulders I could carry to strengthen our guy lines. In addition to the eight anchor points on the freestanding dome tent, half-way up the walls there were an additional six grommets for more guy lines for anchoring in extreme conditions. Our four-season, North Face VE-24 (I found out later) had been wind tunnel tested in winds up to 90 mph.

Throughout the day and into the night intermittent rain and a steady blow kept us inside—tense and anxious. Again, sleep was only a waking dream. The following dawn all hell broke loose. Temperatures dropped near freezing. Gusts in excess of 60 mph made us pray for the integrity of the tent. How much longer could this last?

And then at noon the rain stopped, the wind calmed and the sun peeked out. Still, conditions didn't feel right. At least we were able to cook a hot Mountain House freeze-dried meal.

At 5 pm the wind reversed 180° and began to slowly pick up. We prepared for another awful night. At 9 pm all hell, purgatory and the wrath of God hit us.

"Fiona, this is a hurricane." Fiona remained grimly silent as if no response was required for a statement of the obvious. We had our hands and feet full pressing up against the walls and ceiling to keep the tent from imploding due to the combined sledge-hammering of the wind and the accumulated weight of the wind-driven sleet. Our limbs acted as improvised—instead of center—multi-location poles. Had one of the aluminum poles snapped, we faced a grim reckoning. The winds must have neared if not exceeded 100 mph.

"No, I mean that in a technical sense. It's good news." When the going gets tough, Fiona, normally garrulous, clams up. To me, a withdrawn, silent partner *in extremis* is a sign of trouble. But with my observation I had managed to pique her curiosity. She glanced at me inquiringly. It was midnight. In spite of the thin layer of gravel we'd pitched the tent on, the rate of precipitation was such a deluge, it had created a pond under us, while the pressure of our hands and feet on the fabric from the inside against the inch-thick sheet of sleet on the fly was causing drips and rivulets everywhere. We were quickly getting soaked. The temperature was 32-34°.

149

"Think about it. This latest storm hit about 4 am this morning, with winds from the east and about 2" of rain until it let up at noon. About 8 hours. Then we had 8-9 hours of relative calm —the eye of the hurricane. Tonight, at 9 pm, the storm resumed, but this time from the west. It's a typical hurricane pattern. The good news is that it'll only last until 5-6 am tomorrow morning. The bad news is that this second half is typically worse than the first half."

All night we fought the collapse of our tent. I kept a chatter going to keep our morale up; difficult for a man not given to chit-chat, but necessary—what about, I haven't a clue, but I must at least have speculated about our bad weather luck. Not a word from Fiona.

Like Siberia east of the Urals and north of 60°, Arctic Canada east of the Rockies is susceptible to extremes of weather. I always wondered what made those regions different. Global weather always moves eastward, due to the earth's rotation—the Coriolis Effect. This causes prevailing winds to blow from west to east. Oceans are heat sinks. They act like fly wheels, but with heat instead of energy. They tend to remain at the temperature they're at and, unlike land masses, change very slowly. Land masses just east of large bodies of water—northern Europe next to the Atlantic, and the Americas' Pacific Northwest, adjacent to the Pacific—benefit from their moderating influence when winds carry the steadier temperatures over the land.

Land masses, such as the vast arctic flats of Siberia and eastern Arctic Canada, east of continental mountain ranges, which sap all the beneficial effects of the heat sink, are consequently subject to wild temperature fluctuations. With the Pacific Ocean and Hudson Bay downwind from them, these provide no moderating influence. The resulting extreme temperature gradients can cause in havoc in any number of ways. Fiona and I were getting the show-and-tell version of this lesson.

Two days later the winds abated enough for us to venture out in our kayaks. The rain had stopped the morning the hurricane had relented, but the winds had continued. In spite of being unable to build a fire, we managed to dry our clothes. But we were running low on food.

Qamanaugaq Bay Inuit archaeological site

Around noon we reached the end of Aberdeen Lake. Eight-hundred-foot hills squeezed the Thelon's exit. At Qamanaugaq Bay an Inuksuit beckoned. We pulled in for lunch. Up on the low bluff an old Inuit settlement, eerie and foreboding, conveyed the rigors of life in this country. Stone circles, niches and depressions that at one time must have been deeper and had been laboriously and incrementally dug to allow the permafrost to thaw, both spooked and welcomed us. How old was the settlement? All the rocks were well covered with lichen, as was a hand-carved, very simple wooden tobacco pipe, cracked and aged—the only organic remains we found.

As we ate our p-nut butter and crackers—the only food we had left—the wind turned ominous. I stood, walked over to the bluff and studied conditions from the edge. Fiona, however, complacent in the progress we were finally making, got stoned and turned on her Walkman—an unexpected displacement response: she'd had enough stress. Was it safe to proceed? Should we take the chance? I needed to talk it over with my partner: to stay or to go—that was the question. If we went, we both needed to commit 100%. I didn't want to make the decision for her.

I asked Fiona to come take a look. She was uninterested. I explained that I needed her input and advice. But Fiona had checked out into her own private world. I pleaded and cajoled but got no response. So, WHACK! I slapped her. That got her attention. She was stunned. I had never struck her. She immediately realized the gravity I perceived. We walked back to the bluff together and talked things over. We agreed to get going and got in another half day's progress. Now into Schultz Lake, the last of the big three lakes before Baker Lake, we had only 80 miles to go.

The next day, around lunchtime we spotted a strange apparition, what looked like five giant white sugar cubes at the mouth of a shallow canyon. Man-made structures, obviously. We bee-lined in. Each plywood box was elevated on short stilts. The doors were secured but unlocked. Inside bunk beds lined the walls. Except for one larger sugar cube: the kitchen and mess hall. We figured this was a wilderness lodge camp for fishing and hunting clients.

The author at fishing camp feasting on canned beans

We made a beeline for the open-shelved larder. Cold, canned beans with BBQ sauce never tasted so good. Fiona slurped straight ketchup with a coke chaser. Sated, we contemplated staying there. But this being late August, the season was over. And the day was nice and we had miles to go.

We headed out. Another half day's progress, maybe eight miles. This vast, empty land, instead of magnifying sounds, absorbs them. Out of nowhere a small motor launch appeared next to us. Four Inuit hunters stared at us. "Have you seen any caribou?"

"No," I answered.

"Any musk ox?"

"Nothing since we got to Aberdeen," I said. They looked disappointed and slowly motored away.

We carried on in the unrelenting but paddle-able blow, which kept freshening. By the time we made camp it was obvious that we were facing another serious storm. We secured the tent for an arctic holocaust.

Storm-bound for another four days. Thankfully it was no hurricane and dropped scant precipitation. We were down to chicken noodle soup packets. Fiona finished her *One Hundred Years of Solitude*, a title that reflected our feelings. We were totally out of reading material. For tent-bound times such as these I often carry difficult crossword puzzles to help pass the time. I'd completed all of them. Fiona was lapsing into a funk; she'd run out of pot. I suggested we compose a crossword puzzle from scratch. The idea grabbed her imagination and we spent the rest of the day engrossed.

On the fifth day we once more launched, hoping to hit the end of Schultz Lake. But turning the corner of a hilly peninsula the full brunt of an eastern head wind hit us. We headed in. Shortly afterward the Inuit we'd met previously landed. Their kicker couldn't fight this wind either. We all pitched in to erect their canvas wall tent. Guy lines everywhere and a continuous line of rocks along the tent's edges. They even had a radio and antenna that required a tall pole for use.

A successful hunt: caribou legs

We told them we'd run out of food. One of the men hopped over to the launch and, grinning like he had good sense, pulled out the two forelegs of a tuk-tuk. Their hunt had been successful. But he added that, with all the storms and search for game, they'd run out of gas. All six of us needed some sort of rescue.

That evening we contacted the RCMP in Baker Lake. Our friends prefaced the call by saying that the RCMP would not help them, but might offer us assistance. The Inuit did the talking. Fiona and I were way overdue, out of food and still had 64 miles to go in very questionable and variable conditions; the Inuit needed 12 gallons of gasoline to get home. Hoping to ride on our coattails, they explained the situation of the six of us. The RCMP offered Fiona and me a rescue, but it did not include gasoline for the Eskimos. We said we'd call back.

Plan B. One of the hunters radioed his father, an old man close to seventy. He offered to bring gasoline and take Fiona and me back with him as soon as there was a break in the weather.

We accepted the offer and radioed the RCMP back. Score one for self-reliance; zero for the RCMP.

Rescue canoe

Afterward we feasted on barbecued caribou, cooked inside the wall tent on a hibachi-type brazier. Out of consideration the Inuit spoke English in our presence, a courtesy that made us feel welcome and warmed our hearts just when we most needed it, especially since they were a generally taciturn group and we were an imposition.

The following day offered no respite. Fiona and I took our collapsible kayaks apart and packed them compactly. The rest of the day we all hung out in the wall tent snacking on caribou bits. Though conversation was in short supply, quiet conviviality wasn't.

The next morning we awoke to a visitor in camp. The dawn was windless and the Inuit's dad had taken advantage of the lull to motor up for the rescue. He was piloting a large green canoe with a transom that held a small kicker. He must have headed out around midnight. His motor was modest and the 64 miles separating us had good current. Introductions were cursory but warm. Papa Eskimo spoke no English. He was short, bowlegged and had a faced so lined with time and wrinkles he resembled a Shar-Pei. At his age I wondered if he was one of the forcibly evacuated people of the land. Probably. He was one tough but sympathetic stalwart.

Our hosts unloaded the gasoline and we loaded our gear—now somewhat reluctantly that we weren't getting to Baker Lake under our own steam. We lost no time in heading out.

Baker Lake, just a village with an airport, held less than 1,000 souls from 11 different Inuit groups. After arranging for a room and getting cleaned up, we weighed ourselves. I'd lost 40 pounds. Fiona...well, it's not polite to comment on a lady's weight. At the cafe—the only eatery in town—we stuffed ourselves on burgers and fries. While eating, one of our camp hosts showed up. They'd all made it back in one piece after striking camp. We bought her a burger, took a photo and booked the once-a-week flight back to Yellowknife.

The trip took its toll on us, and not just physically. Fiona and I argued and fought all the drive back to Arizona. In an attempt to save our relationship, we tied the knot soon after our return. But within three months we divorced, both sad and heartbroken, oddly enough because we still loved each other.

Epilogue: The Mackenzie

In the fall of 1968, the late Charles Kuralt, host of CBS' *On the Road*, came to Prescott College to find out what this new, "outdoor" college was all about. Roy Smith, the 28-year-old Lancashireman who'd designed the college's outdoor program, immediately stuck him in a Klepper double kayak and sent him down Diamond Creek Rapid in the Grand Canyon with a 19-year-old Cuban refugee at the helm—me. Kuralt was hooked.

Smith, never one to lack ambition, imagination, or the gift of gab, was soon leading Kuralt on imaginary journeys to the uttermost ends of the earth with wet-behind-the-ears students discovering their potential through character-steeling adventures. And so, Roy's idea of descending the Mackenzie River, portaging over the Richardson Mountains to the Yukon watershed and running clear to the Bering Sea—all with a bunch of kids who had barely gotten their driver's licenses (and still couldn't down a cold beer)—found fat sponsorship from CBS. I was put in charge of the menu.

Meanwhile, I read everything I could get my hands on about both rivers. One story, in particular, stood out way above the rest. Alexander Mackenzie, after whom the river was named, never intended to descend it—he was looking for a route to the Pacific Ocean not the Arctic. Yet once woefully off-route on its waters, he made short shrift of its 1,000 mile length in record time as if it were little more than a speed bump on his race across Canada. Still, he was much bummed.

All the other extant accounts were triumphant. Like the admiring populace in Hans Christian Andersen's *The Emperor's New Clothes*, they praised and romanticized a river whose charms shine ephemerally, if at all. Ironically, it was Mackenzie who, playing the part of the innocent young child in Andersen's fable, declared the river (albeit for different reasons) less than it seemed by naming it Disappointment River.

The Mackenzie is the Western Hemisphere's 3rd largest river, after the Amazon and Mississippi, and drains nearly the entire Northwest Territories; yet, in terms of population, it's pretty empty. The NWT had 40,000 people. Half lived in Yellowknife, the capital, on the north shore of Great Slave Lake. Another 7,000 were split between Hay River (commercial doorway to the Mackenzie's promise), and Inuvik at the opposite extreme, near its mouth and deep in the delta. The remaining dozen or so villages and towns in between had fewer than 1,000 inhabitants each (often much fewer), mostly First Nations natives whose primary contact with the outside world was along the water or by air.

There is spotty and very distant road access at various points along the river in summer. But the river is so big and wide, and the spring ice break-up so violent that it remains unbridged. Three ferries connect the sometimes 2-mile-apart shores: at Fort Providence, Arctic Red River and at the new connector spur near Wrigley. In winter, the frozen river itself becomes a highway. Barges out of Hay River service the oil fields at Norman Wells and supply the settlements with heavy cargo. One solitary tour/cruise boat plies the river. It seldom fills.

Six months later, in early May of 1969, with the 12-student expedition ready to fly up to Fort Providence, NWT, Canada along with a raft and motor for Kuralt's camera crew, CBS pulled the plug on the whole enterprise. A last-minute corporate re-organization left us low and dry.

But a missed expedition to a budding adventurer is more anguishing than unrequited love to an adolescent and, like a character out of a William Faulkner novel, I was haunted by the lure of the Mackenzie and Yukon Rivers for the ensuing 30 years.

Now that I'd inadvertently kayaked both the Yukon and the Thelon, the Mackenzie beckoned, not only as a vehicle to tie the two previous rivers into a water crossing of the North American continent but also to fulfill an old dream from college days.

Tina, my post-Fiona wife, was game. She had once rowed a sixteen-foot raft—solo—down the Colorado River through Grand Canyon without any prior experience on any river—did well and loved it. She was a very old acquaintance and sometime lover, who had, ironically, introduced me to Fiona many years before. Built like a 5'3" feminine Terminator and skeptical of everything, she'd uncharitably acquired the nickname "Teflon brain" as a young girl because—as a good friend once put it —"she woke up in a new world every day," the result of unfortunate, in-utero trauma. But it was a happy world. Nothing could dislodge Tina's positive attitude or sunny disposition. She was ADD, OCD, argumentative (yet expert at avoiding conflict), and given to concocting Lucy and Ethel schemes...in other words: fun. Though she couldn't remember names, dates or places; often confused time sequences, and played fast and loose with pronouns that, in stream-of-consciousness conversation, referenced vague, free-floating antecedents, she could talk her way out of any mishap, especially traffic tickets. Tina had grown up "street smart," sussing situations through intuition and body language—and always prevailing.

Great Slave Lake is the source of the Mackenzie River. We'd launch in Hay River on its south shore, not far from the source of the Thelon, and end at Tuktoyaktuk on the Arctic Ocean, passing by the Rat River portage over the Richardson Mountains, the path to the Yukon watershed. Though a bit short of an exact tie-up to both rivers at both ends, it would be good enough for us.

At 56, but feeling like a 19-year-old, I arrived at Hay River, NWT with Tina and two Feathercraft Expedition K-1's. We were ready to jump out of our skin and into the trip of a lifetime's anticipation. We made arrangements with a local outfitter for storing our vehicle and logged a float plan with Coast Guard Canada and the Royal Canadian Mounted Police.

The RCMP corporal, an avid kayaker, talked of his favorite northern rivers. The Mackenzie wasn't one of them. The Coast Guard Rescue Coordinator told us to be careful, particularly at Sans Sault Rapids; that the river gets a handful of Mackenzie wanna-bees each season and to make sure to visit the Coast Guard cutter on its patrol for a shower and meal as, "It would relieve their boredom".

While the Yukon is a civilized wilderness experience and the Thelon is a truly wild wilderness journey, both are compellingly attractive, worthy and, yes, fun expeditions. Not so much the Mackenzie. Yes, it's a giant wilderness river of great historical significance but, for a variety of reasons, we in time found out why it wasn't one of the RCMP corporal's favorite rivers.

Tina and Woodland Bison

Launching from Hay River—we thought—would allow us to experience the grand majesty of Great Slave Lake. We set off on a glorious June 1st day with light winds and little chop. It didn't take long to discover that, **There's no shore**. Yep, that's right. Great Slave Lake and the entire mighty Mackenzie River are shore-challenged. Less than 20 miles out of Hay River, the shores disappear in a miasma of shallow marshes, reeds and mud extending impossible distances toward some, doubtlessly existing *terra firma* beyond our reach. Where the marshes abated, deep, glutinous, unstable mud ruled. For the unwary, this had "personal" consequences.

Both of us were clad in dry suits with relief zippers. For a man, relief was just an un-zipping maneuver and a baggy away; for a woman, extraordinary contortions became the norm. At first, we'd find shoaled trees. Tina would scuttle out, carefully balance on the trunk, and whip out her Lady-J while I stabilized everything. Then she'd compose herself and let 'er rip.

Bladder relief on a floating log

In places, especially along the south shore of Big Island (on Great Slave Lake) and the north shore of Beaver Lake, 18-20 hours in the boat is the norm. Now, Feathercraft seats have a well-deserved reputation for being *the* most comfortable seats in the industry. But on the unlandable Mackenzie they turn into iron maidens. The sling design nestles your bum like a water-worn cobble in a slingshot. It's impossible to shift your position. When you attempt it, the hammock just follows your shift and, over many long hours, constipation, seat sores and even hemorrhoids sprout.

With a shortage of shore comes its inevitable corollary, **There's no camping.** But I exaggerate...a bit. Winter road landings and built-up ferry clearances of compacted gravel were god-sends. Shore-side detritus, offering solid footing across the mud, sometimes provided access to firmer ground. At the villages, well-maintained landing spots were the norm. And wherever the river narrowed due to resistant strata, a dry, sloping pediment provided firm campsites.

So how did the doughty Mackenzie cope? With giant voyageur canoes manned prow to stern, he just bore full-steam ahead covering about 100 miles a day. At that rate, campsites miraculously materialized much more often. We had a map of Mackenzie's campsites, compiled by Robert Douglas Mead in his book, *Ultimate North*. One interminable day, with zero camping prospects, we decided to have a go at one of Mackenzie's overnight stops. It was located at the junction of the river with a minor tributary coming in on the left. With such a large group as his, we were certain of pay-dirt. But 2006 is not 1789. Over the intervening years, the junction had morphed into an endlessly muddy swamp.

Mud-bedaubed banks are a clear indication that, **There's no current.** The faster a river flows, the more—and bigger—suspended stuff it carries. Whereas fast, high gradient rivers can tumble car-sized boulders down their channel, medium gradient rivers can only carry gravel, sand, and lesser-sized particles.

As rivers slow down, the larger particles settle out in decreasing order of size. Slow, low gradient streams are limited to carrying silts, clays and organic sludge—in other words, mud. As the water stills to a nearly complete stop at a delta—or anywhere along its course where a river pauses to meditate—all of that mud is liberated.

Once, when the mud looked deceptively stable, I jumped out of the boat for a desperate pee. Big mistake. I was sucked, in slow motion, all the way down to my crotch. But with my plumbing muscles already relaxed, I surrendered to the moment. Luckily, my hips stopped my disappearance and, since my boat was within reach, I was able to pull myself out (though I couldn't convince one of my boots into following me).

In its 1,077 mile length, the Mackenzie drops only 515 feet: a gradient of less than $1/2$ foot per mile. Who would have thought that Canada's largest river would be such a slug? Right at the start, between Fort Providence and Mills Lake, the Mackenzie seduces the paddler by blowing most of its wad in a powerful burst of current—for all of 20 miles. Afterward, it alternates between still and stiller.

A cursory glance at the map shows the Mackenzie flowing out of Great Slave Lake and coursing unbound all the way to the Arctic Ocean except, that is, for tiny Mills Lake near Fort Providence. A closer look reveals additional Beaver Lake, just where the river is supposed to be girding its loins to bust through the great Canadian Shield. But no amount of eye-crossing examination discloses the true extent of "tiny" Mills Lake. What looks like a 10-mile long gulp on the river's course is actually just the pig inside the 100-mile-long anaconda that is Mills Lake, making the Mackenzie's actual gradient about 20% less, or .4 foot per mile.

What little gradient remains is further blown in a pair of **Killer rapids** (3 if you believe the map, which labels the actual bit of real current near Fort Providence 'Rapids').

The Ramparts Rapids are just another bit of fast current, more the result of a Venturi effect than an actual drop in river bed level. Here, the 3-mile wide Mackenzie funnels into a low but impressive sheer-sided canyon less than half-a-mile wide. Though the roar intimidates, sticking relatively near the right-hand shore precludes any sign of turbulence.

Sans Sault Rapid (literally, "rapid without a drop") *does* have a drop—over an erosion-resistant ledge deep in the river's bed. Hugging the left-hand shore as we'd been advised to do, we paddled on absolutely flat water.

We'd budgeted a month, or about 38 miles per day (average), on the assumption that a 2-mile per hour paddling rate atop a 4-mile per hour current would yield about 40 miles a day in 6 hours of paddling. As it turned out, we spent endless grueling hours paddling against still waters and contrary winds looking for campsites and trying to stay on schedule.

Rivers with little or no gradient usually traverse pancake-flat landforms. Topographically relief-free terrain is a hint that, **There's no scenery.** For the first third of the entire distance, except for the high bluff that holds Fort Simpson, the channel is the only view. Of course, the bank-to-bank promenade is not without some charm, but with the banks sometimes 3-miles apart, the farther shore usually lacked detail. At about mile 300, the Mackenzie hits the Camsell Mountains at Camsell Bend and turns due north. The glorious Camsell wall is a great relief—in both senses of the word.

In the interests of full disclosure, I must admit that the Mackenzie River's middle 300-400 miles have exceptional scenery, even *grand* scenery and relief commensurate with any-one's expectations: the Franklin Range, Roche-Qui-Trempe-A-L'eau, the Upper & Lower Ramparts, Great Bear Rock, and the Norman Range opposite the Mackenzie Mountains. But once past Arctic Red River, except for one colorful, distant bluff, the terrain reverts to parking-lot flat. Up by Tuktoyaktuk, North America's densest pingo field dots the landscape. These per-mafrost-heaved carbuncles, 3-400 feet high, resemble mini-vol-canic craters and never fail to lure a summit bid.

Not 230 miles into the trip, we discovered that, **Navigation is not always what it seems.** Fort Simpson, situated just be-low the junction of the giant Mackenzie and Liard Rivers, is sur-prisingly difficult to access. Here, the combined channels span nearly 2.5 miles and require hard, determined ferry gliding across almost the entire distance of both rivers against a decep-tively strong current.

Recent name changes, from Anglo to Native, sometimes caused confusion—in a counter-intuitive way. When we asked about downstream villages, referring to them by their "new", aboriginal names, First Nations residents would often look puz-zled: they were used to the Anglo names they'd grown up with! On the other hand, Anglos almost always knew the new and 'old' names.

But we still completely by-passed one village. Wrigley had had the audacity to switch locations: it moved 5 miles upstream to a barely visible new site, so we missed a much-needed resupply

(I must admit we were relying on my 1969 maps which I was too cheap to replace).

Even the locals get lost on the Mackenzie. We were awakened up once at 3 AM from a very deep sleep between Fort Good Hope and Arctic Red River, a particularly isolated stretch of the river, by an insistent whisper. "Excuse me, excuse me!" susurred the woman's voice.

Now, aside from the very occasional tug and barge, there is no traffic on the river, so we were particularly alarmed. Outside our tent, a small inboard power boat, looking like the Grapes of Wrath all filled to overflowing with boxes, household items, children, a dog, two women and a man at the wheel lay nosed up on the shore. From the high bank down came another woman grasping a roll of TP. "Do you know how far we are from Fort Good Hope?" asked the whisperer.

They were traveling upstream. Groggy and disoriented, my downstream-to-upstream and miles-to-kilometers conversion rules-of-thumb deserted me. I blurted out some distance totally unrelated to reality. I just hope they made it.

Somewhere between Arctic Red River and Inuvik we missed the inflow of the Rat River, gateway to the Yukon River portage. We'd been looking out for it. For me it would have closed a circle of sorts, connecting the Pacific and Atlantic Oceans via kayak. I suspect that summer ice break-ups and the fast regeneration of dwarf willow change the landscape so much that landmarks are ephemeral unless elevated.

On the other hand, we were, however, able to help a large outboard skiff, with two men and a dog, grounded in the delta. It was about 100 yards off the south bank of the Middle Channel, in a stiff beam wind. We wondered what was going on. "Do you need a tow?" I asked mischievously.

Author helping beached Inuit

Embarrassed, they explained that the wind had shoved them into the shallows. They were unable to lift the motor, straighten and hold the boat into the wind, push the boat forward, then drop the motor into deeper water, get it started and move forward while at the same time preventing back-drift from the gale. Tina and I jumped out of our kayaks, tied them to us, straightened their boat out and pushed it into deeper water while they cranked the motor and set off. Score one for kayaks. Had we not come along, they would have been stranded indefinitely.

The Mackenzie delta covers 5,000 square miles. On a topo map, it looks like a close-up detail of a Jackson Pollock painting (see photo). Getting lost here is a kayaker's worst nightmare. We'd been reassured that the East Channel, leading to Inuvik, was well-marked with buoys. Someone should have notified the buoys. Not only were they missing, the channel's entry wasn't marked either. A few hours of white-knuckle map reading reassured us we were in the right place.

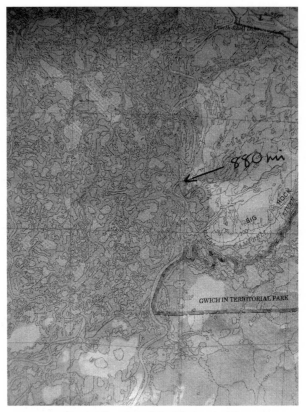

One small section of the Mackenzie delta

One of the joys of sea kayaking or running rivers in the northwest is the endless supply of fresh salmon. And one seldom has to catch them—fishermen always offer kayakers a fish. But, on the Mackenzie, **There's no fish.** Salmon require both a suitable stream and a suitable ocean. The Pacific Ocean is great salmon habitat; not so the Arctic Ocean. We'd never quite consciously realized that, because the Mackenzie disgorges into the Arctic Ocean, there wouldn't be any salmon. Additionally, we'd heard so much about the mouth-watering delectability of Arctic Char (also members of the salmon family) that we didn't really care.

So we asked about Arctic char at every village. Every time people would just shake their heads, responding either that *now* was not the time or that they were *only* found closer to the Arctic Ocean or that the river was *too* muddy.

When we arrived at Arctic Red River, gateway to the delta, looking for a much-needed resupply, we were told that, unfortunately, the only grocery store had closed. No one knew if or when the store would ever re-open. Desperate, we asked at the village council building if we could buy enough food from anyone to get to Inuvik. One employee volunteered local frozen fish. "Arctic char," I ventured?

No, "whitefish", he responded, "But it's just as good". Now, we beamed, we'd get to try the Mackenzie's best. That night we boiled some up and salivated for a great feast. It *was* edible—albeit tasteless (with a fishy bouquet) and a tad oily. We ended up seasoning it with lots of curry. We never got to taste Arctic char.

After dinner an old native motored over to our campsite. He'd brought his granddaughter to chat with the white kayakers. Tina engaged the little girl and made her visit special.

One bit of wildlife the Mackenzie teems with is, **Vicious bugs.** Now, all northern rivers have their share of bugs and they all proceed through a predictable cycle of mosquitoes, gnats, black flies, "whitesocks", horse and deer flies and every sort of annoying, biting, flying insect imaginable. But the Mackenzie is the only river we'd run where some bugs were so bad that the natives actually looked forward to the emergence of certain bugs over others. "Choppers", a slow, vicious, biting type of horse fly —and harmless dragonflies—ate all the other bugs, so they were welcomed.

With deet, bug shirts, head nets and even a 12'x12' screen tent, we thought we were prepared for the onslaught. But it was much worse than that. The bugs were so thick that simply pointing the camera and taking a photo would inevitably capture some on the image. And, again, it got way personal. On a good day, defecation was a 2-person project requiring an assistant to fan the exposed bottom. On a bad day, defecation took place inside the screen tent. Again, we wondered how Mackenzie, lacking our modern conveniences, had dealt with the nasty buggers. We should have guessed. At particularly dismal and bug-infested camps, Mackenzie's men would resort to spending nights submerged in shallow water smoking their pipes.

Alexander Mackenzie wasn't looking for fame and glory—he was just trying to make an honest buck. And he was doing it as parsimoniously as only a true Scotsman could, *and* without government grants, royal commissions, military support or any other sort of official recognition or help. Mackenzie employed voyageurs (French-Canadian for grunts) and cajoled natives with *per diems* and promises of a piece of the fur trade action. Though he sought the Pacific Ocean as a possible conduit for the North West Company's furs, he was also seeking new lands with fur-bearing critters. That's why his little detour down the Disappointment River didn't completely discourage him. Three years later he went back west and kept a beeline heading west, becoming the first European to cross the North American continent from the Atlantic to the Pacific.

His determination, speed and accomplishment were truly phenomenal especially when compared with Lewis & Clark's Discovery Voyage. It's no wonder that Mackenzie has gripped the imagination of many a long-distance kayak voyageur. Still, in a thousand miles of river, we didn't see or meet up with any of these latter-day Mackenzies, but for one notable exception.

One fine day, about halfway down the river, around noon, we caught up with four large canoes and joined them for lunch. They were well and elaborately equipped, particularly with fresh produce, which they generously shared with us. While trading trip reports, it slowly dawned on us that, maybe, we were on different rivers.

No shore? No camping? No problem!—voyageur canoes are big and stable; you can even nap in them. No current? No silly time constraints for this group. Bugs? To Northerners they're like sunshine to Arizonans—just part of the landscape. No scenery?

Why, to these plucky Canucks the Mackenzie was the eighth wonder of the world! Navigation problems? Impossible with a local guide, 2 GPS's and a full set of the largest scale, most up-to-date, topo maps available. Jamie Bastedo, a Yellowknife-based writer, and his crew were on the 'best of all possible' rivers. The Canadian government was *paying* him to write a river runner's guide to the Mackenzie River

And who can argue with that?

We never reached Tuktoyaktuk. Because of time constraints and travel arrangements, we had to cut the trip short at Inuvik.

But don't get me wrong. Knowing what I now know, do I regret any of the aforementioned excursions?

Absolutely not! After all, I'm an incurable romantic, a hopeless optimist and an obstinate kayaker whose idea of a good time in no way precludes the vicissitudes of the Yukon, Thelon, and Mackenzie rivers. Fortunately, long distance kayakers have a redeeming tendency to gird themselves for the worst and savor whatever they get. They revel in the rhythm of the paddle, the solitude, the grandeur, the time standing still, the in-your-face wildlife encounters and the opportunities few others ever get to experience—even at the expense of divorce, potentially deadly wildlife encounters, atmospheric disasters, hunger, sleeplessness, constipation, piles, endless itching and scratching, and every sort of discomfort and indignity imaginable.

There really is no such thing as a bad paddling trip.

Layton Kor Agonistes

By Robert H. Miller with Rusty Baillie

Rock climbing: *An activity in which participants climb up, down or across natural rock formations or walls. The goal is to reach the summit of a formation or the endpoint of a usually pre-defined route without falling.*
—Wikipedia

One hot weekend in September 2011, Layton Kor drove to Las Vegas from his home in Kingman, Arizona, to repair Jorge and Joanne Urioste's brick flower box. At age seventy-two, he was on twice-a-week dialysis for renal failure, yet he continued to work in the 100 degree heat. Salty sweat poured down his face and arms, saturating his shirt. Dehydration was dangerous for his health. "Get a little more water in the mortar mix," he instructed his wife, Karen. "Everything is drying out under this glaring sun." Layton's trade was masonry, and he was a perfectionist.

As a young man, Layton had been on the cutting edge of American rock climbing. He climbed with such tireless speed and dexterity—his partners said—that it seemed as if he were out-running the shouted demands of the construction foreman at his day job. He was driven to climb huge, scary walls, towers, and peaks with sheer, featureless rock that appeared unclimbable to the lay person. These quests relied on a hammer to bang in pitons and bashies, along with rivets, studs, and once in a rare while, a bolt—anything that would stick in the trifling irregularities of nearly featureless rock to allow for upward progress.

The latter three required holes drilled into the rock manually with a hammer and drill bit, after which permanent metal shafts were hammered in. According to the unwritten rules of the sport at the time—the interpretations of which were often subject to dispute as vehemently as if they were biblical passages being considered by the faithful—they were supposed to be resorted to only as a last resort.

Layton was working on the flower box project as a "thank you" for Jorge's and Joanne's recent fund-raising slide-show in Boulder, which helped with his medical expenses. On this day, Layton set neat rows of bricks, without the usual level guide-strings, relying on his skill, intuition and eye. His big fat thumbs adjusted the sometimes wayward mortar back inside imaginary confines.

But this visit wasn't just about bricks and mortar; it was a chance for old friends to hang out together. And new friends. Joanne had invited me and my wife, Tina Cobos, climbing friends on a rest day from scaling the crags, to breakfast with the Kors.

Over the course of nearly 45 years, the Uriostes, a unique and prodigious husband-and-wife climbing team, had almost single-handedly developed the Red Rocks outside Las Vegas into one of the world's destination climbing areas—a sandstone Yosemite—and compiled its first guidebook. Brits, French, Spanish, Canadians, Germans, Poles, Bulgarians—even New Yorkers—climbers from all over the world flock to Nevada's Red Rocks. The Uriostes themselves epitomize the diverse mélange of alpine pilgrims at Red Rocks. Jorge, a Chilean of Basque stock reared in Bolivia, is a Catholic priest, once a Jesuit (yet forever a priest)—but now with permission to marry. He is fluent in English, Spanish, French, Latin, Catalan, Italian and Quechua. His love of the Andes turned him to alpinism; his love of its people, to anthropology, which he taught at the University of Nevada, Las Vegas. Joanne, by trade a nurse, is a native New Yorker.

My goal that morning was to make Layton Kor laugh. But I'd just met him and, afraid of making a complete fool of myself, didn't know what to say. Meeting the architect of some of my most memorable climbs was humbling; meeting a living legend was intimidating. It didn't help that I too was a mason, but one always dependent on level, line and tape measure. Such encounters are fraught with awkwardness. In turn, his reticence—was he just shy or was he taking his measure of me?—reinforced my muteness. I couldn't tell. Joanne had warned me that he was in poor health; and added that, years before, he'd become a Jehovah's Witness—a sect I didn't associate with a sense of humor.

Gatherings at the Uriostes are a non-linear, improvisational experience—part Monty Python, part graduate seminar, but always seasoned with a dash of Julia Child. At one get-together, giggling female climbers mused about the virility of the gathered male climbers based on the pump of their forearms; while at another a spirited discussion on epistemology developed into an inquiry on the nature of free markets. Not to be outdone, Jorge and I once debated the merits of the various regional Andean hot sauces. I expected nothing less at this gathering.

Jorge Urioste, Joanne Urioste & Tina Cobos

After a breakfast of sausage, eggs and fruit, Jorge brought out his new pride and joy: an extremely light and compact, rechargeable, battery-pack electric drill. He placed it at the center of the table, the better for all to admire. Jorge, a tiny man with an impish streak reflected in the gleam of his eyes, seemed to be trying to stir something up. Layton, a climber about as fond of bolts—especially power drill-driven bolts—as Dracula was of crucifixes, looked at it guardedly.

"In sandstone, it'll drill fifteen 3/8-inch by 3 inch bolts on one charge!" Jorge proudly boasted, as if extolling a newborn son's manly virtues, possibly hoping to goad Layton into a reaction.

Climbers have a love/hate relationship with bolts. Before their adoption into the sport, featureless stretches of stone that did not provide a crack or a seam in which to place a protective piece of gear that would arrest a fall, could only be climbed with skill, confidence and testicular (or ovarian) fortitude. It was a measure of the climber's ability to deal with fear and risk, and a feat that made other climbers wonder in awe. But then, when finally introduced, and when no other option was available—and the consequences of a fall fatal—climbers might resort to a hand-hammered, tiny bolt to allow for upward progress.

Layton was not averse to hand drilled bolts when he believed they were absolutely necessary; but he remained a staunchly traditional alpinist eschewing the new wave tendency to place bolts at will, spaced five- to fifteen-feet (for safety—*and for fun*—not to test one's fettle) with a power drill. Modern bolts are often placed while the route creator dangles safely from a rope anchored above a prospective route, instead of "boldly, from the ground up" as it was done in the "old days."

I sensed an opportunity opening up. Sitting next to Layton, I reached out for the drill to admire it, cradled it in my palms, turned it over and gestured left and right to share the wonder of this votive offering. Then I set it down, placing it subtly closer to Kor, and I asked him if I could get a photo of the two of us together.

"Of course," he replied, pursing his lips tighter into a lopsided, ironic grin. Layton's lanky arms, legs, and torso, like a

Scooby Doo skeleton's extremities, had a rhythm all of their own, which the tiny dining room chair he'd landed on was challenged to contain. The remainder of Layton, led by knobby elbows and king-crab hands, sprawled over the table seeking composure.

Robert Miller & Layton Kor, sans drill

Throughout the meal Layton had kept his blue baseball cap on—a demeanor that punctuated his guardedness. It was pulled tightly over his head and about halfway down his brow; a cap that, like the Gadsden flag, sported a coiled cobra ready to strike if trod upon. I edged my chair next to his and tried to look natural while Tina set up the shot. As inconspicuously as possible, I drew the drill closer to us, all the while keeping up a disarming chatter of small talk ("Nope, that's not vegetarian sausage") to distract Layton from the *mise-en-scene* I was engineering. But his gaze darted back and forth, while the cobra's jowls seemed to swell and flare in support.

"No you don't," declared Layton, breaking into a broad grin. "I know exactly what you're up to," and he pushed the drill away to prevent contamination of the photo. We all burst out laughing.

* * * *

Layton Kor was one of America's great pioneer rock climbers from the late 50's to the late 60's, during which time he climbed like a freight train, with such urgency, speed, and hunger for new and "impossible" routes that many of his climbing partners compared his energy to that of a caged lion. He climbed with the best climbers in the world at that time, doing hundreds of seemingly-impossible first ascents on the crags and mountains of his home state of Colorado (on the Wisdom Roof, the Diving Board and the Naked Edge); on the sandstone towers of Utah and Arizona; on the sheer granite walls of Yosemite; and on the peaks of The Alps and The Dolomites.

It's ironic—his reaction to the drill. But far be it from me to point out that while modern climbers seek simplicity—an ethic Layton strongly espoused—he banged his way up routes using direct aid, hammering in piton after piton and yes, whisper it, bolts when necessary, to get up routes now often climbed without artificial aids. "Pitons!" Layton was once overheard shouting, "I love pitons!" Yet as Bob Godfrey has observed:

> *Times have changed, attitudes toward climbing are different, and styles which were suitable for one decade are not appropriate for another. The style of Kor...in the sixties, was absolutely appropriate to that period of time...Paradox after paradox.*

Bob Godfrey, mountaineer, writer, photographer, reluctant raconteur, was Layton's first biographer. I first met Bob in 1972 as his student, just before Layton captured his imagination. When Godfrey approached Kor in 1976 to suggest a biography, Layton kindly demurred. He was happy laying brick for the Adolph Coors Brewery; writing a book seemed like too much work. But then in1981, Layton changed his mind.

Back then I was working as a climbing instructor for Challenge/Discovery in Crested Butte, Colorado. One evening after work, I walked into my boss's home to cook a pot of Cuban black beans. There sat Godfrey, motor cap on his thinning scalp, tete a tete with Roy Smith, another notable Brit alpinist and now my boss. They stopped talking and looked at me. I invited Bob to stay for dinner and the conversation took a different tack.

The next day Roy told me that Bob had just been diagnosed with Parkinson's. He was planning on taking his own life. But his interest in Layton had become an obsession. He was training to climb Layton's Naked Edge, 5.11b, first put up in 1964 in Colorado's Eldorado Canyon. It was a fitting bookend to his life. Bob Godfrey committed suicide in 1988.

* * * *

Now that we'd broken the ice, I told Layton I'd survived a fall on his Castleton Tower route in the Utah desert back in the '70s. His wry smile twisted even more. I'd just bought a new Mountain Safety Research (MSR) helmet designed specifically for climbing and had resolved to wear it. Back then, the few climbers concerned about their noggin wore all-purpose Bell helmets. Newly-founded MSR decided to design climbing-specific safety gear. Their helmet was bright yellow and was reinforced around the rim by a half-inch protrusion. It was not form-fitting and a bit ridiculous looking, a bright yellow cabasset. As I was leading, the damn thing wedged into the off-width crack a third of the way up, immobilizing my head.

Off-width cracks are notoriously difficult to climb: wider than fingers or a hand—denying those extremities secure jamming inside—but not wide enough for a person's torso, like a chimney, which allows the full insertion of a body for security. The off-size width requires snake-like contortions of arms, legs and shoulders variously known as "arm bars" and "shoulder bars", "knee locks", "stacked feet" or heels, "fist stacks", "Gastons", where palms are placed on opposite sides of the off-width, pushing out sideways as if attempting to open a jammed sliding door (named after their inventor, the famed French Alpinist Gaston Rebuffat)—with butt, torso and chest precariously insecure out in mid-air. Wiggle as I might, the helmet refused to be dislodged. With knees and half a butt cheek securing my stance, I freed my arms and smacked my head outward to free the helmet. Out I flew, arrested by the single ¼-inch bolt Layton had inserted on the pitch. I dumped the helmet and completed the pitch shaking like a dog shittin' apricot pits.

Layton choked on a guffaw, as if torn between laughing and inadvertently vindicating a bolt—never mind that it was *his* bolt. As for his *Yellow Spur* route in Eldorado Canyon outside of Boulder, Colorado, Tina and I groused about the start—indistinct and shaped like an S, incut deeply at the bottom and followed by an overhanging, unprotected, braille puzzle. The lead fell to me.

In rock climbing, one person leads, the other follows. The follower is always protected by a rope from above—a rope that the leader has taken up. The leader doesn't have it so sweet. As he goes up, he places something solid in the rock, threads the rope through it and, if he falls, the protection he's inserted will catch him.

While Tina and I generally swap leads, she always takes over on the difficult, unprotected starts that require a solid "spot"— someone with arms outstretched ready to temper a leader's fall from the initial ten feet or so of a climb—from a burly partner. I complained that I was forced to surrender the lead to Tina, the lighter team member, to provide a suitable cradle under her lovely glutes in case she fell—a situation, I pointed out, that Layton surely had never encountered, with his all-male climbing partners and gorilla reach. We all roared, save for Layton. Uncertain about the propriety of the innuendos, he first glanced at Karen before joining in.

Tina, wiping sausage grease off her chin, then had her own comments about Layton's *South Face of Washington Column* route in Yosemite Valley. She'd had to climb the Kor Roof, a section of overhanging rock, twice—once retreating because of a battle with the elements; the second time retreating because of a battle with her partner—a battle that could be heard all the way across Yosemite Valley's floor to the base of Glacier Point Apron. She was about to thank Layton for the closely-spaced bolt ladder on the Kor Roof (he'd initially placed only two and was infamous for his unreachable bolt placements) when he fixed her with a penetrating look and asked her why she climbed.

Unaware that Layton's decade-long, manic obsession with perfervid climbing was fueled by an unknown, inner quest—one that may have been more metaphysical than physical—she replied guilelessly with a shrug and a smile that belied any intro-spection, that she, "just loved everything about climbing."

* * * *

Joanne first met Layton in 1986, through the climbers' grapevine when he and his then-wife, Joy, were travelling through Vegas. Layton had his eyes on a new 1000-foot route up the North Wall of Rainbow, in the Red Rocks just outside of town. Joanne had just given birth to a daughter and invited Joy to stay at her home.

It would be 20 years before Joanne met up with Layton again. During the interim, he had lived and worked in Guam, Hawaii, and the Philippines, where he met and married his sec-ond wife, Karen. He gravitated toward warm climates. Eschew-ing the cold, snow, and alpine rigors, they and their teen-aged son, Arlan, settled in Kingman, Arizona, a two-hour drive south-east of Las Vegas. As Joanne recounts:

The family would come to Vegas a few times a year to stay with us for the weekend, during which Karen and I would go grocery shopping at The International Market, and I'd set up top-roping climbs for Arlan, while Kor watched from a folding chair. Layton and I would occasionally climb together, in The Valley of Fire in Utah and in the Nutt Wilderness in Arizona, but by 2011, climbing was no longer possible for him.

Layton & Joanne, Valley of Fire, Utah, March 2009. Photo by Alfred Newman

That spring back in 2011, Joanne and her son Danny climbed several Layton Kor routes in the Front Range of Colorado with Layton's 19-year-old son, Arlan, who wanted to sample what his dad had done in his youth. By then Kor suffering from kidney failure, was too weak to join in. But he watched from a comfortable seat in a car parked nearby. Jorge, who was seated next to Layton, noted that the old climber scrutinized his son's every move. As Danny, Joanne and Arlan jammed their way up the steep cracks, protecting their progress with cams—spring-loaded, triggered protection devices placed and removed in seconds—Joanne wondered how Layton back in the 1950s, still just a teenager shod in clunky boots and armed with a hammer and a few pitons, had managed to get up such exposed, unknown and improbable places. Even before his prefrontal cortex was fully developed, Layton was driven by a relentless commitment and tenacious imagination. Managing the razor's edge between life and death seemed to draw him, like a passion or a personal sense of aesthetics.

One evening in Boulder Layton told Joanne a story:

He'd bivouacked on a north face in Switzerland many decades ago, surviving a night of crazy electrical storms. At dawn, the weather calmed and he continued upward with his partner. Close to the ridge top, they stumbled over a tiny niche filled with freshly-charred human remains—undoubtedly, a fellow climber singled out by that night's fulminations. Layton's summit had suddenly become that much dearer.

Yet that didn't stop Layton. Well into the mid-1960s, he continued to pursue "risky ascents of improbable summits and big, sheer walls, such as The Diamond on Long's Peak, El Capitan in Yosemite, The Black Canyon of the Gunnison, the Desert Towers of eastern Utah, and the north walls of the Alps, including the Eigerwand—one of the Alps' great north faces—in winter", as Joanne puts it. Who knows what drove him? But he was impelled to explore the seemingly impossible, and raised a bar that would elevate standards for years to come.

* * * *

Rusty Baillie, Rhodesian ex-pat and prolific first ascentionist (including Scotland's Old Man of Hoy, a sea stack in the Orkneys, with Chris Bonnington and Tom Patey and immortalized in a BBC documentary) recalls that when he first met Kor he "was scared off by the light of fanatical mountaineering in his eye." But he was also drawn to him "because he was so very different to me. So frantic! Such wild energy".

RUSTY: *Back in late fall 1968, I had a phone call from Joe Nold, my Colorado Outward Bound boss:*

"We have Layton Kor here. He wants to climb the Painted Wall with you. Why don't you take some time off and go play..."

*Rusty Baillie (white helmet) & David Lovejoy finally get high on the
Painted Wall, 1972*

This was actually the second time I've had a boss send me off on a crazy first ascent, and of course I was quick to be of service.

Hours later Layton picked me up at the Colorado Springs airport. He had also recruited "Wee" Brian Robertson (another Brit immigrant) and a very young looking Alaskan bush pilot who was hoping to whisk us over the Rockies in a remarkably small Cessna—which was grossly overloaded with metal big-wall climbing gear.

That wild and borderline flight was just the startling beginning to what was probably a fairly typical Kor outing.

The Painted Wall is a part of the North Rim of the Black Canyon of the Gunnison on Colorado's West Slope. The Black is not as big as the Grand Canyon but it's more compact and the walls are steep-to-overhanging. The Painted Wall itself is dramatically beautiful—shot through with pegmatite intrusions that look like a series of Chinese dragons in full flight. The rock quality is atrocious.

On a previous recon I had approached from the North Rim but Kor had a Plan. He had located an "easy" gully on the more accessible South Rim, directly opposite the Painted Wall: we would nip down this, cross the Gunnison River, and be right there, at the foot of our wall and ready to climb.

Kor had good credibility. He had already made a serious attempt, getting up 6 pitches, including the Kor Roof (Kor was known for his roofs) and the shallow grooves above...all in a day! Each pitch stretches the full length of the climbing rope so that's close to a thousand feet of new, extreme, climbing in one determined push! It doesn't matter that the whole Kor Roof—thousands of tons of rock, eventually fell away, thankfully with no one bivouacked on top of it.

To me those six pitches are one of the most magnificent climbing efforts ever achieved. Really! On his first, on-sight visit he got higher, faster, than we eventually did over many days—hauling all our equipment and agonizing over the steep rotten rock. I never could perceive, understand, or even conceptualize how a mere mortal could do that...

Naturally, the "easy" gully turned out to be an epic in itself. Patches of water turning to slippery ice in the late fall weather, steep waterfalls where we had to rappel...lowering ourselves on our ropes...and some dense and impenetrable brush. But, in the dark, we finally got to the river, even found a nice snug cave. With a good fire roaring and some food in the belly things began to look promising...although I had learned that neither Layton nor Brian were happy swimmers, so I would be handling the river crossing in the lead.

But that night it snowed and the river flooded.

In the foggy morning I went over to check out the river. I thought I could see a way through the boiling eddies and over the snow-covered rocks, to find some places to fix a rope for our non-swimmers. I went back to the fire but Kor had quietly packed up and left, heading back up the canyon wall, into the mists. Brian, a dour Scot and not given to flowery language, said that Layton looked like a grey wolf, loping after his prey.

*We were actually in a bit of a pickle! Snow still covered the rocks and new ice was forming everywhere. The steep waterfalls we had rappelled down would have to be re-climbed. And our packs were huge: climbers call these big wall duffels **Pigs**...they are cumbersome and awkward, full of steel pitons and hammers, heavy ropes and vertical camping gear. We would have to carry them on our backs, not having the luxury of winching them up with pulleys.*

Brian and I had climbed together in the French Alps in challenging weather. We had done a new route on the Brouillard Pillar of Mt Blanc (with Chris Bonnington and John Harlin); together we had forged a winter route on the Aiguille du Plan and we had escaped from a severe storm on the Grandes Jorasses. We were also happy with the challenges of famously frigid Scottish winter climbing...but this was ridiculous!

Layton by now was long gone so we set off too. He had left scuffles on the snowy slabs and we started following these. All day we followed those bloody tracks, often with clearly printed fingerprints where Layton had crimped a particularly technical hold. Of course, we refrained from roping up, at least until we could catch Layton and tie him into the safety of the rope, too. There were a lot of cruxes, lots of places where he had cleared all the snow from tricky friction holds, lots of places where we 'shat bricks'. Several times I was all for dumping the pigs—no matter how much it would cost to replace them...but those damned paw prints kept challenging our manhood and forcing us on.

When we finally escaped from our tomb and doom, there was Layton and a ranger, waiting in his heated truck, with hot coffee and burgers, collected after their leisurely lunch in town.

But he was human too. He endeared himself to me when I saw that he was incredibly fastidious about flecks of charcoal in his tea...in a rough bivy situation, where any kind of comfort was a luxury. With Layton you didn't seem to have a chance to breathe, or feel the need to take a breath even. He had a knack for sweeping you along quite smoothly—always smiling, gentle, considerate and companionable—except of course when he got shit in his tea…

* * * *

In spite of Layton's working class roots, he was a dedicated aesthete. From the little glazed fruit tarts he'd eaten at a café below the Eiger, the creamy brie cheese with crunchy fresh bread, the golden, frothy local pilsner—none available in Podunk Kingman—to Salvador Dali's psychedelic paintings with elephants and suggestive goddesses, Layton had a taste for the extraordinary, the exquisite, manifested especially in his art: elegant alpine lines up impossibly seductive rock formations.

Most climbers suffer from/thrive on OCD—Obsessive Climbing Disorder: an irrepressible drive that combines the intellectual challenge of chess, the sensuality of sex, the physicality of gymnastics, and an emotional roller coaster of fear, ecstasy and transcendental meditation…all at the same time. A heady brew.

When fear engulfs us, we're tempted to panic—shake all over, lose mindfulness, fall and hurt ourselves—or alternatively, to focus on the situation and work out a solution. The more often we succeed in getting out of harm's way, the more we grow. And growth is addicting. The higher the stakes—the prospect of a dangerous fall—the greater the growth…and the greater the satisfaction at resolving the problem. Still, somewhere in our subconscious we keep a tally of how often we succeed (or luck out)… and the burden is a bitch.

In 1966 during a winter attempt on the North Face of the Eiger, Layton's climbing partner and close friend, John Harlin, died falling 4000 vertical feet when their ¼ inch fixed line snapped. It was too much for Kor. He fell into a deep depression and experienced debilitating respiratory problems accompanied by a profound fatigue. Doctors were unable to help. So Layton entered an "alternative" medicine health retreat, where his roommate happened to be a Jehovah's Witness.

Did Harlin's death bring home his own mortality in a way nothing else could? Joanne Urioste, a registered research nurse, speculates:

> *Had the auto-immune kidney failure that would later kill him begun to take hold? Could the relentless cold and wind of that exceptionally vicious winter have been overwhelming? Cold often worsens auto-immune flare-ups and fatigue is a common symptom. Who knows what combination of factors affected Layton when, sometime in 1968, in his early 30s, he left high-intensity climbing and joined Jehovah's Witnesses.*

Mary Stewart, a Glaswegian active in the 1960s Chamonix climbing scene—and to whom Layton gifted his duvet—commented that Layton "took to hanging around street corners, trying to gather up souls for redemption, or at least for membership in the Jehovah's Witness," his faith was so strong.

Layton didn't completely leave climbing, though he married twice and raised two families. For many years he dabbled in "recreational" climbing. But then, in the early 2000s, something gripped him and he returned to seeking first ascents. The Black Mountains of Arizona near Kingman, where he'd retired, became his canvas.

RUSTY: *The next time I met Layton was in Arizona, in about 2000. Much had happened in the intervening thirty-two years: we had travelled around the world, raised families and found new gods.*

Layton and his wife Karen were just back from a mission to the Philippines with the Jehovah's Witness church, living in Kingman, a great center for rock and climbing. I had just been enjoying some Kingman sport routes with my own wife, Pat, and we had been camping high above the town, in an area of squat volcanic pinnacles. Layton and Karen were sorting their gear and getting ready to climb.

We had retired to Idaho but were back for the winter, as snowbirds. I loved this remote and uncluttered area of Northern Arizona and was always looking for desert climbing partners so, after we had caught up on idle gossip, we got down to the real business of climbing prospects.

First I tried to interest Layton in my favorite local projects on the superb granite slabs and faces of nearby Walnut Dome and Hackberry Wall, two remote, undeveloped crags…hardly climbed and a welcome exception to the typically loose and crumbling desert rock.

*"Sounds like **just** rock climbing" was his rather disdainful comment.*

I was a bit shocked at this indictment of those acres of iron-hard granite. Maybe he considered this indulgent: soft and effete? Maybe his heart was still in thrall to those fierce, remote and crumbling desert spires he had once ruled over?

So I tried to suggest we use some of the New Technology to make those fierce desert spires a little less lethal: we would use a compact battery drill and long sleeve-bolts to rig solid anchors in the soft rock.

*But he was even more disgusted by this blatant cheating and the abandonment of his cherished and dearly-won climbing ethics. The famous story of Kor rigging a hanging belay on a single, postage stamp-sized, rurp piton may be apocryphal, but there is no doubt that he survived many loose, unprotected and runout desert leads. Maybe he actually **liked** that stuff?! Sorting **that** riddle was not on my agenda and so I sort of sidestepped out of the picture: saddened but greatly relieved. We parted and I never met the Kors again.*

* * * *

On April 18, 2013, Jorge invited Tina and me to climb *Sugar Plum*, one of his new routes in Red Rocks, up Pine Creek Canyon (at 76, he was still putting up new multi-pitch climbs). We met at the parking lot and hiked in with Pepper, his dog. For some reason—at the last minute—Jorge decided not to climb that day, but said he'd accompany us to the start and ensure we ended up on-route.

While scoping out the climb's line, a fellow climber overheard our Spanish-inflected discussion. He interrupted and asked if Jorge was *the* Jorge Urioste. Proud as punch at being recognized, Jorge smiled and said yes, he was Jorge. The climber praised Jorge's accomplishments, and asked if he could take him and Joanne out to dinner—"if that didn't inconvenience them too much." Before the toadying got too deep, I warned the interloper to check Jorge's ID. Taken aback, the climber asked Jorge again if he was really Jorge. Jorge pulled out his driver's license and handed it over. When we found out the petitioner was a doctor and not some dirtbag, Tina and I inveigled ourselves along for a free meal—a meal scheduled for the following evening.

After completing *Sugar Plum*, Tina and I headed into Pine Creek Canyon the following day to climb *Valore*, an obscure route next to the popular classic *Birdland*. On the approach, the scant desert ponderosas swayed gently in the cool air beside the rippling creek. Hummingbirds darted to-and-fro amid waxy-pink cactus blossoms in the warm sunshine of the spring day. A few hundred feet above the creek bed, was the ominous black grotto of *Valore* where the climb heads up out of the grotto for a couple of body lengths, then traverses right, over a giant, buttressed boulder—which creates a cave—for ten feet, and continues traversing right, out on a bottomless ledge over an increasingly yawning overhang before heading up an arête. It was Tina's lead.

The Spectrum Wall, where *Valore* is located, glowers threateningly. Varnished to an obsidian black with eons of manganese and iron oxides, it camouflages its many charms. And, depending on the season, it can sear flesh like a branding iron or paralyze fingers and rattle limbs with shivers during cold snaps. With the added penumbral oppression inside *Valore's* incunabulum, a vague sense of foreboding unnerved me. I shook off a shudder as I uncoiled our ropes.

Not Tina. Oblivious to the penumbras and emanations that a more reflective and insecure psyche might intuit, she perfunctorily surveyed the route ahead with a wham-bam-thank-you-ma'am glance, geared up, checked her knots, gave me a first pitch kiss, announced confidently, "climbing," and headed up the leaning boulder to the ledge.

At the junction of the ledge with the arête, she placed her first piece of protection, a solid, large #3 cam. She was out of sight, hidden by the giant boulder leaning against the wall. Suddenly, she screamed. Not ten feet away from me, like a Goya grotesquerie, I saw her dangling upside down, her head six inches from the ground, out cold, bleeding profusely; the rack splayed like a tutu around her head and shoulders.

How had this happened? There had been no tug on the belay I was providing.

She'd been holding a sandstone plate with her right hand—which felt solid when she whacked it—while pulling rope slack with her left hand to clip the #3 cam. But the hold broke before she could clip in, launching her backwards and upside down. The V-slot formed by the junction of the boulder with the wall had caught the rope and stopped her—but with only fifteen feet of rope between her and the snag, she had suffered a factor 1 fall, causing a severe impact when the rope became taut, snapping her backwards at the waist.

The safety of a falling climber depends on the elasticity of the rope and avoiding hitting obstacles—such as the ground or protruding rock—on the way down. The more rope out, the softer the catch. But with little rope out there is almost no elasticity, and a falling climber who nears terminal velocity is jerked viciously to a stop.

Nearby, other climbers who had queued up for *Birdland* rushed to lend a hand as I struggled to right her, bring her to consciousness, untie her knot, and lay her down right where she'd almost landed. The ground was sloping and uneven, she weighed too much, was in too much pain and there were no better choices. With a possible broken spine, moving her wasn't a good idea. Someone cradled her head, checked her vitals, and determined that the sources of her bleeding—now much reduced—were minor scalp wounds from the upside-down rack of protection devices—usually donned bandolier style—whacking her forehead.

Someone called for a rescue. A helicopter was being deployed. When she came to, she asked, in between moans and cries, what had happened. She didn't even remember we were climbing. I told her, but it took a few repetitions for the story to sink in.

"How hard was the climb?" she asked.

"Five seven (a very moderate rating)," I replied.

"Five seven!?!"

The indignity of falling on such an easy climb rankled. She swore me to secrecy. I repeated that it wasn't the difficulty that got her, but that a hold had broken, adding that a helicopter was on the way to evacuate her. Further outraged, she insisted on cancelling the chopper, that she didn't need "the fucking thing," that she was walking out, that she couldn't afford it—until she tried to move and screamed in agony. "Maybe a chopper *is* a good idea," she muttered.

By the time the helicopter arrived forty-five minutes later, Tina was fully conscious and in even fuller pain. It couldn't land, so she was evacuated via a cable that dangled from the chopper, a handsome rescue medic attached to the Stokes litter that cradled her—a detail she savors to this day. She was flown to University Medical Center in Las Vegas, where she was diagnosed with a broken back, concentrated in two vertebrae, the result of being jerked backwards at the waist where she was harnessed to the rope.

Meanwhile, I hiked out alone, carrying our two packs, over 50 pounds of gear. Halfway to the parking lot, sobs wracked me unpredictably and intermittently but stopped just as abruptly. In between, a million disjointed thoughts vied for attention—Oh god! Oh god! Oh god! What comes next? Does Joanne know? How is Tina right now? What's for dinner? Where is she? Will she be OK? My life was no longer my own; it had become the instrument for Tina's redemption.

Other than the Uriostes, we knew no one in Vegas. After checking on Tina at the hospital, I phoned Joanne and told her answering machine what had happened. On Friday afternoon, Joanne later recounted, she found this message on her cell phone: "Tina took a lead fall and was evacuated by helicopter. She broke her back." Joanne felt like vomiting. *"My friend, so pretty, so charming, so kind...could she now be paralyzed and in a wheelchair??"*

Joanne opened her heart and home to us offering whatever was necessary, including her skills and knowledge as a nurse and said she'd be at the hospital first thing in the morning.

She never made it.

* * * *

On Saturday Joanne got a call from Karen, Layton's Philippine wife. As a native Tagalog speaker, her English was difficult to understand. The fuzzy phone connection didn't help. So Arlan got on the phone. He was distraught. Joanne suspected it was the call she'd been dreading for years. Layton had had a hemorrhage that morning. He'd lost so much blood he couldn't continue dialysis. Hospice was requested to take over...immediately. "Then, to my amazement," Joanne later told me, "Layton took the phone and told me to bring him some Brie and French bread before he died. I said I would."

That Saturday evening Jorge and I downed half his stock of twelve-year-old Cragganmore single malt. The next morning when I was back at the hospital, Joanne rang. "Layton's dying. Jorge and I are driving to Kingman to be at his side. We'll leave the door open. Make yourself at home. Give Tina our love."

I didn't see the Uriostes again until late Sunday evening after they'd returned from Kingman. While Jorge and I finished off the rest of the whiskey, Joanne recounted their visit with Layton:

George and I, driving the two-hour stretch from Vegas to Kingman on Sunday morning, had no idea what we would find when we got there. Arlan had given me the address of the hospice the night before. Will our presence be intrusive or helpful? Will Layton be awake or asleep...alive or dead? We faithfully toted the Brie and French bread, as if on a mission. The hospice turned out to be a quiet sanctuary surrounded by neighborhoods of exploded meth-kitchen trailers. We entered a spacious, clean, chapel-like facility where Layton was the only occupant, amid Karen's and Arlan's red eyes and tears.

The nurse part of me kicked in and I suggested that we work together massaging his cramping muscles, lubricating his dry lips, and bringing cool sips of lemon soda to his mouth. Layton thanked us for coming but said he could no longer handle the Brie and French bread. I became aware that there were no IV fluids, no blood transfusions, and no plans for dialysis. With so little kidney function, he was dying from dehydration and electrolyte imbalance.

Joanne asked Karen why he wasn't receiving a blood transfusion. "Surely," she thought, "this could allow him to continue with dialysis, extend his life and perhaps even allow him to see his son graduate from college next year". They replied softly, "Jehovah's Witnesses prohibit blood transfusions." Joanne was stunned; absolutely floored. She was silent, incredulous. She'd always assumed that Layton was not extreme in any ideology.

Though she was well aware of his religious conversion, she never thought it would trump his practicality. Joanne continued:

The muscle cramps came harder now, making him scream. No medications were administered, so we worked together with our massages. A church elder and his wife entered the room. They whispered with Karen, their backs to Layton, then darted out without any acknowledgement that he still was conscious and alive.

At a few minutes before 5 pm, George and I said goodbye to Layton. I kissed him many times lightly on his right cheek. I lingered a long time before breaking away. He said, "Thanks for coming," kind and straightforward until the end. We drove back to Vegas through the glorious golden gloaming bathing the desert mountains and crags that had brought Layton to Kingman in the first place.

I took in Joanne's account half in sympathy—for Layton and the Uriostes—and half incredulous. I, an infidel, with at least one sheet to the Cragganmore wind, sick for Tina, and impervious to the fact that both Layton and his family had chosen their convictions out of a deep faith, vented my stress in choleric fulminations against the apparent coldness, obtuseness, and lack of empathy displayed by Kor's co-religionists. Jorge, a former Jesuit priest, listened sympathetically.

After Joanne finished recounting their visit with Layton, I updated them on Tina's condition. Tina was tested, probed, interrogated, evaluated, X-rayed, MRI-ed, CAT scanned, pampered and drugged to drooling. Late in the day, a neurosurgeon recommended surgery to fuse four vertebrae, two of which were squished like marshmallows. Miraculously, there was no serious nerve damage. We agreed. The surgeon scheduled surgery for 5 am the following day.

* * * *

That Sunday night at 10:35 Karen called the Uriostes and told them that Layton had just passed away. Arlan added that his dad had refused palliatives, wanting to fully savor the final course of this brief repast. He wanted to spend every conscious moment with his wife and son.

Layton Kor died on April 21, 2013. He was 74.

Joanne spent a restive night (if she slept at all). She was terribly upset. To ease her distress, the next day she walked out to Pink Goblin Pass. The April flowers, heightened heart rate and dripping sweat began to ease her feelings and put Layton and Tina into perspective. She thought of the irony of how Layton had so often outsmarted death. Of how Tina was "doomed as she flew through the air. Fate had saved her, while Layton chose his check-out."

She burst into a torrent of tears.

The next morning, Monday, I was at the hospital by 6 am. Tina's surgery had gone well. A surgeon had fused four of Tina's vertebrae. With the two connecting rods and supporting standoffs, the center of her spine now looked like the cable route on Half Dome. The following day she insisted on walking, even if it was just around the nurses' desk—which she did, in great pain and with even greater pride. It was a no-negotiable demand.

A week later I drove her home in our van to Prescott, Arizona. She lay flat on her back, on the camper van bed, wrapped up in a body brace, moaning periodically.

* * * *

RUSTY: *I had originally found in Layton a kindred spirit. Someone who could inspire me. I saw in his wild spirit a connection with Nature and access to its raw energies. I had built on that connection and found comfort and reassurance. But Layton had then chosen a new and different path, one* *that was strange and alien to me. He had travelled this path for the rest of his life and had died a terrible death upon it.*

Tina had held fast to her natural roots, her simple and sincere beliefs. She had created an authentic life that had no need of contrivances. She was happy and spontaneous. And then…she had fallen on a climb, betrayed by an unexpected loose handhold, and was now facing paralysis and desolation.

Both our friends had followed their dreams with total commitment, trusting in their very different support systems to provide balance and, if necessary, reconciliation. Both had been treated harshly and had their convictions tested to the utmost.

I was shaken.

It was not an abstract, objective situation. I too had lived this life, was still playing this game. My confidence, the wellsprings of my courage, my sense of meaning, all demanded a successful resolution.

* * * *

Twelve months later, Tina was on her way to a full recovery, though she might never again touch her toes without bending her knees or sit in a kayak for long periods of time.

Halfway through her convalescence, still strapped into a half-body brace and looking for some inspirational reading, she picked up Tom Patey's book *One Man's Mountains*. While reading the chapter on Patey's, ascent of the Old Man of Hoy, the sea stack off Scotland's north coast, with Rusty, she burst into tears. She was afraid she'd never climb again.

I piped in that though she might never lead again, she'd at least be able to climb *via ferrate*, an easier and safer sort of climbing.

"What's a via ferrate?" She asked.

"It's via *ferrata*; *ferrate* is the plural," adding that these were rock routes in the Italian Dolomite Alps that were protected by continuous steel cabling to which you attached yourself with a pair of short lanyards, thereby rendering them extremely safe.

Now curious, she further inquired, "Who put them up?"

"Most were established between 1900 and the First World War to train alpine troops and to establish defensive positions along the Austro-Italian border where both countries had territorial claims," I continued. "It's boutique climbing at its best. They're very popular with older climbers."

In an instant the tears disappeared and a big toothy smile burst forth, incisors leading the charge with bright-beam headlight-eyes illuminating her *café au lait* face. Suddenly the future looked bright—for both of us.

Somewhere inside that fragile stalk there was perhaps a lot more than "just loving everything about climbing"—as she'd once told Layton—something much stronger and deeper.

* * * *

RUSTY: *Climbing, especially close to The Edge, requires clear and concise judgement, a discipline based on careful factual analysis and self-reliance. In climbing situations, blind faith in anything is usually catastrophic. Most of us are more interested in surviving our adventures to quaff a few more beers, than in relying on promises of a sublime afterlife if things go south.*

This society we have cobbled together is surprisingly free. So long as you don't break an actual law, you can believe anything you like, follow any lifestyle you choose. And so I tried not to be judgmental—but, try as I might, I could not see a Happy Ending to Layton's story. Even in the short time we had spent together, and in spite of our different climbing inclinations, we had shared too much together, traveled too far into a more vibrant world not to bemoan the path he'd chosen.

So, no matter how hard I worked on empathizing with Layton's final moves, no matter how hard I tried to appreciate his final sacrifice, my mind kept going back to that magic day in the Black Canyon of the Gunnison and how we chased him up those snowy slabs...

Layton and Tina faced their mortality in different ways: On the one hand was Layton, who had started off as a primal force of nature, but had then given his life over to one of the christian gods. His last moments, though tragic, were an affirmation of his new faith.

On the other hand, was Tina, who had no sympathy with any kind of intellectual daydreaming or ethereal promises. Tina had jokingly denied being a spiritual person at all—but had pulled herself back from the brink of death, paralysis and desolation. She was climbing again...steel parts and all!

* * * *

A year later Arlan Kor stopped at the Uriostes' while visiting Vegas and told them of his Yosemite climbing adventures with his friends. Now leading, his brown skin and dark eyes glowed, his grin the exact duplicate of Layton's.

Finally, Joanne recalled, "I'd rappelled near Valore several times in the past year, but had not wanted to swing over to actually see the site of Tina's accident. Soon after Arlan's visit however, I found myself in that area. As I rapped, I swung over to the untraveled hollow and saw the bleaching blue nylon sling on the abandoned #3 Camalot wiggling in the updraft. I pulled it out to return to Tina the next time we rope up".

Buying Gasoline in Ethiopia

By Robert H. Miller

...there are also unknown unknowns—
the ones we don't know we don't know.
—Donald J. Rumsfeld

Buying gasoline is usually a simple task. We might ponder the causes, effects and solutions to the world's energy problems. But on a day-to-day basis we generally figure that we can buy gasoline pretty much at will.

Not too long ago, I was nearly defeated in an attempt to buy 20 gallons of regular in Addis Ababa. I was there to complete the plans for a river trip intended to be an adventure for the participants and a source of profit for the organizers: me and my partner. As a condition for our rafting trip, one branch of the government wanted us to supply another branch of the government with gasoline that only a third branch of government produced and sold. Fair enough.

I put my gasoline-buying algorithm in gear. Step one was finding a gas station. I rose early, ate a breakfast of raw hamburger with chilies and a cup of thick coffee. At the door of the hotel I turned right and headed north up the street. Intuitively, I reckoned I'd encounter a gas station within 20 minutes. I passed government buildings, the Hilton, the Cuban and East German compounds. I took mental notes of the streets (most unnamed; none straight; few in a grid pattern). I wandered into a residential slum area. I got lost. I decided to call or hail a taxi, return to the hotel and start over. Addis Ababa had no public phones (these were the mid-1980s); I knew no Amharic except for "good morning". If only I could get directions to a public landmark I could start over.

The Imperial Palace of the deposed Haile Selassie seemed like a good bet, so I accosted a passerby with *tenayistilign* and with my best "I'm lost" body language queried, "Haile Selassie?" The poor woman's face turned white with corneas and teeth. I may as well have asked for Che Guevara in Miami's Little Havana. News travels fast in the slums of Addis. A policeman soon approached, asked for my papers, and with barely intelligible English escorted me back to my hotel where I prepared for a second attempt.

This time I turned left and headed south down the street. I encountered a commercial district. Lots of shops, kiosks, schools, cafes and bookshops. I couldn't help myself. I had to sample the delights of a "people's" bookstore. Did you know that the collected works of Joseph Stalin run to 20 volumes and that Bulgarian farm collectives publish a monthly journal in English? But I was no closer to finding a gas station, although I'd acquired an Amharic/English dictionary that I thought might help.

Ethiopia is predominantly Christian. So I began to feel quite nervous as I discovered I was in the midst of the Moslem quarter, outside the gates of the Addis mosque. No gasoline here—just cold penetrating stares. Being of Cuban extraction, I tried exuding an air of Cubanness to cover my aura of lost gringo tourist. It was a subtle distinction lost on the average Ethiopian, but it made me feel better.

I wandered into the largest open air market on the continent. Flies buzzed a welcome. No gas here, but I made the best of it. Perhaps jerry cans were available here. I kept an eye out for a pots, pans and containers vendor. I should have watched my step. Rivulets of raw sewage flowed over the ground in complex dendritic patterns under and around beggars, drunks and amputees. Distracted, I walked into the breasts of an Aunt Jemima look-alike. Time to retreat. I had the will to continue but my nose's endurance faltered at the over-aged, raw meat stalls.

What had gone wrong? Surely, a determined random walk in one of Africa's largest cities ought to produce a gasoline station.

Several warm beers later at the hotel bar I made a tactical re-evaluation. I'd entrust my fate to a taxi. Addis Ababa had no mass transit at that time—no buses, no trams, no rental cars, no rickshaws, few bicycles or mopeds. No taxis as we know them. But they did have collective taxis, all painted blue and white, most of them Morris Minors. If you wanted a ride, stand on a main street, wave frantically, and one might stop. Tell the driver where you're going and if he's going near there, you've got a ride. If not, repeat the procedure. I tried my hand at it. A tiny Peugeot with six people pulled over. The driver looked at me searchingly. My Amharic failed me. I lost that ride.

I hopped into the next taxi without asking about the destination or negotiating a fare. The driver beamed with pride at his foreign passenger. After several other passengers had been dropped off and new ones picked up, I worked my way up to shotgun and made him understand where I wanted to go. He drove right up to a gas station with a long queue of taxis. I beamed with success—prematurely. The station had no containers. None. Of any kind. Anywhere.

* * * *

I never did want to go to Ethiopia. As a Cuban refugee and a staunch free marketer, a river trip in Communist Ethiopia wasn't my idea of a good time. Wilderness adventures and socialism are incompatible. The wilderness is freedom and self-reliance; Marxism is regimented and paternal. But I like a challenge, and I love adventure. And my partner, Roy Smith, offered me 40 percent of the take. I couldn't refuse. His job was to sign up ten paying customers; mine, to do everything else. Fair enough.

Roy came from a venerable British explorer tradition with a target fixation on Africa. Since the reign of Queen Victoria, the African bush has drawn these men like stray dogs to a landfill. As a soldier in the Lancashire Fusilliers, Roy had left his mark during the Mau Mau uprising of '52, the Suez Crisis of '56 and—on the side—had managed a little private gun-running operation to Somalia. He also boasted various first ascents on peaks in East Africa. Together we had led mountaineering excursions in Kenya and Tanzania. Now the Omo River beckoned. But while I considered myself expert with river currents, eddies, weirs, keeper holes and the arcana of ferry gliding vector forces, Roy had never rowed a raft or paddled a canoe or kayak—but he was a good swimmer.

The Omo has its source in the mountainous plateau 120 miles south of Addis Ababa. The forty thousand square mile watershed in the rugged highlands of western Ethiopia is shaped like an oversized question mark and guarded by fortress-like mountains with precipitous cliff faces and gorges, unlike anything anywhere else in Africa. Flowing south for 600 miles (and down 9,000 feet) through some of the wildest and most inaccessible terrain in Africa, the turgid brown waters enter Lake Turkana (formerly Lake Rudolf) on the Kenyan border. It never reaches the sea. Only one road (virtually impassable from either side) crosses the upper gorges; the middle reaches are nearly inaccessible and not fully under the control of the central government. There are no accurate maps, only WWII-vintage British cursory military surveys.

A California outfitter, Richard Bangs, and his company, Sobek, had pioneered Omo River trips during the reign of Haile Selassie. But since his overthrow by the Derg under Mengistu Haile Mariam, whether raft trips even made it on to the river were a roll of the dice. Only a handful of trips had been successfully completed. Sobek's rafts were gathering dust. We contracted to hire their rafts. I was to precede our expedition by a few weeks and organize food, equipment, transportation, logistics and the absolutely essential government permits—the reason why Sobek's trips had become a crap shoot. My contacts in Addis were the National Tourist Office (NTO), and Conrad, Sobek's representative.

Conrad had been teaching mathematics at the University of Addis Ababa since before the revolution. He spoke Amharic well, a language related to Hebrew, and coordinated Sobek's Omo trips in Addis. Our contract with Sobek, besides the basic raft rental, included our use of Conrad as a liaison and general information factotum. Lacking maps—except for a trusty Michelin road map of N.E. Africa—Conrad would supply us with a written description and log of major rapids and tributaries along our 350-450 mile descent. But Conrad was suspicious and guarded his turf like a building inspector scrutinizing an owner-built home. Ethiopia had allowed me in as a tourist leading a group of tourists with dollars to spend. I could not engage in any business other than as a retail consumer. Though I bristled at the restrictions, we fulfilled the letter of the law by contracting with Sobek in the US and signing on our passengers in Colorado. Still, the transfer of equipment and consummation of the trip would take place in Ethiopia.

For purposes of dealing with the government, Roy and I saw ourselves as Sobek sub-contractors. Not so Conrad. He would have no part of it. To him we were potential competition, or at worst, unlawful commercial adventurers that might imperil Sobek's de facto monopoly. I begged; I cajoled; I tried to reason, all to no use. My dad used to say that if you ignored a problem long enough it would go away. I decided to follow his advice.

* * * *

Ethiopia has few parallels. Coffee and honey were first domesticated there. Archaeological discoveries confirm it as a cradle of mankind. The Ethiopians have always rallied to repel foreign invaders, from the medieval hordes of Islam to the Victorian English. Aside from a short and brutal foray by Mussolini in the 1930s, Ethiopia has never been colonized. But its isolation and sovereignty have nurtured pride and equanimity of character along with a variety of *sui generis* religious beliefs. Besides animistic traditions, it is home to an ancient sect of Judaism born of the very first stages of the Diaspora. Most Ethiopians are members of the Ethiopian Orthodox Church, itself a branch of the Coptic Church, one of many pre-Reformation Christian traditions that do not recognize the suzerainty of Rome. The Ethiopian Church is an amalgam of Jewish and early Christian practices.

About the time of the Italian invasion, a revivalist sect called Rastafarians made their appearance in Jamaica. These people worshipped Haile Selassie under his pre-coronation name (Ras: prince, Tefari Makonnen) as the son of God, the true Messiah. The cult eschews white dominance, pork and second-hand clothing. They are noted for their dreadlocks, long disheveled peppercorn curls, and use of cannabis.

Ethiopian cuisine revolves around raw meat, sourdough pancakes made with tef, an indigenous grain, chilies and mead. Pasta dishes, introduced during the Italian occupation, remain popular. Before the Revolution, the imperial family and nobility owned all the land. Peasants belonged to the land. Afterward, everything belonged to the Derg, or Central Committee, chaired by Mengistu Haile Mariam (Mengistu, might of Mary), a vicious Marxist dictator whose government had (at the time) killed more people than all the wars with whites in African history (or so says Denis Boyles in *African Lives*).

* * * *

But back to the gasoline. We were due to terminate our trip at the newly established Mui National Park and Game Preserve. The park had no road access, no accommodations, no campgrounds and no game save for scattered Cape buffalo and some zebra. The animals were being poached by marauding Sudanese and local bandit bands. The park had three rangers, one thatched hut, a landing strip, a wind sock and a tortile observation tower made out of twisted albeit stiff vines, the function of which, one ranger assured us, was to "watch for enemies of the people". Several years earlier, the park had been endowed with a massive six-wheel drive Volvo flatbed truck. We were hoping to employ this vehicle to transport us the 30 miles between the Mui/Omo Rivers junction and the wind sock where an Ethiopian Air Lines DC-3 might pick us up. The availability of the Volvo was contingent on our supplying gasoline and a mechanic.

I was able to obtain four heavy-duty plastic jerry cans from a government hardware store after securing the necessary permits. The permit ensured I had a valid need and wasn't just indulging in impulse buying. I went back to the gas station. No sale. Frustrated, I went to the National Tourist Office. They informed me —after the requisite wait and red tape—that I needed a permit and a ration card to buy gasoline. Fine; would they supply me with these? No, they would like to comply with my request, but it was not within their jurisdiction. Where could I get the necessary papers? At the Ministry of Transit. I went to the Ministry of Transit. I waited in socialism's ubiquitous queue. Sorry, the Ministry did not issue gasoline ration cards to foreigners unless they possessed a Certificate of Necessity issued by the Ministry sponsoring their visit. I got angry and ran back to the NTO. If they knew I needed a Certificate of Necessity, why did they send me chasing paper all over Addis? They apologized. They issued me a Certificate of Necessity and even called up the Ministry of Transit to obviate my need to stand in line. With my three documents in hand, I decided to call it a day and retired to eat and drink too much—way too much—at a Syrian restaurant.

John Harrington's 1596 contribution to civilization is a perfect example of form following function. It is ideally suited for the purgative functions of both sexes, though very young children sometimes fall in. Whether by design or happenstance, the rejected contents of a sick stomach seldom miss the bowl. A sober vomitee can bend over and steady himself on the tank. A drunk can settle down on the floor, relax and hug the commode. But there was no position I could take when both amoebic dysentery and too much grappa attacked my gut that night. Every orifice in my body had to disgorge something, and if one went, they all would go. I needed a bathtub with a four inch drain.

Hotels in Ethiopia were either for locals or foreigners. My hotel, the Tourist, was the cheapest of its class. In keeping with the new regime's political proclivities, each floor had one communal toilet and shower facility. My room was 2 by 3 meters and was finished in a bare rose stucco, with a single light bulb dangling from a ten-foot ceiling. For atmosphere the management piped in the capital's all-news radio station: items on the latest milk production figures in Romania and the progress of Tanzania's rural self-education brigades. Hot water was sometimes available between 11 a.m. and 2 p.m., electricity only in the evenings. The clientele were mostly Djiboutians.

After a night of Ethiopian toilet hugging I showed up at my favorite gas station with my four jerry cans, Certificate of Necessity, Purchase Permit, Gasoline Ration Card and cash. Again, no sale. The permit was dated yesterday and was good only on the day of issue at the gas station specified on the back; this station being for taxis only. Back to the NTO for a translator and the Ministry of Transit for a new permit. Three days after beginning my quest, I stood satisfied but helpless on an Addis curb with 20 gallons of regular.

No taxi would convey 20 gallons of gas as this was against the law. I had to hire a lorry. Lorries could be hired between 5 and 7 a.m. at the southern edge of Addis. I turned back to the gas station and, passing a few Birr note (the local currency) to the harried attendant, asked him to keep my gas canisters overnight.

My hotel was on the northern extremity of Addis. I needed a good run, so I rose early the next day and jogged to the industrial area, found a 2-ton Benz flatbed with an eager conductor and was soon on my way. We stored the gas at the NTO since my hotel would have nothing to do with it—against regulations.

* * * *

I badly required a rest from bureaucrats and rules. At heart
I'm an anarchist. It runs in my family. My brother was drafted for
the Korean War but soon discharged for being "temperamentally
unsuited to taking orders." I have always been self-employed. At
the time, my home had no electricity or phone. It had its own
well and no street address, just a sectional description.

To avoid the bureaucrats for a day I concentrated on securing provisions. Before leaving Arizona I sought out one of
Sobek's boatmen who, luckily, made his home in the nearby town
of Jerome. Star—my cynicism blossoms when confronted by individuals who affect a single name—agreed to meet me at a
roadside vegetable stand.

"Take plenty of food", he cautioned. Star had a disconcerting way of answering in vague, Sixties freak-speak banalities.
Everything was "heavy", "far out" or "cosmic". But he did focus
concretely on food.

"We lost all our oranges in the first rapid", he declared.
Sobek, catering to a young, health-conscious clientele, tried to
provide a diet of fresh produce and meats. To accommodate this
culinary philosophy in the wilds of central Ethiopia required extraordinary effort. Rafts were stacked with boxes of fruits and
vegetables. Giant ice chests were constructed of imported plywood and Styrofoam and stocked with ice from the Addis Hilton
to keep slabs of meat from putrefying in the humid heat. Midway down the river, Sobek planned a four-wheel drive resupply
of provisions, including more ice and meat, sometimes made
contact as scheduled, sometimes not, depending on the vagaries
of weather, bureaucracy, rapids, hippos or any number of unpredictable contingencies, but always at great expense and trouble. Star had gone hungry or dined on rotting fare, and the experience had never left him. I decided on a regimen of dried and
canned goods with no resupply.

I went shopping. Twelve people for 21-28 days. No ice, no fresh food. All canned and dried. Addis had no Safeway, and the open air market looked like a dangerous way. I made the rounds of the neighborhood grocers. Once they had been thriving, cutthroat concerns run by East Indian or local entrepreneurs. Now they were franchises of the Derg with identical stock and prices, managed by bored and surly attendants. I bought dried lentils, black beans and rice, coffee and English tea, canned Russian mackerel (complete with scales and bones) and tinned ground pork parts, Eritrean wine and Italian spaghetti, dabo-kolo (a deep-fried, potato chip-like snack), berbere (a spicy gravy base) and Ethiopian peanut butter; and, of course, Cuban sugar. From the US I brought spice and gravy packets, dried vegetables and two pressure cookers. Winston Churchill, in the midst of the Battle of Britain, sought relaxation in the tedium of bricklaying. I spent the rest of the day sequestered in my hotel room measuring food portions into Zip-Lock baggies I'd brought from home. I hope Churchill found bricklaying as relaxing as I found this prosaic activity.

Before Roy arrived, we had our first financial crisis. One week prior to launch the NTO raised their fees by 300 percent. Visa, MasterCard and American Express couldn't have helped. I had to call Roy and have him bring more money. At the Ministry of Communications I was able to snare an international phone line after a two-hour wait. Roy answered the phone out of a deep sleep. When it comes to money, Roy is parsimonious to a fault—he's from Lancashire. Instinct took over and all he could say was "NO".

So I said I'd cancel the trip and come home. This woke him up. Would I lend him some money? "No," I said (he must not be fully awake yet). So I spelled it out for him: "You must raise the fee we are charging each customer by a commensurate amount to the NTO's extortion." Since he and the customers were flying separately, the additional funds would be given us in Addis. Although this solved the NTO problem it left us holding lots more dollars than we had entered Ethiopia with. It's the only time in my life too much money has posed a problem. Currency violations could be a capital offense.

Money is freedom. So Ethiopia had strict currency control laws. At the time, every dollar brought into the country, every dollar exchanged into Birr ($1 = 2 Birr), every Birr spent had to be declared, receipted and tabulated on a currency control ledger. Roy and I are honest men, but we ran afoul of the system. Intimidated by the Uzi-toting guard at the customs desk at the airport, Roy under-declared his bankroll by 50 percent. Ethiopia had a very simple formula for tourists: you could take out as much foreign currency as you brought in, minus $50 per day, every day, whether you spent it or not. Birr could not be exported, and they could only be exchanged for foreign currency within these regulations. Roy had got himself into a muddle.

Travel within Ethiopia was strictly proscribed without permits. My most important chore was to ensure that all the requisite travel permits were issued and in order for every member of our group. For this we paid the NTO over $1,000. Yet each day, like a baroque courtship ritual, I would have to oil the gears of officialdom. "The permit applications are being processed, Mr. Robert" (in Ethiopia the family name comes first). Sobek cancelled many a trip for want of permits.

It was on one of these daily trips that I met our tour guide, Efrem. All tourists must be accompanied by an NTO guide. Efrem was 24 years old and hosted a tape worm. This assignment was punishment for a bookkeeping infraction on a previous excursion with East German big-game hunters. He spoke English well but none of the languages we expected to encounter along the banks of the Omo. For $2,000 we were getting two parasites in one. Our safari guide could neither swim nor cook nor handle a gun. But he was a natty dresser, with pointed leather shoes, sleeveless cardigan and stylish afro.

* * * *

The day Roy and the rafters flew in, I cancelled the expedition. The Ministry of Parks and the NTO were feuding. The six-wheel drive Volvo, according to the latest memorandum, would henceforth be used only for game management and not for tourist transportation. With nothing to lose, Roy and I stormed into the NTO minister's office and demanded our money back. Unintentionally and without forethought we played good cop/bad cop: I ranted and raved; Roy begged and bribed. We were lectured on business ethics and our organizational acumen was impugned. We threatened bad publicity. Finally the NTO minister phoned the minister at Parks. We got the Volvo.

The day we left for the Gibe bridge over the Omo gorge I celebrated by getting drunk and belligerent on Eritrean wine in defiance of the rules for riding in a bus. At the Gibe crossing, a detail of soldiers armed with Baby Thompson sub-machine guns guarded the WWII-era truss bridge. At that time, at least six separate rebellions hounded the Derg. In the north, Eritrea, an Italian colony until 1952 but at this time a province of Ethiopia, was trying to strike out on its own. In the Ogaden, ethnic Somalis wanted to join Somalia. Between Eritrea and Somalia, the Tigre People's Liberation Front and the Oromo Liberation Front held sway. On the west, Sudan gave sanctuary to Ethiopian rebels and poachers. Addis retaliated by supporting Sudanese guerrillas. Nationwide, a nascent anti-Marxist resistance was exhibiting birth pangs. Consequently, our seditious little group of tourists was met with lock-and-load skepticism. Efrem rescued our cameras from confiscation.

We set to work ferrying our gear down the steep embankment and kitting up our two rafts. I personally carried the gasoline. By late afternoon we were ready to launch. It was late November with only a couple of daylight hours left, but we were busting a gut to head downriver. Besides Roy, myself and Efrem, our group of twelve consisted of an MD from Sweden, Anita, who specialized in tropical diseases, another MD, Dean—a general practitioner from Texas with his wife and son—a Colorado divorcee, and four other Americans.

Roy recounts our first, the following morning on the river:

In the early morning when the noises of the night are finally overwhelmed by the first raucous scream of an Adaba Ibis and the shriek of a fish eagle, a fine mist will sometimes hang over the Omo River creating an atmosphere of timelessness and mystery. The bellowing of a bull hippopotamus echoes quietly across the valley. The noise is lost in the emptiness of the tall Hyperrenia grass-covered hillside and cloudless sky.

The thin strip of dark green vegetation that clings to the river's edge appears sinister and dangerous in the early morning...A crocodile swims lazily towards the center of the river, slowly turns and looks towards my tent through the transparent, drifting mist. High in the branches of a sycamore fig a colobus monkey begins the day with a defiant sounding call like that of a monstrous tree frog, and is answered from across the river by another colobus whom he will never meet. The message of the colobus, whatever it might be, is passed on by a succession of voices that finally recede around a distant bend in the river. Dawn was breaking in Africa.

Hippo gauntlet at a rapid's entrance

Hippos fleeing into the river upon spotting our rafts

In addition to miles of whitewater, the Omo presented movable gauntlets of hippopotamuses. One day we counted 300. Hippos don't like rapids. They congregate in the pools above and move around seemingly randomly. Unlike most animals that scatter when startled, hippos instinctively plunge to the center of the stream, either seeking the safety of deeper water to avoid our rafts, or attacking our rafts if they felt threatened. Suckling mothers and bulls in rut know no fear. Predicting their movements as our rafts entered the pools above the drops at first seemed impossible. To improve our chances, incentivize the hippos and, if necessary, defend ourselves, Roy took to accumulating a hundred pound arsenal of shot-put size cobbles on his raft. The kumbaya contingent in our group strongly objected to resorting to violence against wildlife. Finally, we also resorted to hugging the shallow shore where few hippos were likely to be wading, arcing our way around a pool instead of heading directly to our preferred opening. But this strategy wasn't always successful, as Roy recounts:

One time I noticed what looked like a large lava boulder in an eddy by the east shore. It became immediately apparent that the rock was the badly scarred back of a large hippo. Half its torso, legs and head were submerged. With no perceptible movement other than the gentle lapping of water along its bulbous battle-torn flank, I decided to move in for a closer look at what I was fairly sure was a dead hippo. It seemed strange that there were no crocodiles on hand cleaning up the carcass. I was beginning to feel a little nervous and slapped my oar down on the water to see if the noise would bring the carcass to life. It did, and with alarming speed the hippo performed an underwater pirouette on its hind legs, wheeled, and charged directly for the raft. It was the largest hippo I had ever seen and the meanest. I instinctively pulled on the oars to get into deeper water where it would have more trouble climbing on board and biting the crew. There was no way we could outrun it. "Stand by to repel boarders!" I shouted and grabbed an oar as a weapon. With the benefit of negative buoyancy the hippo was narrowing the gap in a series of underwater sprints and spectacular surface lunges.

Armed for hippo

At twenty feet I could smell his breath and looked directly down his pink throat as he blasted out a mouthful of water and lungful of air. Together we hurled fist-sized rocks at the gaping head and jaws. One of the rocks was a direct hit and disappeared down its throat. He must have known by now that we meant business, but he kept on coming. A trail of bubbles and a surface wake created by his large bulk traveling fast under water, made it clear he was

212

coming and meant to attack. His final lunge was directly alongside the raft. The orchestrated screams of a very scared crew along with a battery of rocks directed at his head were our last resort. At the very last second when disaster seemed imminent he lost his nerve, dove under the raft and reappeared in deeper water.

Hippo teeth

We did encounter one dead hippo a few days later. He was badly battle-scarred, but not yet bloated or scavenged. He must have died within the previous 24 hours. We spent half-an-hour examining him: his dentition, proportions, genitalia, facial features, etc. I took particular notice of the muscles at his tail. When hippos defecate their tiny tails spin like a fan on high speed, spreading the feces in a wide area.

During the night these overgrown porkers (to which they're reloated) grazed on the hillsides. Their trails to and from the river resembled eight-foot bowling ball chutes. While the hippos monopolized the sandy, sylvan beaches, we camped on rocky, sloping promontories. The first priority in making camp was to gather large piles of driftwood so we could keep a protective fire burning all night. Camp routine included all-night watches in two-hour intervals. It was a good time to read, write or reflect. As we boiled the next day's water supply, we'd watch the parade of curious eyes at the perimeter of light. High, large and far apart eyes precipitated frenzied spurts of fire feeding. Lion, hyena and leopard stalked the shores, tracks and scat of which we'd often discover in the morning; and it wasn't unusual to find the deep grooves of crocodile tracks made during the night only a few yards from camp. Crocodiles, unlike alligators which are shy and retiring, stalk human prey.

Crocodile

There are three cardinal rules in the sport of river running: always wear a life jacket; tie everything securely to your craft; and never descend anything you can't see. John Wesley Powell, on his first descent of the Colorado River, had an oak desk chair strapped to the high deck of a dory as a makeshift crow's nest. Sometimes only stopping and climbing the banks will reveal the severity of a drop. Most rapids are caused by the damming of the current either from accumulated debris or resistant strata.

While the speed of river water varies from nearly stagnant to NASCAR fast, rapids are stationary phenomena with fixed obstacles. Typically, in a pool-and-drop river such as the Omo, the rapids are formed by boulders deposited by tributaries at flood levels. This creates a lake effect upstream filled with very slow water. At the downstream end of the pool, the water weasels through openings in the damming detritus and rushes downstream through, over and against the obstacles. The first key to a successful run through a rapid is to identify the opening with the most water flow and fewest downstream obstacles. This can be like threading a needle. A good run avoids all the obstacles or, if that is impossible, uses them like caroming billiard balls. An excellent boatman will employ all his English skills when forced to work with, instead of, to avoid obstacles. Sharp rocks and pointy snags must be avoided at all cost.

Some rapids have so many dangerous obstacles that it's too much of a crapshoot to attempt running them—especially far from civilization where dire consequences are difficult to correct. The choices are portaging—carrying everything on terra firma, however convoluted, around the rapid—or lining, a cumbersome in-between technique of walking the crew and some gear around the rapid while using the bow line, muscle and sticks to nudge the raft around shoreline obstacles. We decided to line Gypsy's Bane Rapid.

Portage of Gypsy's Bane Rapid

A full half day of struggling with two heavy rafts, pushing them out and wheeling them in repeatedly, often up to our waists in treacherous, boulder-strewn waters with Spitting Cobras and Black Mambas potentially hiding on the verges, and with conflicting orders shouted back and forth, finally got the rafts below the obstacles. At the end, bloody shins and one lost shoe later, our Colorado divorcee was missing her life jacket. She didn't seem concerned. Irritated at her nonchalance, I lit into her—albeit in a somewhat feigned anger—telling her she couldn't ride in my raft without a life jacket: I didn't want to be responsible for her irresponsibility. Of course, we weren't going to abandon her on the banks of the Omo. Good cop/bad cop again; Roy took her.

Since the beginning of the trip I'd become aware of a certain dynamic exhibited by paying customers that I'd been blind too: Hiring a guide provides a certain sense of security. In their minds all risks are minimized when they pay an outfitter. After all, a truly dangerous undertaking is not for tourists, but only for the experienced—sharing organization and hardships, with full knowledge and common consent. I had to convince them that running an uncharted, isolated river in Africa replete with objective dangers was a very serious undertaking, in spite of Roy's salesmanship and my organization...and the remuneration for our efforts. Night watches, hippos, crocs, bilharzia, sleeping sickness, rapids, armed tribes, elephantiasis, river blindness, lions, deadly snakes and who knows what else were not window dressing to a boutique float trip in an exotic destination—they were the hard and harmful realities of our situation. That evening I emphasized that we had to be at our tip-top best; that we relied on each other to see us through to a successful completion of this venture; that they weren't merely tourists, but intrepid explorers (however novice).

Efrem

All of this puzzled Efrem, our Ethiopian guide. "Why do people like you Americans do things like this?" he asked Roy when they were alone.

Roy only smiled. "I didn't really have an answer," he confided to me later.

Efrem was a kind, gentle soul resigned to his assignment without resentment. He was never in bad humor and exuded an endearing transparency. Somewhat reserved, we tried to draw him out as the days passed and we spent all our time together. We were especially curious about his political perspective. But Efrem breasted his cards. I'd brought along Shiva Naipaul's *North of South: An African Journey*, a scathing account of African dictators' venality and cruelty. Efrem was an intelligent, thoughtful young man, but had not brought along any reading matter. I offered him Naipaul's book.

Thereafter, at every lunch stop and campsite, Efrem, eyes wide with wonder, couldn't put the book down. Although he didn't actually express any anti-Derg sentiments, we sensed that his reactions to the book's revelations were a proxy for his evolving political judgements about his own government.

First descenders usually get rapid naming rights, but not always. While scouting a rapid just before the confluence with the Gojeb, Roy found a 1780 Maria Theresa silver dollar jammed between two boulders. Wondering under what circumstances that coin had come to lodge between those boulders deep in the inner Omo gorge, he re-named the rapid after the Habsburg Archduchess of Austria in spite of most of the serious rapids having been named by Richard Bangs on his first descent in 1974. The largest and most violent rapid, at the confluence of the Omo with the Denise River, had deposited boulders some thousand cubic yards in size, the result of floods of such volume and velocity, they are nearly impossible to imagine. Bangs named that rapid Potamus Plunge after a young hippo that, perhaps a little too curious and following a raft too closely, was sucked into the maelstrom but survived its turbulent descent.

One day we encountered one lonely couple in the upper Omo gorge. The man was barefooted but wore a tattered shirt and pants. He carried a sewn and inflated goatskin—a flotation device for crossing the river. Both he and his wife looked terrified at the prospect. With good reason. Most can't swim. But more importantly, the location of a crossing couldn't be in still water: hippos and crocs abounded. So fairly swift water (short of being a rapid) was preferred in spite of the danger of being swept downriver. This day he was in luck. We ferried him across after taking leave of his mate.

Procreation will kill us if it doesn't save us. Living organisms multiply and spread without regard to consequences. In this part of the world, wall-to-wall people is the rule. Yet for 200 miles down the upper Omo we only saw that one couple. As romantic adventurers we reveled in the absolute wilderness; as a skeptic, I wondered: Where are the people?

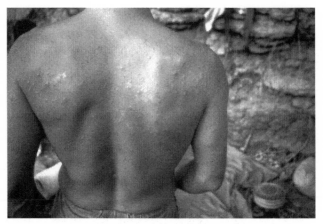
Tsetse fly bites

I have never been able to pronounce tsetse fly, but I certainly felt its sting. About the size and color of a deer fly, the bite is slightly milder than a hornet's and the itch of the welt is comparable to a black gnat's. The insidious effects are not apparent immediately: sleeping sickness and elephantiasis. After a short stint lightly clad in the hot and humid clime, we opted for no shorts or bare backs on our rafts.

Cooling off with river water was no antidote for the heat and humidity. If the crocs didn't snare you, the Schistosoma would. Entering through the pores, the parasite usually lodges in the liver, lays its eggs and, years hence, brings about its host's demise. Often there are no initial symptoms. I was beginning to understand why the upper Omo was unpopulated.

* * * *

But it was not to last. Two weeks down the river a Bodi hunting party waved us over—eight tall, handsome Nilotes armed with WWI Italian carbines and a gourd, no clothes or hair. As we approached shore, Anita, our Swedish doctor, warned us against disembarking barefooted. River blindness, transmitted by a beach-borne parasite that travels up the sole of the foot, was endemic to the area.

Roy and Bodi hunters

The Bodi couldn't tell whether we were male or female. I assume our hair, clothing and white skin confused them. So they felt for our genitals. At first this was a bit disconcerting. We'd heard that a Bodi male's coming of age ritual included cutting the testicles off a male from another tribe and hanging the desiccated scrota around the newly-minted man's neck. Roy later heard from the chief of another village that, "The Bodi are bad people...and they eat people."

Bodi home

Their innocent arrogance, however, was so disarming we took no offense. One woman was flattered when she was invited to a tryst in the bushes. Another, our recent divorcee, was disheartened no Bodi hands touched her crotch. Apparently we weren't fair game for their rituals. I think that instead of perceiving us as members of another tribe, they looked upon us more as aliens from another world.

But most of their stroking they saved for our rafts, so we obliged them with a ride down to their village, a colorful grouping of spherical straw huts. We traded razor blades, fishhooks and empty tin cans for eggs and jerked hippo meat, which I pressure cooked with beans into chili. They knew money had value, though they could not differentiate between denominations and preferred coin to paper.

Sobek, in the interest of preserving the native cultures (and, I suspect, keeping them 'primitive' for subsequent Sobek trips) had developed a set of guidelines for trading with the natives. Anything the river peoples had was fair game. But in return, trip participants could only offer items already in use by them: fishing line, salt, razor blades and such. No Sierra Club T-shirts, Swiss Army knives, baseball caps or such. Although Roy and I were sympathetic and conveyed Sobek's guidelines to our group, we neither endorsed nor rejected them.

When one proud Bodi warrior eyed my yellow rain jacket and expressed an interest in obtaining it, it precipitated a flurry of self-doubt. I was conscience stricken. I can't patronize another human being. Who was I to decide what that man should or shouldn't have? He, rather than I, is in a better position to decide his needs and wants. I pointed to his hand-forged dagger. We closed the deal.

Navigation on the river was "by ghesse and by God." Our Michelin road map for NE Africa supplied the broad strokes (we didn't even bring the British WWII maps). Sobek had compiled a pilot describing major tributaries, rapids and landmarks with running times between them at low, medium and high water levels. Interpreting their descriptions and differentiating between major and minor tributaries, or guessing as to whether we had low, medium or high water according to their estimate (I immediately thought of my stoner informant Star) required lots of Zen guesswork and accurate timing. Did Sobek row in stretches of calm water or just laze in the river's current? After a few days of loosely noting our progress, we opted for eight-hour days full on the oars closely calibrating landmarks with Sobek's log.

* * * *

"Salaam, doctor, salaam!" yelled the Mursi hunter with a penis that hung to his knees and grapefruit-sized testicles. It was the only European word he knew. Both our doctors just shook their heads. We had no way to treat elephantiasis. Anita put on her best bedside manner and gave him two aspirin.

Post mortem on the electric catfish

We were lucky to have two doctors on board. Anita, our expert on tropical diseases, suffered a miscarriage halfway through the trip. Dr. Dean, the GP from Texas, was knocked unconscious while cleaning an electric fish he'd caught, which we mistook for a common catfish. But it was their surgical skills that really saved us. A maverick snag disemboweled Roy's raft. It needed over 100 stitches to become river-worthy again. All for naught. A few days later a hungry croc administered the coup-de-grace to the left front chamber of his Avon Pro. With six air chambers, the raft could still float. We folded the bum chamber back on itself, tied it off and loaded all the gear on my raft for the run out. There went our raft deposit; that crocodile swallowed all our profit.

Croc attack air chamber casualty

Mursi country presaged the end of the trip. The river broadened as it entered drier lowlands, and we encountered no more rapids. Along the banks the tropical forest was thick, but inland it resembled central Arizona. Crocs became much more common, hippos scarcer. Nonetheless, one behemoth surfaced under Roy's crippled raft lifting the entire boat and crew five feet up in the air and knocking Efrem into the drink. The panicked non-swimmer precipitated a rush of would-be humanitarians into the water, which in turn precipitated a frenzy of crocs off the banks after them. Entering a raft with 18-inch round air chambers from the water is not easy. Roy performed miracles pulling everyone back in expeditiously.

Dr. Anita with Mursi women with a labret

The Mursi differed from the Bodi in the females' use of labrets, some a full 6 inches in diameter…and they herded livestock. The presence of cattle marked the edge of tsetse fly territory. Log dugouts with live chickens displayed with pride would periodically glide out to trade. Though unlike Star's Sobek trip, we did not run out of food, we did run low and were glad for the live fowl. Roy, having grown up poor in rural Lancashire following WWII, was the only one among us that knew how to turn a live bird into a roaster.

Mursi chicken traders in dugout

At first we felt confident we wouldn't miss our take-out at the Mui River junction: "a small tributary on the right preceded by a right bend just past a left bend marked by a prominent pink cliff with a white streak and a Mursi village on the opposite bank". How could one miss such a detailed description? As we neared the Mui tributary doubts beset us. The first was a discrepancy in the description of the Mui. Was it a "river" or "a small tributary"? And then there was that "Mursi village". Mursi villages, we discovered, are seasonal. Their location is changed periodically in search of agriculturally productive land. The "pink cliff" was a band of loosely consolidated conglomerate strata extending throughout the entire region and exposed at every bend. The "white streak", which I originally pictured in my mind's eye as a water-deposited, vertical lime stripe, turned out to be a horizontal caliche lens—every cliff was endowed with one.

Somehow, we found the right spot.

Loading the 6-wheel-drive Volvo truck at the Mui Game Preserve

Logistics at the Mui Game Reserve went as planned. The six-wheel drive Volvo met us on schedule and was operational. I personally fed it the 20 gallons of gasoline we had nursed down the river. But our DC-3 was delayed by two days, precipitating a massive depression among our crew. Now that the adventure was over, we wanted it to be definitively over. Marking time in the forest was tedium verging on despair.

"It's a staph infection," announced Anita prescribing an antibiotic ointment. I was skeptical. It had taken a modicum of courage to take the beautiful blonde Swede aside and show her my privates. My testicles had never been so swollen, raw and painful. I pictured in my mind the Mursi hunter with elephantiasis. Dr. Dean declared that it looked like herpes and prescribed fresh air—no ointments. I *knew* it wasn't herpes. The tropics sure breed some strange critters. Our raft decks sprouted large mushroom colonies out of the layers of the plywood. Upon our return to Addis Conrad told me I'd been bitten by a Blister bug. I'd be back to normal in a week.

On the appointed day we hoisted the wind sock and, with the help of the Volvo, chased the Cape buffalo off the landing field. Our DC-3 lacked bulkheads and real seats. We piled in with all our gear.

Back in Addis the real hardships began. My visa had expired while on the river, and Roy and I had to repair two rips on his raft seamlessly—a three-foot slash on an air chamber from the croc and a two-foot rip along the floor from the snag—so we could get our $6,000 security deposit back. The visa extension proved easy—Efrem accompanied me to the Department of Immigration and explained why I'd been unable to renew on time. But after a full day's stitching, gluing and patching, Conrad wouldn't accept the repairs. We understood; the damage was just too extensive and critical.

Our biggest challenge was to devise a way to smuggle the $4,000 (which we'd collected when our crew arrived) out of the country. Part of it was in Birr. We could legally convert some to dollars at the National Bank, so we did. And we got every member of our group to help out. The rest of the Birr we traded to our crew so they could buy last minute mementos. We then consolidated the remainder into $100 bills, which we now wondered what to do with.

We paced and brainstormed for half a day in the hotel room. I love my life. I categorically refused to smuggle any money out. The consequences were just too dire. But Roy and cash are hard to part, and he had experience smuggling guns in Africa.

Roy hiding money in the sole of a shoe

I suggested making a neat incision along the edge of one of our sleeping pads, placing the money inside and gluing it together again. Too much work thought Roy. Instead, he sliced the built-in arch supports from the Nikes he'd worn daily on the river, stuffed the folded bills inside, and glued the sliced soles over the wad of bills. Then he placed the rancid shoes in a stuff sack with his dirty river clothes and stuffed the lot in his duffel bag. He was lucky he opted not to wear them.

At the airport, I didn't even enter by the same door as Roy. Wherever he went, I went the other way. The first hurdle was baggage check. Two armed guards ransacked our luggage for contraband. Roy was three booths away, nonchalant as he could be. The guards pulled out his dirty clothes bag, opened it, pulled out his shoes, took one cursory glance at them and told him he could repack his belongings. I still didn't relax.

Just before boarding the plane we had to pass currency control. We lined up. The white, telephone booth-sized cubicles had a quick-draw curtain for privacy. Each departing passenger was subject to a strip search and a full accounting on his currency control ledger. One well-dressed East Indian looked terrified as he was motioned into the booth. Some long minutes later he was escorted at gunpoint out of the booth and back into the airport. He was all eyes, sweat and terror, punctuated by the humiliation of unshod feet. The guard carried the shoes in his hands.

Roy and I, separately, passed muster and boarded our Lufthansa flight. When the plane took off and finally entered Sudanese airspace we exhaled lungfuls of Ethiopian air in a big sigh of relief. We yelled and hugged...and counted our money.

* * * *

Most of us developed a variety of strange symptoms about six weeks after our return home. Roy's were the worst: loss of weight and appetite, dizziness, intermittent fevers of a violent nature. His doctor referred him to the Centers for Disease Control in Atlanta, part of the National Institutes of Health. The NIH took a very solicitous attitude toward our group and began running extensive tests immediately.

"Why don't you mail that in Prescott?" Asked Fran, the postmistress in Chino Valley, my home town.

"Because this is a US Post Office and I'll be sending out one a week for the next six months and Prescott is a far drive away." Fran had never dealt with Overnight Express Mail, and the prospect of reading reams of instructions and filling out new forms set her to quivering. She had become postmistress through a complex process of political patronage. Her brother-in-law had been a one-term state legislator and the job had been offered to her husband. The regimentation ill-suited him, but they needed the money so she accepted the post. Fran worked hard and had a good heart but complexity overwhelmed her.

"What's in there that's so important?"

"Fresh biological material that must arrive in Atlanta within two days." In fact, I was mailing small ice chests with stools on ice and in formaldehyde, and blood samples.

Eight of us tested positive for schistosomiasis and two for amoebic dysentery. Anita had told us that while the Omo was Schistosoma laden, the side streams above waterfalls were parasite-free, since the bugs couldn't travel up cataracts. She failed to realize that the side streams might themselves harbor Schistosoma, which had no trouble floating downstream. The Deans were not infected. They had taken to towel drying immediately after bathing. Apparently, the bugs only enter the pores as the skin's surface water evaporates; towel drying catches them before they burrow.

Hunter, a Texas attorney, and I caught the dysentery. While I was symptom-free, Hunter spent months in a Houston hospital fighting for his life. In spite of my warnings, he'd been the only one to eat the hippo jerky before I pressure cooked it. I'd probably caught my dysentery at the Syrian restaurant in Addis.

For me, the cures were worse than the symptoms. Bayer had developed an experimental schistosomiasis drug the NIH prescribed for us. It was a one-day bad acid trip. A week later the dysentery drug followed. In spite of showing no symptoms, I was urged to submit: the long-term effects were extremely deleterious. This cure was a milder bad acid trip, but it lasted a week.

A few years later Roy returned to Ethiopia under the auspices of the National Geographic Foundation and with sponsorship from the Ethiopian government. He ran the Omo all the way to Lake Turkana. For the former he conducted a team of scientists for a variety of environmental studies. For the latter he acted as an agent of the government to help extend the central government's control over the lower Omo basin.

Mengistu Haile Mariam was deposed in June of 1991.

Learning by Falling

By Rusty Baillie

I love to lie in the shade of a gum tree
And listen to the night birds sing...
I love to sit at night by my smoldering fire
That's where a man can dream
Dream of the great deeds done long ago
By men who were brave and true...
Dream of the deeds that are still to be done
By lads like me and you...
—Anonymous

Us Africans were always proud of owning humanity. Every single human being originally came from Africa. And I was actually born there. In Rhodesia. I have a white skin, with red hair and freckles, so dermatologists love me. As an indigenous African, the Immigration and Naturalization Service (INS) classified me as an **Afro American** which led to confusion when I started working with the Black Panthers and Afro American Education.

Unlike most white young Rhodesians, who wanted mainly to hunt, play rugby and maybe find a gold mine, I just wanted to climb. This was not altogether unusual; after all, it was not so very long ago that humans came out of the treetops to seek our fortunes on the savanna floor and trees are still dear to kids, of all ages.

Our group, The Parrot Outlaw Gang, had its clubhouse in the branches of an immense and ancient fig tree, growing out of a cleft in a huge granite boulder. Each member crafted for himself an elaborate and comfortable chair, as far out in the branches as he dared—where they became thin and whippy and swayed in the faintest breeze. Our initiation rite consisted of taking a dump from this airy perch. Perhaps we had realized that any lack of daring would tighten the sphincter muscles and prevent such defecation. Perhaps we needed to go. But probably we were just being boys.

Parrot Outlaw Gang member high up on a fig tree

Not all prospective members passed our entry test but, if you succeeded, you were helped to make a fine bow out of hibiscus wood (pruned from some kind donor's prize hedge at dead of night) and a quiver of reed arrows—tipped with a flattened nail and fletched with another unsuspecting neighbor's turkey feathers. These shafts might not have penetrated the plate armor of a

French Knight at Agincourt, but they could pierce quarter inch ply. We used them to hunt feral cats. These escaped domestic pets created havoc with the local poultry, and folks, white and black, were happy to pay us a few shillings to clear them out. Some of these cats died hard and some fought back, teaching us the difficult lesson between play and real life.

Meanwhile, an anxious community was hoping we would soon grow up a bit, join the army or at least be persuaded to become Boy Scouts. The Scouts were not such a bad way to get going. Parents seemed to trust them and you could go off camping and overnight hiking with minimal fuss. You also learned cool skills, like how to fix broken legs and build rope bridges high in the trees.

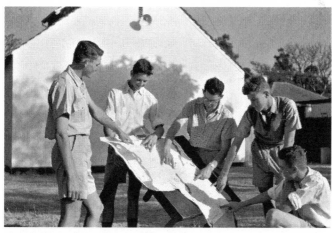

2nd Salisbury Senior Scouts, Kilimanjaro planning, 1955; L to R: Dave Walker, Mick Lowe, Ken Nortje, Brian Clarke, Rusty Baillie

All this rugged outdoor action led us, in 1955, to decide to climb Kilimanjaro. It was the highest mountain on our continent so that seemed the obvious thing to do. It was also two thousand miles away, over atrocious, corrugated roads. But fortunately our scoutmasters seemed fairly willing to demolish their personal vehicles for the cause. We did not realize it at the time, but scoutmasters are just overgrown kids who have not lost their sense of wonder and adventure and are real nice people.

So, there we were at Hans Meyer's Cave, halfway between the last hut and the summit rim of Kibo, the volcanic peak that is the highest point of Kilimanjaro at a lofty 19,560 ft. We had left hours before dawn and I was now puking up my entire gastrointestinal tract, battling the pounding in my head and trying, with only partial success, to avoid immersing myself in the growing pool of my vomitus. I had felt almost as bad when we left the hut but my scout troop had a motto: POR: Press On Regardless. The question was now not whether I would make the summit but if I would ever leave this cave? Sharing my misery were most of my friends, and Ken Nortje and Dave *"Mufad"* McFadden, the scoutmasters.

Ken was wiry, fit and enigmatic. He had a somewhat acerbic wit and this, coupled with his boundless energy, served him well in the maelstrom of teenage dynamics. He was to become my first climbing companion and a trusted friend. Mufad was rather more droll, with an artist's sensibilities and a dry sense of humour. He taught me basic photography and was subtly tactful when I attempted to court his beautiful youngest sister. Our two Last Men Standing, Dave and Mick, had gone on to the top with our giant Chagga guide, whistling and chatting merrily…

At that particular moment, if you had told me that, ten years later, I would return to these equatorial ice mountains and, with Barry Cliff—an English buddy—set a still unbroken record by racing from the top of Killy to the top of Mount Kenya, 286 miles away, in under 24 hours, I would have looked around for a big rock to silence you with. Although *that* epic was kind of fun (in a depraved sort of way) it was actually performed for crass profit: Barry badly needed expensive new tires for his Jag XK150 (one of our shuttle vehicles) and Goodyear had promised him five new, state of the art rally tires if he performed a newsworthy "stunt".

Pepsi (John Petheram) & Itch (John Gray)

I did eventually learn to acclimatize my body to hypoxia and other high altitude privations—after all, there was still Everest to climb—but one does not need to be a psychiatrist to see that, in that cold and malodorous cave were born the seeds of a desperate determination to stay as low as possible and climb small rocks. I do love mountains but I have begun to learn that climbing ecstasy is best found moving smoothly over warm solid rock, with nothing but "a rope and a rack and the shirt on my back".

Back in Salisbury (the capital city of Rhodesia) it was time to explore this new dedication. The school library was full of dusty tomes about heroic Englishmen ascending the great peaks of the

Alps, Andes and Himalaya. These heavy volumes were doubtless meant to teach us young colonials stern lessons of manhood and commitment to Empire, but I was wise to that now. I wanted to rock climb, not carry huge packs and trudge over hill and dale for days on end. I had no real idea what exactly I was seeking. I was not trying to break into an established sport or pastime. There was just this feeling in my bones: a way that my muscles were put together, that set them moving up steep places.

The British tend to form clubs for just about everything, even in remote corners of the new Commonwealth...and the people I needed may have been there somewhere. But I couldn't find any trace of a local rock climb—or rock climber. At age 15 I was considered too young to tour the local pubs and bars where such things might have been located and all the kids I knew were quite happy with sports and girls. I would have to do it myself... and that was OK with me.

The one clue I had was "Know Your Rhodesia", a weekly feature in the local newspaper. This usually featured local spots of scenic interest, but one week there was a picture of a small rocky cliff. This looked promising and so I got my gear together.

Boy Scouts are taught to Be Prepared and our Senior Troop was highly organized, very efficient and well led. Our leaders were dedicated men who shared our boisterous adventures while they tried to keep us in line. But they seemed to be dragging their feet on this rock climbing business and so I decided to do a "reconnaissance" on my own.

I had a natty pair of school shoes which had been chosen for their fashionable buckle but which also turned out to have superb "sticky rubber" soles. These were bright red and up there with the best we have in this new millennium. They had proven their worth on small scrambles on the neighborhood boulders and trees and the leather uppers were polished to a high gloss. But I also needed a rope. All pictures of climbers showed a trusty rope, nicely knotted around the waist with a secure bowline—a knot one could tie at lightning speed, with only one hand. This particular rope had been "borrowed" from the scout Pioneer Locker. Normally used for constructing bridges and zip lines, my fifty feet of stout hemp made up a significant load.

Finally there was my bike. The sport of Mountain Biking was far in the future, but that noble (and immensely heavy) Raleigh was my passport to travel and adventure, which began in earnest the following weekend. After an hour of hard pedaling, I was gazing in dismay at my featured "rock climb". It turned out to be an old shale quarry, loose and holdless...so much for the integrity of the press.

But...here I was on the Great South Road, already some distance out of town. I seemed to remember driving that way once with my parents and seeing a good sized granite *kopjie* shimmering off in the distance. *Kopjies* (which include *dwalas* or domes) are giant piles of rock, home to baboons, leopards and other wild things. It would be a bit (lot) further than normal biking distance but, as active kids, we had already learned the time-honoured trick of just "having a look".

A few more hours of pedaling and there it was. As I had remembered. Maybe a bit further off the road than it should have been, with a large *vlei* (swamp) in between. Fortunately it was the dry season and the vlei should be passable, with most of its slithery inhabitants somewhere else.

Eventually I came to the solid rock. It had been tricky. First hiding my valuable bike from prying eyes and then hopping from tussock to tussock to keep my all-important shoes dry. It was also a bit confusing: I wasn't really sure just what a "rock climb" was. The few photos I had seen were of immense cliffs and slabs and I had already learned that granite can be steep, smooth and holdless. But, ahead of me, the main block of the kopjie was split by a huge cleft, and this seemed to promise some sort of access to the top.

Trying out chimney technique

Unfortunately, like many granite outcrops, the base of the rock was overhanging and my "chimney" was too wide to stretch across. Luckily, growing usefully against one wall was a Stinging Nettle tree. These, like the iconic African Killer Bees, pack a hefty wallop—but only in the leaves. I picked up a short stick to knock off any attacking leaves and set off up the thin trunk. I had a vague and uneasy feeling that what I was doing was not strictly kosher in proper rock climbing circles, but kids are expert at ignoring the demands and standards of stuffy but well-meaning adults.

After about thirty feet I could see a nice ledge, the size of a kitchen table, appearing on the side of the chimney. Inconveniently, my tree was on the wrong side and the stinging leaves were becoming quite dense. It was time to jump ship. I reached across but it was too far to stretch my legs and body, and my exertions were setting the rapidly thinning trunk to swaying precariously. It turned out, however, that this sway could be developed into a useful to-and-fro motion. All it needed was to let go at the propitious moment and I was catapulted decisively onto the far ledge.

So much for Pitch 1. From here it looked like I was about to get some real rock climbing at last. The next layer of the giant block, directly above me now, was also somewhat undercut but— surprise, surprise—it was covered in rough, mushroom-like protuberances. Hand and foot holds! Up close, I could see that these holds provided a convenient kind of ladder, up which I swarmed without a second thought. Voila!—Pitch2 (or was it #1?).

I was now on a nice broad ledge, hunched up against a dead end. The only way out of this cave-like situation was to re-cross the giant cleft, over to where a pretty slab led upwards into the sunlight. There were more of the solid holds sprinkled across this far slab and it looked as though I perhaps wasn't trapped after all.

The only problem was that I would have to climb down a bit before I could cross over. By now it was a long way down that cleft and I would have to gaze down into those dark and ominous depths. Bummer! It didn't seem like a lot of fun.

Suddenly, childhood exuberance was no longer sufficient to mask the horror of what I had done—deliberately seek out a dangerous and potentially lethal course of action. Time for another scout motto: GAG: Get A Grip!

I expect that was a moment where my life did one of its hiccups but I didn't have time to ponder what was happening—I was too busy lowering myself back over the chasm. This time I could just stretch one foot across and get it firmly set on a nice foothold at the bottom of the slab. It felt solid, but it was too far to stretch a hand across as well, so as to have secure holds on both sides at once. I would have to brace my legs, let go with both hands, and let my body "fall" across the gap. Child's Play! A quick scramble and I was on the summit plateau.

But not the tippy top. The True Summit was two giant rock pancakes now looming above me. Again, the start was overhanging but my resolve, wavering slightly by now, was boosted by the discovery of a marvelous jug handle, high up but reachable with a small jump. It was such a good jug (although it was some time before I learned the proper name for these most wonderful of nature's gifts) that I swung up the overhang without a care or doubt. And there were lots more jugs, all positive and solid, and I remember distinctly thinking, perhaps for the first time, Wow! This is fun!

Now I was on top of the first pancake, squeezed into the narrow ledge between the two, on my back, gazing up apprehensively at the last stretch, right above my head. This last rock challenge was even more overhanging and had now become smooth and holdless. Bugger!

The low, sloping ledge I was on is called hereabouts a *"dassie* traverse". Dassies, or Rock Hyrax, are cute and furry rabbit-like critters who live in suchlike sheltered spots. Over the millennia the scampering of their little paws polishes the rock to a high gloss. At least their droppings had all rolled off the ledge so I could scoot myself along smoothly to look for some more of those fine holds. Still lying down, I inched my way around the corner until the traverse closed out. I was wedged securely in place but could not lean out far enough to get a good look around above. The best I could do was to reach up one hand while using the other to keep me wedged in the traverse slot. This desperately grasping hand found…smooth granite and some shallow pocks! So near and yet sooooo far.

One last trick. I squirmed my body and rearranged my inside shoulder until it was just beginning to lose its purchase and reached up again…a little higher this time…and there it was! My beloved jugs had not deserted me after all. I was so pleased to curl my groping fingers over that sharp, iron-hard edge that I gave it no further thought–just pulled up and pasted my sticky rubber soles onto the smooth dassie ledge, giving only a brief and passing psychic belch at the exposure, which now reached all the way down to my bike.

239

A few more jugs, not so perfect but now quite adequate, and I was on top. The view was, of course, spectacular. Out beyond the fringes of the kopjie, beyond the vlei, into the blue distance and the savanna of the hinterland. There was the way I had come, there a native village—probably the same people who had built that nearby grain storage bin—safe from marauding Matabele raiders.

Eventually, as to any and all who summit, came the realization that "You cannot stay on the summit forever". How on earth was I going to get down?!

Rusty Baillie with Hillary hat displaying "modern" abseil technique

Those overhanging moves could not happily be reversed and I now obviously had to do what the books called an "abseil":

slide down my fixed rope. At last those feet of hemp, hauled along with great labor and discomfort, could pay their way. But fixed to what? No convenient nettle tree up here. But over there…that super jug, just below the highest point; that looks kind of hooky, that might snag a rope. And sure enough, the final jug turned out to be a perfect abseil anchor! I quickly had the rope halved and "bent" around the anchor, my final piece of equipment, a pad for my rugby jersey, deployed—and I was ready to teach myself how to abseil.

I don't really remember what I thought of all this at the time. Re-living it for the writing, it seems surreal and miraculous. A gift! Back then of course there were other things to think about: how to unjam that top abseil…I daren't leave my scout rope behind…how to get back across the scary chasm…recrossing the vlei in the dark…wading past those slithery sounds…arriving home ridiculously late and presenting my loving mother with a pair of waterlogged and scuffed best school shoes…

Mazoe

My next move was obvious: recruit some partners. I talked up my newfound "climb", mounted an anti-sports campaign, and by sheer persistence and will power soon had a curious team assembled. The PTA of our scout troop were horrified at the prospect of lowering their beloved sons on an old, tatty, hemp rope and so they funded the importation, across three oceans, of a lovely, snow white, Viking nylon climbing rope. The scoutmaster claimed that we now knew what we were doing, and that it was based loosely on rumours that "there are climbs at Mazoe". On his annual holiday Mufad had watched some South Africans abseiling and so we were now doing proper carabiner-sling descents. Ab-ing out of our second story clubhouse had become all the rage.

The Mazoe cliffs of the Iron Mask Range are visible from the main road north to the Zambezi and are composed of Banded Ironstone, an extremely hard and smooth metamorphic rock. I wasn't sure if this rock would have any of my favourite "jugs" but was told that the local Mountain Club loved it there. So... here we were.

Mufad, as our most experienced adult, tied onto the rope and set off up yet another likely looking chimney. He did well, working his way up about thirty feet to a large chockstone, firmly jammed in place. This chockstone formed a small but nasty overhanging roof and stopped him dead. We knew nothing of running belays so Mufad was faced with the awful necessity of leaving the snug security of his deep chimney, to launch out into space over the "chock". As a responsible adult he was reluctant to be hasty about this.

On the whole, we were polite and well-behaved kids and so we stood around, encouraging our leader...for a while. But we *were* kids—and I could see my Grand Scheme to finally snag a real rock climb grinding to a halt. I thought I could perhaps climb up a little way to his left and see if there were any good jugs up there that might help him out. The face itself was quite broken and, seeing that Mufad was not getting one iota of safety from his fine nylon rope, it didn't seem too impetuous or irresponsible to also scramble up a bit. I didn't consider myself stupid but I hadn't got to the stage of wondering if I was maybe a bit headstrong.

Sure enough, just to Mufad's left, one short move from his cramped impasse, was a big flake. It was a strange shape, quite different from my wonderful granite jugs, but hey—a jug's a jug! I reached across and swung onto it, just to show Mufad how easy this was going to be but, with a sigh, the flake detached itself and toppled over into my grasp.

I have remembered and reconstructed these moments so many times that they have become engraved into the membranes of my mind. First the awareness that I was airborne—so quick, so easy. Then Mufad's face, concerned and a touch horrified, streaming past. Some concerns that I had to get rid of that flake, still clutched in my grasp. Then, somehow, I have twisted round to face outwards, as though I am jumping out of a tree on some dare. Then the lip…I am not quite so sure of this one. I fancy I have sensed that I am headed for the lip and will need to raise myself up a bit to clear it. This of course is physically impossible, and many years of doctoral study have yet to reveal True Levitation, but pass safely over it I did. The final moment is the landing and here I was certainly lucky: The slope was smooth, soft and steepish. I landed neatly and continued tumbling down the grade a ways. As I stopped I bounded to my feet in relief or triumph… or guilt? Later I would learn to inventory myself for injury before moving but now I just spat out the dirt and leaf mold I had ingested and looked around. Several pairs of startled eyes told me that my spellbound audience had still not fully registered the improbable fact that I was still, apparently, alive.

I didn't have time to worry much about my pain and embarrassment, or the blood streaming from my mangled face. I was more concerned about what my mother would do to Ken when he delivered me home. As the scoutmaster "in charge," Ken would, unfairly I thought, be held accountable for my sorry state. Mum had been born on the Indian Ocean island of Mauritius, still spoke her native creole French fluently and was highly Gallic by temperament. She loved us kids totally and absolutely and was highly protective of her family. However, she did not consider her responses at length or try to soften her strong emotional reactions. My brothers and I (and my Dad) had learned that, if we could somehow divert the first lethal reaction to trouble, it would soon calm down, peace would return, and no grudges would be held.

The trick would be to keep Ken safe during those first critical seconds. So we stopped by his house first and his mother washed the worst of the grit from my face and pried away the congealed blood and snot where my teeth had come through my lips. And then we lucked out: my elder sister was visiting and knew all about rambunctious boys (she had five brothers). She grabbed my Mum before things got bad and reassured her in French:

"C'est rien—seulement des garcons" (It's nothing—boys don't feel pain).

The only thing that upset me, and I held it against my mother for years, was that she washed out my bloodstained Hillary Hat. I had been wearing this cap and it had absorbed most of the blood and gore. I had been looking forward to wearing my "Red Badge of Courage" proudly but casually around my friends…

Much later, with the continued education of future trauma and revelation, I have wondered about the resources I had to draw on back then, as my face slowly healed, and I picked up the threads of my dreams and ambitions. I may have been shielded by childhood naiveté and youthful arrogance, and I can't recollect much mental anguish—but I think deep down I was hurting. It's not that I can't believe I could have gone it alone, but that I am now beginning to fully appreciate how close my path came to my father's…

When he was eighteen, my Dad left a secure job as an apprentice joiner in London and joined the Royal Marines. When I asked him why he was so impulsive he started singing:

> *I joined the Navy*
> *To see the world.*
> *And what did I see?*
> *…I saw the sea.*

If he was looking for adventure, he certainly found some action! The year was 1914 and his ship, *HMS Collingwood*, was in the battle line two years later at the pivotal Battle of Jutland in 1916. Although the Brits lost 14 ships and 6,000 men to Germany's 11 ships and 2,500 men, they gained command of the sea and so they redeployed their Marines to the trenches of France and Flanders.

Royal Marines tended to be used at the front as trench raiders and my Dad was just in time for Passchendaele. Having been a carpenter he was most comfortable with hand tools and such folk traditionally favored a heavy ball-peen hammer for denting-in enemy helmets during night attacks. They would pick up their hammers and home-made clubs, sharpen up a cut-down bayonet and creep into the enemy trenches. There is something startlingly primeval about such crude combat, something brutally honest. Something, perhaps, that demands, and awards, total responsibility.

I once saw my Dad, braced in the skeleton of a roof he was helping my eldest brother build, pick up a long 2 x 6 timber, hold it in place against the ridge and scribe a line on it with his thumb nail. He then gripped it firmly in one hand, took a crosscut saw in the other and cut accurately along the compound angle cut… which then fitted perfectly into place.

The thing was—although he was 6' 4" and still immensely powerful when I came along—he was the most gentle man I have ever met. I never heard him raise his voice to anyone, even us rowdy kids, and he never so much as laid a finger on us in anger. He just didn't have to…

Like so many who served their country, he was eventually wounded in action by mustard gas and shrapnel. He sometimes had coughing fits and, when we all bathed together, us kids used to admire the dramatic scars on his legs. We pressed him for gory war stories but he would just sing old naval songs:

Hearts of Oak are our Ships
Hearts of Oak are our men…

After the armistice and a spell in a military hospital he was demobbed in Durban, Natal, South Africa, then still a part of the British Empire. There, close to some of the best surfing in the world, he met my mother, just over the sea from Mauritius, and, after a whirlwind romance, they were married. Eventually the wanderlust returned and they moved north to Rhodesia where my own story began.

In Rhodesia he moved into an office and worked for the government, keeping the unions content, the workers working happily, and Southern Africa out of the Axis forces during the Second World War. His trick was being able to see across classes, races and nationalities. This gave him a knack for keeping things peaceful, without having to crack heads, and The Queen rewarded him with the Order of the British Empire when he retired.

Sitting around a warm, desert campfire in Arizona, on a cold winter night, as I approach my 80th birthday, 60 years after my Dad died, yakking about such things with climbing friends and a full wineglass, I suddenly realize: ***that's how it worked! That's why it all came so easily, why healing happened so quickly, why it seemed to flow so naturally...*** Thanks Dad.

And so I didn't wimp out. It simply was not an option. I found the route description for a climb at Mazoe and pestered Ken until, against his better judgement, he agreed to try it. We took our nylon rope out of storage, worked our way around to the back of the ridge, and found Bee Buttress. This was supposedly a moderate route—though it had a traumatic history: the first ascent party had run into a large bee's nest halfway up. These were the dreaded African Killer Bees and they attacked ferociously and immediately. There was only one good way off, by abseil, and three people to wait their turn. One distraught member of the team could not wait: he was driven frantic by the stings and took the direct route into the void. Amazingly they all survived.

So, we listened carefully for a buzzing sound. A large hive makes a sort of faint roaring sound and the air seems to vibrate. Sometimes there is a subtle waxy smell hanging around. Today the air seemed peaceful: my own adventures with African bees were scheduled a good decade into the future...

This time we both tied on and I led off. It was steep but fun climbing—big holds and occasional trees. Trees we knew. When the rope ran out I was lucky to be near a robust fig tree, growing horizontally out of the rock. I clambered into the branches and made myself comfortable. Ken soon joined me and led through. He was still traditional—in nailed boots with triple hobs around the edge and softer, single hobs inside "for friction". The nails made a *crinching* sound on the hard rock and I could follow his progress via the soundtrack.

Ken was definitely a neat and meticulous climber. His footwork was clean and precise; every time he moved onto a new foothold there was a crisp *crinch* and then a pause. The rock was steepish but the holds were nicely incut. He made steady progress and was soon out of sight.

After a while however I realized that the *crinching* sound had slowed down…and then stopped altogether. It was obviously getting tough up there. People talk about the "umbilical cord of the rope" and it's true that climbers are preternaturally connected to this safety line…I could just *feel* the tension and anguish flowing down that cord. Then the sounds started up again, only this time they were hesitant and discordant. There was no more harmonious rhythm and soon some painful, drawn out scratching. Then finally there was one long sustained shriek of iron and rock and I knew that poor Ken was sliding down—and into space.

I was a rank novice but I knew that he would be coming fast, and that he would be generating a huge force. Our new nylon rope would not break conveniently and leave me safely in my tree, as had happened to Whymper on the Matterhorn (thank you school library). As I was not tied in at all, we would both go flying.

And so I took the rope leading to my waist and wrapped it round and round my tree, at about the same time that Ken arrived, crashing through twigs and small branches. When he finally snapped onto my improvised belay there was so much going on that I never felt the faintest jerk…and Ken was, amazingly, unhurt. We abseiled off and went home. One fall each.

Time passed and we went back to studying for an Astronomer's badge and building bridges. I normally loved "pioneering projects"—lashing poles together and tensioning cables with block and tackle. We built some structures that a car could drive over and our favorite was a cableway high in the canopy. But I just had the feeling that we were moving on here. I was worried that all this mayhem might have finally convinced our scoutmasters to stick with knots and lashings but this is where Ken showed his mettle: soon, he was asking me how I was feeling after all our adventures, if my mum had calmed down—and how we might securely lash ourselves to the mountain in future. POR!

He also got himself some nice rubber climbing soles.

Bari

We needed a survival edge. Running belays and leader protection hadn't been invented yet in this part of the world, but we found an old adage in another library classic: "The Leader Must Not Fall". We had no quarrel with that.

By luck (good luck, we hoped), I found another "Know Your Rhodesia" article—this one about Bari, a big granite lump up north, halfway to the Zambezi River. It seemed that some climbers from the elusive Mountain Club had actually climbed it —and that the locals believed that if the brush on top caught fire they would have bumper crops. Being kids, we wanted to help with that but worried about how we would get ourselves off without being fried, and how our nylon ropes (we now had two) would manage in the heat.

And then suddenly…there we were! Bari! Real rock climbing. No easy way to the top and a lot of steep, blank, granite. We were a bit young for a "sober" silence, but there was certainly not much idle chatter. The side facing the road was totally intimidating. There had to be an easier way, right? And so we set off to walk right around and, sure enough, on the remote back side was a ridge of off-vertical rock, leading straight up to the summit plateau. It looked easy to our recovered enthusiasm, and we quickly established ourselves at the base.

Ken Nortje, Lake McIllwaine Kopjie on the Great South Road

There were four of us. Some hard-core and some perhaps not yet fully aware of the lethal potential of this "interesting" new activity. There were Ken and I and then "Muk" McGarett and "Ichabod" Hendrikz, appropriately but maybe not auspiciously, members of my Mallory patrol. Perhaps appropriately, we all carried anonymous nicknames onto this immense slab of rock. "Muk" was the younger brother of a six foot "Mac" (a rugby player). He too was also strong, quiet and reliable, the usual way out of any physical problem. Ichabod wore spectacles and assembled radios for a hobby. If intelligent thought, de-coding, record keeping or comprehension was needed, Ichabod was your man. I did indeed used to be auburn-haired (Rusty); and Ken, well "Ken" was as far a parody as we dared.

Lake McIllwaine Kopje

We surged off up the first pitch—this was getting to be old hat now. The climbing was straightforward and fun and soon we were all ensconced in yet another fig tree. This time each one of us tied in securely. Ken now took the lead and set off in his new, silent rubber boots. The moves soon became a bit more challenging and then a small fig let him hang on and get his bearings. The angle was steepening uncomfortably. Where did this overhang come from? Another few tentative steps and he was shut out completely. What looked so simple from below was turning out to be smooth and blank, with a nasty bulge blocking the way. He worked some tricks with the small fig and came down, a bit miffed.

Now it was my turn. I'm not sure Ken was totally thrilled by the thought of me out on the sharp end again, but he sucked it up like a champ and sent me on my way with a cheery word. I didn't waste time straight up. Watching Ken's progress carefully, I thought that the angle might ease a bit over to the left, so I made my way up the other side of our tree. Sure enough, a hidden break in the overlap revealed itself and I was soon established on

the upper slab. My new position was a long way from home! The
fig tree seemed to have faded into the hazy depths and I was now
surrounded by a vast sea of wide-open granite. Very much
alone... Where to go? I looked around, somewhat desperately,
for a workable direction, something to aim for.

Ken's Groove

Way out right, almost on the horizon, there seemed to be
some grass growing. Maybe there was a ledge there? I decided to
make that my destination and tiptoed off.

The gods were smiling...there were small but positive holds
on this part of the slab and my Commando Soles were gripping
really well. I was beginning to enjoy myself again when I heard a
voice drifting out of the void: "no more rope—you'll have to
stop".

Damn! Another new experience. I was still a long way from the possible ledge, balanced on my small holds. The climbing had been tricky enough that the thought of climbing **down** just didn't compute, so I yelled back: "I need fifty feet".

Lesser mortals may have called up to me that this was a physical impossibility—or distracted me with valid arguments and advice. Not Ken. He put his considerable stubbornness and resolve to work and in a surprisingly short time yelled up: "go ahead".

He had untied the others from the tree and tied our two ropes together. Seeing there was no troublesome leader protection to thread the rope through, this would work just fine, and on I danced, getting ever closer to the supposed haven of my elusive ledge. The last few moves stopped me cold.

Separating me from the grass was a drainage smear that looked shiny and holdless. Water flow had polished the rock and my nice smooth granite had been worn to a slippery sheen. I tried a few places but could find no way through.

So near—and yet so far! By now I was getting tired, and a bit strung out. I was looking forward to relaxing on that ledge and letting Ken figure out the next moves. I wondered if I could sort of spring across the gap and grab a sprouting tuft of grass? Surely I had "Done My Best", as the Cub Scout Promise demands!

But No. I immediately discounted such lunacy. If there was one thing we had learned about this rock climbing business, it was that you do not mess around. This *fun* could, and would, kill you if it got a chance. We were growing up…

I took a deep breath and a closer look. There were actually some dents and divots in the stone, and even one not-bad small flake that could maybe provide a fingertip hold. I tentatively moved across the rugosities but stalled out when my following left foot had nowhere to go. I carefully climbed back—another first in this momentous day. On my next try I almost made it, but, once again, got my feet tangled. By now I knew the reverse moves well and was beginning to feel a new confidence. Back on my slab "rest" I took a moment to think things through: I had to make one less-than-perfect move, and that would feel more controllable if it was off my right foot. If I could pull off a holdless, friction dab with this right foot, that would put my left foot on an actual small roughness and I could then step through carefully with my good right foot.

When I finally did it, it seemed ridiculously easy. And that **really** confused me! So near—and yet so far. But what was I getting close to, in this crazy business?

And then there was the unsettling fact that The Adventure was not letting up. My "ledge" was sloping steeply and there was nothing I could tie myself to. It was tempting, once again, to think that this was most unfair. But it was also exciting: the stuff we trained for with "venture journeys" (Scout initiative tests).

I started yelling back to my arboreal friends and we soon ascertained that I had moved over enough so that I was now more or less above the big fig tree. I would be able to throw the joined rope down, directly to the others. I kicked big holes in the tussock grass of the slope, braced myself firmly and brought up Ken and Muk.

Ichabod was still perched in the fig. He had analyzed what was happening and calculated his chances of survival as better down below. Little did we all know that he was destined to end up as the hero of this whole escapade.

When Ken looked around our anchorless belay, his cheery words had chilled somewhat: "Well done…it seems you accomplished that feat not without a fair measure of risk".

It was entirely appropriate for him to adopt a somber tone as he was leading the next pitch, a steep groove, and if he fell, all three of us would be reunited in the tree with Ichabod (If we were lucky).

"Steaming Jim" Jan McMorrin on the hand traverse a few years later

He stepped daintily up, with his trademark careful and considered moves, and moved steadily towards yet another small fig tree halfway up the pitch. By now, in this atmosphere of experiential learning, we had quickly figured out that, once Ken crossed over that tree trunk, we would all be safely protected by the pulley action of the rope over the trunk.

And...it was so. A great sigh arose to the heavens. The rest of his pitch seemed a scamper by comparison and we were soon all on the summit plateau.

But any celebration was premature. This rock was a gift that kept on giving.

A final overlaying layer of rock barred us from the top. But... splitting the overhang diagonally was a beautiful hand traverse flake and up this Ken was soon swinging. He made it out to the end of the flake, resting his weight on friction holds, getting his money's worth from that fancy rubber. And...that was it!

He now had to reach over the rest of the bulge into a shallow finger crack and pull over the final steepness without any protection whatsoever. But without ever having seen or experienced a finger lock, either in the flesh or even in a picture, he wisely came down.

Years later we would return and place a homemade angle iron piton here, still finding this crux move challenging and intimidating. But now...I was of course eager to try my luck before we gave up completely. Yet now Ken had a worried look on his face. "We should go", he said. "We've pushed our luck far enough".

That made an unhappy kind of sense and prompted us to think about how we were going to get ourselves off this rock. We quickly realized that some worry was in order.

We could not simply abseil down the line of our climb—there were no anchors on my grassy ledge and even our joined ropes would not reach from that top tree. In any case, if we left our ropes fixed in place, we would be stranded at the big fig tree. On the way up Ken's top pitch, I had studied the cliff to our left and noted a groove with some saplings sprouting out of it so I suggested this as a possible abseil line. We peered over the edge, trying to decide if the small bushes were sturdy enough to take our weight and we could see that, further across, the rock steepened, and was even blanker. Besides, Ichabod was still waiting patiently somewhere down there, to be rescued by us.

So, down we went. The groove worked well. The trees were OK and our (first) multiple abseil proceeded smoothly. Soon we came to a place where we could shout across to Ichabod and promise him that all was well. Though it quickly became apparent that our confidence was somewhat premature: the groove we had been descending ended abruptly on the lip of a large, very overhanging wall which had been hidden to us from above. We were still far above the jumbled rocks of the talus slope that formed the base of the wall. One of our proficiency tests was estimating distances and we all agreed that we were a good two hundred feet from safety. The hundred and twenty feet we had been managing with our doubled ropes would certainly not reach to the ground.

Another "venture discussion" ensued: what if we tied our two ropes together and abbed on a single strand? Would the sheet bend knot, used for such joinings, pass through the carabiner on our abseil slings? This new kind of abseiling that we had adopted was safer and (marginally) less painful than the old classic body wrap. Testing showed that the knot jammed every time at the carabiner. If we wrapped the rope directly around the body in a traditional Dulferzits—with the single strand going straight through the crotch (really bad for males!) and over the shoulder—that would pass the knot—but could we control such an abseil for two hundred feet of totally overhanging space? No! For sure. And what about poor Ichabod!

It was pretty clear that if someone jammed on the rope, out in space, they would quickly suffocate...and the ones above would be trapped. Although we would name our climb **Fleur de Lys**, after our gentle Boy Scout symbol, the climb was a real "Scorpion"—it had a fierce sting in its tail.

About then our attention was diverted to Ichabod's yells. He was beginning to feel it was time to leave his leafy nest so I went around the corner a bit to call down some "reassurances" to him. While I was trying to think of something heartening to say, I realized that he was actually quite close to us. Maybe we could connect to him somehow and go down **that** way? I coiled our thinnest, lightest, rope and tried for a lifesaving toss. This is a kind of rope throw that lifeguards use to pitch a rescue line to swimmers in distress. For our First Class Proficiency we had to be able to drop that rope between two marks three feet apart and twenty yards away, two times out of three.

Throwing downhill like this turned out to be reasonably simple and I had soon nailed Ichabod in his tree. He was still quite a way around the corner, on the original slab where this had all begun. An abseil down to Ichabod would have to be performed at a steep diagonal angle. If a hapless abseiler came unstuck from this precarious angle, they would swing back over and end up in the middle of the overhang, eighty feet short of rope and with everyone else permanently stuck in place.

To prevent this unfortunate possibility I shouted down that Ichabod should tie the ends of the abseil rope, which he now held, very firmly to his tree. After a bit more back and forth chatter, I stepped into my sling, clipped the biner and set off across the gap. The ropes went around the overhang and were soon snaking down the easier-angled slab. In most places I could grasp flakes of rock or patches of vegetation to keep me in place. As the angle eased I could lean across and friction my feet sideways. I tried to keep my stance solid and not be mesmerized by the deep void off to my left that was waiting to swallow me.

It was going well—until I hit a final smooth section just before the last steep corner, where I could swing around and grab the tree. Try as I might, I could not shuffle around this blank section. I would have to pull on the ropes. I yelled to Ichabod that I was using the ropes and, pulling back on them, I swung around the corner. There was a lurch as my weight came fully on the abseil ropes and then I pulled myself across, hand over hand, into the tree. Whew! Safe at last!

When I caught my breath I called back to the others to start across and then leaned over to thank Ichabod for saving us all.

He was still sitting, wide-eyed, in the tree. In his desperately locked hands he had a death grip on the ends of the rope. He had not received my yelled message to tie the ends to the tree. But, as I looked into the depths of his eyes I could tell there was no way Ichabod would have let go of those ropes…

We returned to Bari many times, to climb this and several other routes. We would climb other routes too, on rock and ice, all over the world; but never again would we have a Greater Adventure than that day on *Fleur de Lys* with the Second Seniors.

Envoi

The mists of time and place swirl apart and we're climbing at the Epworth Boulders, just outside Salisbury/Harare. I'd been a member of the University of Cape Town Mountain and Ski Club for three years and considered myself well up on the latest gear and technique.

Balanced Rocks at the Epworth Boulders

We'd just climbed the famous Balanced Rocks, even today a solid 5.10 rated climb. On the way down, negotiating the complex overhanging blocks, we left a rope loop to abseil from—hooked around a secure knob of rock. Threaded onto the loop were two shiny metal rings, to make sure the doubled rope pulled down easily…better to lose a small sling than the whole rope.

We move off to try another boulder and are soon high above the ground, with a broad bird's eye view. Looking back towards the Balanced Rocks we notice a native *piccanin* ("small" in Shona; from the Spanish/Portuguese *pequeño*; without implications of skin color) creeping through the grass. The little tyke is stalking us, keeping in cover and moving stealthily. He moves with that loose-boned gangly grace that comes so easily to African kids… he's probably playing at being a Freedom Fighter—and looking for mischief.

When he gets to where we abseiled, below the abandoned abseil loop, he bursts into the open and, to our amazement, literally scampers up the bottom 5.9 pitch. We remember all too well some tricky and technical footwork on that steep friction slab but our piccanin just seems to float up it.

He gets to the ab loop and does a little victory swing on it— then, before we can register what's happening, he flips the loop over his shoulder and scampers *DOWN* the route.

We have just abseiled down that pitch, because it was so intimidating, and are literally struck dumb.

We would like to find him and recruit him for our climbing team; teach him to belay, and plug ourselves into that elemental energy—but he has taken his prize and vanished back into the mists and shadows of this Dark Continent...

Learning by Dying

by Rusty Baillie

... when you have reached the mountain top,
then you shall begin to climb.
And when the earth shall claim your limbs,
then shall you truly dance.
—Kahil Gibran

Setting the Scene

Canadians had never visited the Highest Point on Earth—
the summit of Mount Everest. And so, we were going to take the
Maple Leaf flag to The Top. Being proud, modern climbers, we
were going to do so via a new route of extreme difficulty—the
Direct of the SW Ridge—which we had, modestly, renamed
"The Canadian Spur".

But first we had to get through the Khumbu Icefall.

An impressive place: here an ancient glacial ice accumulation
from the massive Western Cwm (Welsh for a steep-sided hollow,
or cirque on a mountainside) is funneled downwards through a
narrow gap in the encircling ridges, at the same time plunging
several thousand feet down a near-vertical rock cliff. The icefall is
always moving, obeying the relentless tug of gravity. The glacial
bed is too steep to allow the ice to use its natural property of uni-
form, fluid flow: it freezes soundly in places and then, when the
internal forces become intolerable, it explodes into huge shat-
tered blocks, which crumple down until the tensions are released.
Meanwhile, unusually deep crevasses try to relieve the residual
pressure and, as they slowly sink and yaw open, they play havoc
with ropes and ladders that have been fixed to establish a "safe"
route.

Basecamp with Khumbu Icefall in background

But we were supremely keen and confident. Working, initially, as equal climbing partners—or so we thought—with our experienced Sherpas, we had found a "least worst" way through, and were all busy ferrying supplies...

Prologue

There are many misconceptions about dying but not too much solid information about what it's really like. A common thought is that our death is a most serious business—the end of our time on earth. But, it didn't work out that way for me.

Then there's the idea that you only get to try it once—so you'd better get it right the first time. Also not the way I found it —though I was always haunted by those lines of Bill Shakespeare's:

> *"Cowards die many times before their deaths*
> *The valiant never taste of death but once...*

...but then, The Immortal Bard had never been to Everest.

Also, I had never been interested in suicide, which might have provided some special insights of its own. My life as a mountaineer, outdoor-pursuits instructor and father all kept me firmly and steadfastly dedicated to living for as long as possible. Life was good. Like Musashi advises, I wished to gallop my steed along the very edge of the sword blade, but not to stumble there. I had, however, sort of realized that dying would not be a solitary affair. True—in theory one's troubles might be over—but there was a whole mess of hassle for those left behind. It almost seems that dying is hardest on the lucky survivors.

Practical administrative problems for one's estate can be softened considerably by careful and proactive planning. The ongoing statistic back in 1982 was that 10% of Everest climbers were killed; and so I made sure to take out extra life insurance for my family (fortunately the insurance actuaries did not have this particular statistic). I also arranged wills and powers of attorney (to ease the path through probate) so that life could go on as normal in my absence. Of course, there is the matter of grieving. That's not so easy to soften.

Such a direct approach to a risky challenge did not go over well with everyone else. The possibility of a climber getting killed was considered bad public relations for expedition fund-raising efforts and I was asked to keep it all very low key. Somehow I got the feeling that planning for a possible death was thought a bit defeatist, maybe like setting up a self-fulfilling prophesy. It seemed that modern western society, considering itself more civilized and sophisticated, had repressed thoughts of death and bound them down with euphemisms and innuendo.

"Come stand to your glasses steady
The thoughtless is here the wise
One cup to the dead already
Hurrah for the next that dies".

Fortunately, my wife and daughters were more pragmatic and seemed relieved to be provided for. They had been involved in family outdoor adventures for many years and were familiar with both the rich rewards and the high prices involved: horses kicking, biting and rolling on you, avalanche potential on cross country ski tours, rattlesnakes and scorpions—all things to be noted and dealt with.

Starting with a short army stint, I had tried to find some professional guidance on how to conduct myself in potentially lethal situations, though I was totally unconvinced by exhortations of patriotism and a duty of blind obedience to orders from "my betters":

"Theirs not to make reply,
Theirs not to reason why,
Theirs but to do and die…"

Bringing in Christian theology didn't help either. I found the promise of Eternal Life for martyrs and The Saved even less convincing. Ideas of heaven and hell seemed just a little too convenient for manipulation by the authorities and didn't hold up in the face of danger and injury. As a youngster I had had a ringside seat in the back of our family car when a nearby truck knocked down a cyclist and scattered his brains over the road: THAT had been real…

Happily there was Bushido.

A rash of Samurai best-sellers had introduced us to a culture of steely-eyed supermen (and women) who had No Fear of death and an overruling sense of honor. It turned out, moreover, that there was a rich and authentic martial arts literature, now available in English. Works like Musashi's *Book Of Five Rings* and Tsunetomo's *Hagakure* were a rational and erudite study of situations that were eerily familiar to us climbers. Combined with the intricacies of Zen and Taoism, such ideas were fascinating and compelling. Someone seemed to understand what was going on here!

Best of all, Bushido is absolutely practical: if you invented an esoteric sword technique you would be politely invited to demonstrate it in a duel—and if it didn't work, you would probably end up without a head.

Two main lessons remained with me after studying Musashi and Tsunetomo: the first was to learn to be calm...

Both in fighting and in everyday life you should be determined though calm. Meet the situation without tenseness yet not recklessly, your spirit settled yet unbiased...

The second was to consider carefully and objectively the possibility of dying during a climb and to have pre-decided what would be an acceptable way to do that...

Only when you live as though you are already dead will you be able to find freedom...

Of course, no Samurai WANTED to die! For them, also, life was valuable and sweet. By breaking away from our western all-or-nothing thought systems I hoped I could combine the best of both worlds, benefit from the synergy of the combined systems and find some inner peace.

And so I hoped, when I finally boarded my first-class (sponsored) Air Canada flight for Khatmandu, that I was ready for the greatest challenge of my life—and that my family would not feel that I had abandoned them.

The Icefall: Avalanche

We had met to devise a strategy for carrying loads through the icefall in bad weather. We knew we were early in this post-monsoon season and that heavy snow storms would have packed the high slopes to create an avalanche hazard. So we decided to send an advance team up before each carry: if those two got up into the lower Cwm and found it to be snowing heavily, they would radio down in time to cancel the main carry. Peter and I would form the first recon team.

We awoke several hours before the rest, did a thorough radio check, and set off up the fixed ropes and ladders we'd previously set up. Our headlamps provided a secure pool of light for us to climb in but, conveniently, did not penetrate the mysterious and intimidating depths of the monster crevasses through which we were threading our tenuous way.

Somewhere along the Traverse in the Icefall; Rusty on ladder

Soon we noticed that snowflakes were intruding into our world of light and the wind seemed to be strengthening. By the time we crossed over the last scary ladder and emerged into the lower Cwm we were in a full-fledged snowstorm. It was time to make our radio call. There was no question—we would have to cancel the carry. The extra new snow, on top of the already heavily loaded snow-pack would make the slopes dangerously unstable.

Just as we called Base to report in we noticed, to our astonishment, a line of lights heading up to join us. How could that be? We were about to cancel the carry.

The lead light turned out to be Gyaljen Sirdar, the head Sherpa. I explained to him that we were cancelling the carry.

"Oh no sahib", he replied, "We were told to carry. By The Leader".

This put the Sirdar in a spot. I had no idea how the system had been bypassed but I couldn't fairly expect him to disregard a direct order from The Leader—whoever or whatever that was. Our first leader had encouraged consensual decision-making, which had served us well, but our new leader seemed to be morphing into an autocratic despot. I searched for a way to persuade Gyaljen to turn back but his team were already filing past, heading for our staging Camp l, in the Cwm above.

"Be careful", was all I could say, "You are the Sirdar. If you feel it is unsafe, then dump the loads and come back down. I'll support you on that".

Soon the occasional "Om Mani Pedme Hun", a mantra the Sherpas chant when they are worried, faded into the murky dawning light and Peter and I reluctantly signed off from Base. Although we were horrified at the breakdown of our carefully-constructed plan, neither of us was ready for a major radio confrontation, which would have been made even more complicated by the fact that the main Leader was up on the mountain somewhere and we were only dealing with the Deputy Leader at Base. I later regretted that I had not been more assertive. I should have found a way to prevent a bad situation getting worse...but I didn't...

Peter and I pondered our predicament and I unclipped from the ropes so I could adjust my own load of 20kg—like our "porters"—a load mainly made up of my ice climbing gear and special clothes for the upper mountain. On these easier slopes I liked to use a tumpline: a band around the forehead that allows you to unweigh the shoulder straps and encourage blood flow to the brain.

While I was fiddling with the straps I thought I heard a strange, sighing noise above us. The early light seemed to be fading and broken-up snowflakes began to dump down hard onto us. Peter was the first to figure it out. "Avalanche!" he bellowed, in his best Ski Patrol alarm voice.

Then the wind hit us: I tried to hunker down behind my pack. I had been in countless small snow slides before but I had never been the one buried—it seemed to be my fate to dig other folks out, not a particularly popular role among one's friends: they seemed happy enough to be excavated but I always got the impression they would have preferred to be the ones doing the rescuing. But this little snow slide was weird. We couldn't see a thing, just hear that ghostly sighing sound and feel the snow crystals raining down.

Just when I thought I'd aced it yet again, the real air blast hit. Now unsecured to the fixed ropes, I was picked up like a dry autumn leaf and delicately transported about thirty yards, totally through the air, and came softly to rest in a snow billow, a few feet from a deep crevasse.

Then the snow began to settle down from above and soon had me covered. I had trained long and hard for this scenario and started doing the recommended back-breast stroke, as I would have done in a normally moving slide. It worked fine, and I was soon back on the surface. I managed, I think, a weak grin but, before I could congratulate myself, more snow started to settle upon me. This time it was heavier and I had to extend myself to stroke back to the surface and gulp some much-needed clean air. No grin now. And, sure enough, more snow…

"Third Time's the Charm", they say—and it was immediately apparent that the avalanche and I would have to fight it out for this particular charm. This was a serious dump! The snow came battering down and my swimming efforts soon had no effect.

And still the snow came down!

Soon I could not move, and felt myself being buried deep. The powder, which had melted slightly in the friction of the slide, was freezing back hard, and packing tight around my chest, so that I was having great trouble breathing.

But I tried to follow Musashi's advice. After all, he had prevailed in a lethal duel—with five strong swordsmen against him. "Keep Calm", he had said. "Don't tense up. Look for the advantage".

So I played it by the book: In extremis—stick your left thumb in your mouth, to keep your airway from having fine powder jammed inside and bite down to keep it there. At the same time, extend your right hand towards the surface (wherever THAT might be?) so that the rescue team can find you (if they are not all buried too).

I resisted the strong urge to try to struggle and gasp for air— that would just waste valuable body oxygen—and focused on trying to slow my breathing way down and relaxing the big muscles that were screaming for action.

I was remembering a crisis when I had been diving for lobsters off Cape Town, in my student days, when my compressor air system failed. I was down about ten fathoms and needed a few minutes, without oxygen, to reach behind me for my attached air hose and pull myself hand-over-hand back to the surface. Under the snow I was feeling that same dreadful terror of suffocation, of needing to Get With The Program...to do something, anything, NOW!

I had managed to control my panic then, but there was little doubt that this time it would not be so easy. There seemed to be no breathable air coming through the snow, my lungs could not expand, and, although I was now "comfortable", I was starting to drift away…

As part of my Hagakure lesson, I had decided that I wanted to die with dignity.

I would do my best to prevail and stay alive but, in the end, I would not panic and make a hysterical final effort.

That time had come. I let myself go. I did not embrace death but I did accept it.

What was it like? Was there a Bright Light? All I remember was that it was sublimely peaceful—no visions, no life-flashing by. Just peace…and quiet.

But I did not die.

I do not think I even lost consciousness. I seemed to stay in a sort of stasis. Eventually, I came to realize that I was still there, maybe ready to take a very careful, small, breath. Very slow, very shallow.

I flexed my chest a bit: a small crack had opened up, melted out by my body heat, and I could take quarter-inch breaths. I flexed my upper arm, which moved slightly. It seemed that I was covered not by deep, compacted, snow-ice but by somewhat fractured snow and ice debris, disturbed by those seemingly futile swimming motions, and by that hand thrust towards the surface.

Slowly and ever-so-carefully I began to develop my advantages; and after an eternity that flashed by in a nano-second, I could dig away enough blocks to reach my chest and free my ribcage for some proper breathing. The hard part was my legs. They were frozen more solidly in place. As I cleared more of my upper body I could sit up a bit and look around, peering out of my shallow grave.

The first thing I could see was the crevasse into which I had so nearly been dumped. It was now filled to the brim with snow. Dull and compact, halfway to ice.

My second sighting was a boot, still on a leg, sticking into the air and kicking desperately. This must be Peter, thirty yards away and still clipped into the ropes.

Time to move.

Peter was tangled in the fixed rope and his belay leash. The wind blast had wound him around his anchor and buried him upside down. When I uncovered his face I could see he was cyanotic (blue lips) and that he was beginning to suffocate from the rope pressed tightly against his windpipe. He was non-responsive and didn't have much time left.

What to do?

It would take far too long to dig him out and untangle him carefully. That rope across his throat had to go! I reached for my rigging knife, usually carried handily around my neck, but it was gone—ripped away by the air blast, as were my mitts, tuque and sunglasses. So far I had been digging with bare hands. I tried biting through the rope but it was yellow polypropylene and rock-hard. My mother bequeathed me good teeth but it was hopeless—the rope was like a taut steel cable.

I was becoming somewhat frantic. Peter was dying in front of me and I was powerless. I needed to think carefully...Maybe two metal things to chop together?

My own pack, with all its ice climbing ironmongery was gone (for now), and Peter's ice axe was nowhere to be seen. I would have to try to see if Peter had a knife somewhere. I was deciding this was a forlorn hope when I heard a voice behind me: "Namaste Sahib".

Another Sherpa with his load! I tried to keep calm. "Namaste...Do you have a knife my friend?"

"Here", he said, and handed over a superb, razor-sharp, Swiss army knife.

A tricky cut, very near the jugular, but the effect on Peter was dramatic. A great deal of coughing and spluttering but we soon had him bundled up and prepared to go down to our nice, safe, Basecamp for a nice hot breakfast, with lots of tea.

Before I had recovered my pack (clipped to a rope somewhere), another Sherpa arrived from above, looking ashen and very worried. "Bad times Sahib", he said, "Sherpas buried up above, maybe some team members (Canadians)".

So much for tea and scrambled eggs! I sent the two Sherpas off with Peter and went up to see who else the avalanche had touched. Not far above a small crowd had gathered over a spot where the fixed rope suddenly dove beneath the snow and ice.

"Three Sherpas buried here," said someone. "Three Canadians, just above, narrowly escaped. Coming down now".

Tim, our National Parks—Canada, Snow Safety Ranger, took over expert control: putting two people up above to look out for further avalanches, with the rest to continue digging from both ends while listening for warnings from the lookouts.

I perked up at the mention of "more avalanches" from Tim's instructions to the lookouts. My mind was telling me to get the hell out of there! More avalanches I did NOT need. But James, our ex-hippie Mountain Center Instructor, was tact itself: he had obviously been delegated to "nurse" me, a standard procedure. Still, I could not help bristling a bit at being patronized. But he endeared himself to me by finding some spare mitts and a natty Inca tuque. And he tastefully let up on the traditional graveyard jokes.

Soon the diggers came to the first buried Sherpa, Pasang Sona. Six-feet down and not breathing. Our expedition doctor was handy and started CPR with vigorous chest compressions and mouth-to-mouth breathing. Pasang responded by strongly throwing up—a promising sign. But unfortunately he did not start breathing. I found a bivvy sack and sleeping bag and got in with him to try some body rewarming, but all our resuscitation efforts failed. Reluctantly we started to bundle him up for evacuation.

After the avalanche. Rusty in sleeping bag with Pasang Sona attempting, unsuccessfully, to rewarm him

Our avalanche observers reported in: the avalanche had come from high on the West Ridge of Everest. It looked like some ice cliffs had been broken away, scooping up the snowfield below and picking up enough energy to cross the entire Khumbu Glacier, climb a thousand feet and travel half-a-mile to nail us in the Icefield. Canada has some of the biggest avalanches in the western world but we were still struggling to appreciate the scale of these Himalayas. We hated leaving Ang Tsultim and Dawa Dorje in the ice, but there were more ice cliffs teetering up there, and it was still snowing. We all paid our last respects and, sadly and silently, headed down.

Another meeting, at which it was decided that a group of Sherpas would set off down with Pasang's body for a traditional cremation ceremony at Lobuche, with its large and sobering collection of memorial chortens. Bill March, who had now established himself as our unquestionable Leader, along with several others, accompanied them to show support. The rest of us took a day off.

I made some notes, tidied my tent, and listened to some tapes my daughters had specially compiled for me and my brand new

Walkman player. I didn't relive my moments under the snow too deeply; after all, my strategy had worked—here I was. Too bad about the failed carry cancellation—but we still had a mountain to climb. This was The Big E—it was going to take unusual commitment from everyone.

Evacuating Pasang through the icefall

The Icefall: Seracs

That night the weather shifted. The Summer Monsoon was finally over and winter started to send its icy fingers probing into the mountains—along with a fine high pressure system. The morning's blue skies and crisp snow promised the beginning of the clear climbing window we hoped would take us to The Top.

But we had to get moving, before the Jet Stream descended and the winter gales arrived. A large carry party headed for Camp 1, together with a New Zealand party that was sharing our Icefall route (but not the danger of rigging it). Along with Dave Read, Pasang Tenzing and Nima Tshering, I went up into The Traverse to secure some ropes and ladders that had become rickety. This Traverse was the place where our route left the right bank of the glacier and plunged into the heart of the jumbled mass of the Icefall. It was a gloomy, shadowy corridor, with high ice walls overhanging an unstable floor. The Traverse ended at the steepest part of the rock step that caused the glacier to break up so dramatically. This was where the deepest crevasses were and an impressive ladder system led up and through the labyrinth. Our job site was near the top.

As soon as I had set foot on that morning's snow, I realized that conditions had changed. All night long the glacier, on which we were camped, had creaked and moaned. I was wakened several times by sudden clicks that seemed to come from right under me. The snow was no longer soft and accommodating. Up until now I had not had to wear my steel-spiked crampons, preferring to press out small steps with my rubber soled boots and to glissade back down in fun, sweeping turns. Now, we all strapped crampons on firmly and watched carefully where we methodically set our crampon points.

What we should have been thinking about was the plasticity of the glacial ice. This cold snap had hardened the ice, and made it more brittle. The hardness was blocking what little fluidity the glacier had to flow smoothly over the rock step; while the unrelenting pressure of gravity was building up inside it.

Dave and Nima worked the bottom of the ladders while Pasang and I fixed new anchors above. Later we were to go up and check the avalanche site, re-rigging the buried ropes. I also wanted to ensure that my pack was still in place up there, waiting for me to reclaim it and move it on to Advanced Base, in the Upper Western Cwm.

It was fun. Soon Blair joined us. He was our official videographer, seconded from the Canadian Broadcasting Company (CBC) to bring our live antics to a waiting public. Young and fit, Blair was a total enthusiast. He had quickly learned to use the fixed ropes and was soon following us up the mountain. He stayed below with Dave, hammering away at snow stakes with a small sledgehammer Speedy, the expedition carpenter, had brought along especially for the task.

Quite soon the New Zealanders passed by. They were on their way down, having completed their carry in record time. Adrian, big brother to our own Alan Burgess, was worried about us working in the Icefall: "Bad place this", he commented, "You need to wrap it up and get a cup of tea down below". Another of their team chimed in with, "You have to learn to move fast up here". I had to work hard to restrain an angry response—after all, he was the son of Ed Hillary, whom I admired greatly. How the hell did he think the ladders he was using so freely got fixed in place! But we were nearly finished anyway. There was just one final guy rope that needed tensioning with a trucker's hitch.

The first I knew of trouble was a loud *craaaack*—like a rifle shot. At first there was no movement that I could feel. Then a cloud of light powder drifted out of a fissure in the serac wall above me, where gigantic forces were beginning to assert themselves.

At times like this eyewitnesses usually report that "Time seemed to stand still" or that "Things seemed to be happening in slow motion". Time is such a subjective thing, even before you start to mess it around with quantum mechanics and string theory...but I certainly felt that there was no rush for me to appreciate what was about to pass.

One of the things I had always been concerned about, when contemplating death in a violent accident, was what the Moment of Impact would be like. What would it actually feel like to have my body ripped apart? Would it be excruciatingly painful? Would the pain be slow and unavoidable—enough to make me break down and cringe? My preliminary evidence, gathered in fairly minor incidents, seemed to indicate that the moment of impact is protected by a sort of psychological anesthetic; that it is the dread of such a thing that causes us anguish. It looked as though I was about to learn the truth of the matter...

Soon, the "solid" ice I was standing on was beginning to undulate and buck. Then, my floor turned into a large slab, which started to rear up, with me having to move up the slope to avoid being tipped into whatever was happening down below. My crampon points gripped the hard ice tenaciously and I could maintain my balance. I gave silent thanks for those sharp points! This seesawing happened several times as my massive surfboard rocked back and forth and we all dropped downwards. For some wonderful and benign reason my slab did not flip over, though at one point it seemed I was on the tip of a pinnacle.

As suddenly as it had begun, it was over. My block was still—and flat, and I was securely on top. It had been a wild ride and it looked as though I had, once again, lucked out.

But...before I could relax and start looking around for my friends, the shivering deep within the glacier began again. Again, it started slowly, though now it seemed to be coming mostly from above me. Towering above were a new set of cliffs: the edge of the ice that had been left behind when my platform dropped down. These cliffs were about fifty-feet high and loomed over me ominously. As they started to shudder and totter, I tried to estimate their trajectory. One in particular seemed to be aimed directly at my happy home. It was probably the one that would squish me.

I cast a speculative eye into the depths of the crevasse below. About thirty feet down was a jumbled ledge, formed by falling ice and snow blocks. Maybe I could jump down there and take shelter from the falling tower. It was a complex decision: Was it better to risk sure annihilation by the tower, or to take a chance of being injured by a jump into the crevasse. And what would I do then? Yell for help?

Eventually I decided that I would rather die quickly (painlessly?), being crushed by the tower, than suffer a slow and unknown future in the crevasse.

Along with this rational choice came the very same calm acceptance of death that I had reached in the avalanche. I was dead. Time to go. *Ave atque Vale*...it had been a good life.

Damn tower must have had a slight twist to it, because it missed me by inches. No respect for my powers of reasoning! There was one final moment of doubt when I hoped that it wouldn't come down hard on the end of my slab and catapult me, like a circus acrobat, into the crevasse after all. But it just pulverized the edge of the ledge and continued downrange, with a great clatter and whoosh.

Now it was—finally—eerily still. The sun was still shining brightly and my existential question was still unanswered. I surfaced from my reverie to realize that there were two people nearby: Pasang, my fellow rigger, was standing a short distance away, uninjured, muttering a few "Om Mani Pedme Huns" in a dazed voice. I was about to join him for some sincere moments of gratitude when I noticed Blair lying down in the ice below me. He was tangled in some ice blocks and it looked bad. He had a serene half-smile on his face but the edges of the blocks enclosing his chest seemed to be just a bit too close together. I wasn't totally positive, but it didn't look completely right. Around his neck he wore an active radio, which was squawking and belching. I lifted it tenderly down and called Base:

"Rusty to Base. A terrible accident. I think Blair is dead"

I wanted to do a more formal assessment of Blair but suddenly an angry voice rose from the mess of jumbled blocks at my feet: "This Sherpa is killing me". Dave had come to rest in a branch of my crevasse. He was stuck in a bottleneck, with the slot opening out below him. He could feel his feet kicking in space. Above him, mixed up in ice and snow fragments, with his face buried in debris, was Nima Tshering. Nima was fighting his way upwards and Dave's head was the only solid stepping stone around. Dave could see himself being plopped downwards into those same depths I had declined to explore.

I needed to get Nima out. I needed a rope—quickly!

Now occurred a pair of miracles that almost persuaded me to give up my scientific pretensions in favor of divine providence. First, I glanced up and there, neatly coiled above me and stuck lightly on the ice, as though on a climbing-store rack, was a length of proper belay rope. I lifted it tentatively down from its small place of smooth order, amidst all the utter chaos, expecting it, at any moment, to dissolve in a puff of purple smoke.

But we all stayed in our present reality. I grabbed it, uncoiled it, tied a loop and lowered it into the crevasse. Nima wriggled into it and Pasang and I hauled him up to the surface. Way up high, on the first ascent of Everest, Sir Ed Hillary had once performed the same service for Tenzing Norgay, just below the summit. Sir Ed had remarked, with rough Kiwi humor, that Tenzing had emerged like a "landed fish" from that summit chimney. Indian nationalists had found this demeaning and lambasted Ed for racism. Back then Tenzing had just smiled; now, when Nima came out of that crevasse—like a landed fish—all he could do was give us both a fierce hug.

But Dave was waiting, still stuck below where Nima had been —not so patiently and not that securely jammed. The icefall was still making unsettling, settling sounds and I quickly dropped the rope for Dave. He was soon securely tied in and we three tried to winch him out too.

No go! He was stuck in that bottleneck more tightly than we had thought. Just above him the crevasse wall bent in and stopped him from "chimneying" his way out, like Tenzing Norgay had done. The only way to get him out would be to enlarge the bottleneck and carve away the crevasse wall. I looked around —no ice axes in sight. Also, Dave said, it would need to be a short ice tool as there was no room to wield a normal long mountaineering axe.

So I sent our Sherpas down to obtain the proper tools. They were sort of reluctant to leave us there, especially after the odd after-shudder from the surrounding scenery. They would not abandon the sahibs, however stupid—or unlucky—they might be. But my triage instincts were strong so I insisted they get down and send back some help. They reluctantly left, picking a careful path through the new Traverse. The Sherpas had done more than a fair share for us already…

I needed to secure Dave but no magic ice anchors appeared for me. I looked around and could see no other way but to clip Dave into Blair's harness. I knew Blair—God rest his Catholic soul—would have been chuffed!

The whole Blair episode was pretty heavy. He had been a popular member, not supposed to go onto the actual mountain but we all ignored that—especially Blair. Later his body was removed for cremation at Lobuche, which precipitated yet another crisis (which I have omitted here). So a simple RIP would not work. It was profound…using him as an anchor…

After a bit of a think and further discussion with an increasingly unhappy Dave, I decided that my best, and only, bet was to find my cached pack with its load of technical ice climbing gear, including my short, one handed, axe. It was somewhere above, not too far from this spot, where the ladders ended in the lower Cwm. All I had to do was follow the fixed rope, to where the pack was securely anchored.

I explained it all to Dave who was not exactly ecstatic. If the glacier moved and his crevasse opened, he would be hanging on the rope. If it closed up…!

"I'm off," I said, "Don't go wandering around down there".

"Bastard!!!"

I started up, trying to follow remnants of the fixed rope. And it was going OK until I came to a sort of flattish, massively disturbed, area with no trace of ropes anywhere. It was a bit like a farmer's ploughed field, or the place where they taught us how to cross minefields...back in the day.

I thought that maybe this was where the ice collapse had originated. The question was: Had it all been filled in...or was it honeycombed and hollow?

I would have to cross this place twice to find my pack and the more I looked at it, the more it all turned into a maze of unstable (and bottomless) crevasses. The distance across varied from 30 to 40 yards...to miles and miles.

I really did not want to dare it. It seemed pure Russian roulette. Enough is Enough! So what, I'm a coward—so sue me!

But what about poor Dave? Your mate! What about honor?! That was easy to justify: that layabout was still single. A limited loss...

It would have been an interesting and educational Personal Growth Experience for me if I had been forced to make—and live with—that decision. But...time for miracle number two.

As I temporized and searched the surface for some kind of inspiration, I saw, half buried in the snow, almost at my feet, my short climbing axe, sans pack of any kind. It was just lying on the surface, still with its nifty wrist loop attached. An old friend from the infamous Craigh Dubh Climbing Club back in Glasgow, now a technician in the geology lab where my wife Pat, worked at the University of Calgary had upgraded that axe for me. He'd cut it down from 70cm to 55 cm, drooped the pick for a better stick in vertical ice and decorated the surface with beautiful whorls. I picked it up and kissed it.

Thank You Sagamartha...or whoever.

I lowered the axe to a very relieved Dave, who soon dug his way out of his trap. We prepared to leave Blair. The ice was still groaning and it was no time to linger so Dave shook Blair's icy hand and we took our leave.

The Reckoning

As we picked our way back through The Traverse, along the route the Sherpas had just salvaged, I prepared to do some serious thinking. This was the most ambitious adventure of my life. It seemed like I had been preparing for it since I started scrambling over that faraway Rhodesian rock. A great many people, a new country and my new friends were supporting our efforts to climb this mountain...BUT what about getting killed up here? *For real*, next time. THAT had become a very real and immediate possibility.

Rappelling down a serac barrier in the Icefall at the end of the Traverse. It was these ice cliffs that collapsed and killed Blair

Then...I realized: My decision was made. I didn't make it consciously and mechanically—it was just there. I never, ever, thought of second guessing it, or even trying to unravel the maze of complicated and connecting paths that twined between the conflicting options. It has served me true. I trusted it truly and unconditionally: I had Faith.

I knew I had died in those icy wastes. All my previous life had been washed away. A new life stretched ahead, unburdened with any baggage carried over from the old. I could now choose whatever path seemed right and best.

First: My family. They had loved me unconditionally and had never tried to curtail my climbing or the risks I took. They had always supported me, although my freely-chosen adventures could well have removed me as their support.

I was going home now. The climb was over for me. I had done my best.

Enough. I was sacrificing nothing. Not one iota. I loved my family. I had played my game and now it was time to move on.

Second: I had no quarrel with The Mountains. They had treated me well, all my life. I would continue to climb them. A New Game would emerge. Maybe I would learn something in the process. I did wonder however...

I had died once, in the avalanche, but that had not seemed to deter me. I had gone back a day later, putting myself, and my family, back on the firing line. All to stand on top of a mound of dirty snow—a mound like an infinity of others scattered over this planet.

And the price had been worth it.

Was that snow mound summit of Everest really the dwelling place, and throne, of Sagamartha, Goddess Mother of the World? Is that what we were so desperately seeking?

Well...maybe not. A goddess mother surely has her home in a diverse number of places. Her dharma is available to anyone, anywhere, at any time...

All it takes is Love.

Aftermath

The warm glow of my epiphany stayed with me. I was happy. Every other problem receded into the distance and became fuzzy. It was just good to breathe in the thin, sun-drenched, mountain air, and watch the clouds roll over the peaks around us.

But...the World was still going on out there. In spite of me. It still had to play out its own, profane, life...resolve its own ambitions and expectations.

The other expedition members had to decide what they wanted to do. I listened to them carefully, and tried to support each of their own decisions; yet, they seemed to have made up their minds about my own case. In a last surge of duty and obligation I tried to volunteer for base camp duties but Bill had decided that all us Quitters should leave as soon as possible.

And still, there was Blair: We had carried him down, with some difficulty, to the place Pasang had been given his Last Rites.

Evacuating Blair from Basecamp to Lobuche. Sundare insisted on accompanying us...he and Rusty (third from far right) carried the litter most of the way

We ordered a load of wood. We came together; to show our respect and affection, perhaps restore some of our own equilibrium. The local lama tried to help us but we were preoccupied with our own needs. I worked long and hard, dipping deep into my new supply of psychic energy, and eventually we had a small bag of ashes to spread on the wind and celebrate the life and memory of our comrade.

The cremation. Rusty facing away while McNab places flowers on the body

The Expedition quickly picked up the thread of its agenda and us quitters set off home.

I was looking forward to a hard-won chance to see my family again and didn't give any thought whatsoever to how the political ramifications of my decisions might impact my career or future.

Bill insisted I walk out with Dave Jones, one of our doctors, who was worried about his heart. Dave was a good companion but Bill did not give us any funds for the extra time our walk would take. We got pretty hungry but the locals took pity on us and bartered nick-knacks for board and lodging. It was not trekking season; there were no "tourists" around and it was a good opportunity to get to know the local people.

Envoi

One day on our way out, fighting our way up a steep, stony ridge, we came around an abrupt corner...and there...washing herself in a small stream was a young Hindu woman. She was naked and standing ankle-deep in the cold water. We were all startled—apparently, us westerners most of all. Before we could reveal our embarrassment, she simply covered up her eyes with her cupped hands, and waited for us to pass by. I tried not to stumble and, thinking perhaps there was a small crack between those fingers, I managed a quiet "Namaste".

She just stood there...silent, still, impassive. She was magnificent. Her breasts reminded me of tantric carvings on the temple walls of Angkor Wat. A goddess...

The mountains have their own way of teaching us.

A family worth living for. Rusty at far left with Pat, his wife, next to him.

Acknowledgements

Without the tales of the departed, the nearly departed and the ambiguously departed this book would never have been possible. Their names are listed in the book's dedication. One stands out for special mention: Tina Cobos, my wife…and, thankfully, a survivor. Tina is our first-line editor. Though no English scholar, her ADAHD ensures that if we can hold her attention, a story has some merit.

For more general editing for the finished book, my sister Anita Hatch-Miller's observations were priceless. But finally, for technical editing—and opinions—our college advanced-Spanish professor Ann Lawrie Aisa was incomparable.

Without the input from Joanne Urioste this work would never have taken the final form it has. Thank you, Joanne. We'd also like to thank Roy Smith, Tom Whittaker, and Terry Beal. I especially thank, Stephen Cox, Professor of English at UC San Diego and my editor at *Liberty* magazine. It was his constant prodding to write an article explaining why I do what I do—inconceivable to him—that led to this book. Finally, I must extend a thank you to Tina Heiple, Martha Reinke, Joe Schallan, and the late Bill Bradford for inspiration, research, photos and constructive feedback.

Collaborations are fraught with collegiality, exhilaration, contention…even explosions. Working with Rusty Baillie, friend, mentor and, at times, sympathetic foil was a lesson in patience, diplomacy and inspiration. Throughout this process Rusty was not just a steady anchor, he was a gyroscope keeping the work moving along through crests and troughs. It was an honor to work with him.

Robert H. Miller

****

In addition to Bob's well-expressed joint thank yous to Ann Lawrie Aisa, Joanne Urioste, Roy Smith, Terry Beal and Tom Whittaker, I'd like to add the following.

In 1974 we went back to Africa, to Kenya, with a Prescott College expedition to climb Mount Kenya with a team of senior students. We planned to climb the steep ice and rock of the Southern Glaciers…a unique experience of snow and ice on the equator. Bob Miller had some of the new American ice tools and a desire for something different from his homeland in Cuba or the sunny Arizona campus.

He graduated Cum Laude, leading a rope to the summit of Batian, and went on to a distinguished career in Anthropology and Constitutional Law. And now here he was, repaying the mentorship with some deft and precise editing of my manuscript. He proved to have a whimsical humor and profound interest in some of the esoterica we were trying to explore. That Bob would become a discriminating writer and meticulous editor, and help me channel some of my own fringe climbing experiences into a coherent and publishable form is a happy and classical reversal of the student—teacher relationship. Thanks Bob…

And thanks Tina—for being such a rock solid example of courage, sound common sense and endurance.

I expect I have always "taken my family for granted". Maybe that's not such a bad thing? But…I would like them to know that, although I did keep climbing, and put them on the line with me, I could never have done it without their very real…and totally appreciated support. Not only have my whole family provided constant support but they have always been normal, active participants in most of my adventures. We have wandered around the world and enjoyed some exciting moments. Thanks folks for being ideal fellow expeditioneers.

Adventurers often seem to end up having to call on personal reserves of strength and resolve to survive a crisis: a lonely and private struggle. But...we "stand on the shoulders of giants"! I have learned so much, from so many people. I cannot thank them all...though I fancy I remember each and every one...

Thank you all.

Rusty Baillie

* * * *

Finally, we'd both like to especially thank Alejandro Ramos, editor and publisher at Cognitio Books for his inspired cover design and his keen interest in this project...no surprise from someone who's logged over 10,000 skydives--a true crank in the best sense of the word.

About the Authors

Robert Miller

Robert Miller grew up in Cuba, learned English in Mississippi, attended high school and college in Arizona, and did postgraduate work at the University of Colorado, Boulder, specializing in primatology and archaeology with an emphasis on the evolution of civilization. He participated in the multi-disciplinary and multi-institutional project to search for the origins of the domestication of corn in Mesoamerica, excavated early man sites in northern Arizona and was a producer for Spirit Expedition Films on their Inca Royal Road project.

Miller has taught at Prescott College, Yavapai College, Outward Bound, Challenge/Discovery, and had many articles accepted for publication in *Liberty*, *The Denver Post*, *The Phoenix Business Journal*, *River Runner*, *Canoe*, *The Arizona Republic*, *Rock & Ice*, *American Atheist*, *Essays in the Philosophy of Humanism*, *Salka Wind*, *Outerlocal*, and *The Alpinist*, on Cuba, Latin America, economics, politics, history, philosophy, adventure and book reviews, and contributed to *Papers on the Archaeology of Black Mesa, Arizona*, edited by George J. Gumerman and Robert C. Euler, Southern Illinois University Press, 1976, as the photographer.

An accomplished outdoor enthusiast in rock climbing, mountaineering, survival, mountain biking and kayaking, he has also taught those skills at Outward Bound, Challenge Discovery, Prescott College and Yavapai College. He is the author of *Kayaking the Inside Passage: A Paddler's Guide from Olympia, Washington to Muir Glacier, Alaska*, Countryman Press, 2005, and its 2nd revised & updated edition, *Kayaking the Inside Passage: A Paddler's Guide from Puget Sound, Washington to Glacier Bay, Alaska*, 2018. In 2015 his *Closing the Circle: A Memoir of Cuba, Exile, the Bay of Pigs and a Trans-Island Bike Journey* was published by Cognitio Books.

Additionally, Miller has been a house designer and builder, specializing in masonry and cabinetry. In his retirement he likes crossing countries by foot and bicycle, and climbing *via ferrate*. He lives in Prescott, Arizona.

* * * *

Rusty Baillie

Born and raised in Rhodesia (now Zimbabwe) in 1940, where he first experimented with rock-climbing as a precocious teenager, Rusty Baillie soon headed down to the University of Cape Town, to train as a teacher, and further experiment with rock-climbing on the massive crags of Table Mountain.

He did well on the rocks, not so well with his BS degree, where he failed a major course over a philosophical disagreement with his History professor and, like many other happy dropouts set off to see the world...and climb in the European Alps.

All that exam trauma was not wasted however as, in 1970, he found himself working an Outward Bound program at the brand new Prescott College in Arizona USA. He transferred to Education, picked up some courses and, finally, graduated with a BA. Modern learning seemed a lot more fun so he went on to earn a doctorate while working a similar program at the University Of Calgary in Alberta, Canada. He received his PH.D. in 1983 from Union Graduate School in Outdoor Education: Sports Psychology & Risk Management. His dissertation *Mental Training for Mountaineering* was accepted for publication.

Jobs in Outdoor Education, back in the last millennium, had a fairytale flavor and included time in Wales, with the National Outdoor Center, Argyll Scotland; at Benmore Outdoor Center, and at the National Outdoor Leadership Center at Glenmore Lodge in Inverness Shire. A challenging post with Colorado Outward Bound, Colorado, in 1968 coincided with the massive Afro-American riots and involved rehabilitating black high school dropouts. This job was approved on the basis of Rusty having been born in Africa, thus an "Afro-American", the program sponsors not realizing he was, in fact, white.

His connection with rock-climbing eventually developed into a love of all mountaineering: snow and ice, ski touring, aid and bigwall, canyoneering, high altitude expeditions...and even whitewater kayaking and mountain biking. He started out becoming intimate with the technical routes on Mount Kenya, did the "First Rhodesian Ascent" of the Eigerwand, new routes on the overhanging big walls of the Sondre Trolltind in Norway and the Painted Wall of the Gunnison in Colorado. He achieved a first-solo of the iconic frozen waterfall, Polar Circus, before modern ice tools made such things fairly sensible. He pioneered the Old Man of Hoy, Scotland's most famous Sea Stack, with two other professionalized "climbing bums"—Sir Christian Bonnington and Dr. Tom Patey.

Quite early on, while resting in a beach job in Malindi, Kenya, Rusty met Pat, a Yorkshire girl, fell in love, got married in Leysin, Switzerland (neutral territory to both families), and started a family.

Rusty published *Thumb Butte: A Climbing Guide* in 1991and *The Promised Land & Lower Sullies* in 1995, both part of a mini series titled "Prescott Rock". Additionally, *Rock and Ice* magazine has published three of his articles. In 2000 the city of Post Falls, Idaho published his online climbing guide to the Q'emiln climbing walls, *The Northwest Passage*. Finally, in 2019, Jordan Halland premiered ***Rusty's Ascent*** at the Telluride Film Festival.

The number of his first ascents are "legion", a biblical word he used when "over 500" was suggested. He is president of the Idaho Panhandle Mountain Bike Alliance and organized the North Idaho Trail Riders Association in 2005.

Made in the USA
Las Vegas, NV
21 October 2020